MAVERICKS,
MONEY, AND MEN

In the series *Sporting,* edited by Amy Bass

MAVERICKS, MONEY, AND MEN

The AFL, Black Players, and
the Evolution of Modern Football

CHARLES K. ROSS

TEMPLE UNIVERSITY PRESS
Philadelphia · Rome · Tokyo

TEMPLE UNIVERSITY PRESS
Philadelphia, Pennsylvania 19122
www.temple.edu/tempress

Library of Congress Cataloging-in-Publication Data

Ross, Charles Kenyatta, 1964–
  Mavericks, money, and men : the AFL, Black players, and the evolution of
modern football / Charles Kenyatta Ross.
    pages cm. — (Sporting)
  Includes bibliographical references and index.
  ISBN 978-1-4399-1306-2 (hardback : alk. paper) — ISBN 978-1-4399-1307-9
(paper : alk. paper) — ISBN 978-1-4399-1308-6 (e-book) 1. American Football
League—History. 2. African American football players. 3. Discrimination in
sports—United States—History. 4. National Football League—History. I. Title.
  GV955.5.A45R67 2016
  796.332'64—dc23

                                                                    2015031425

♾ The paper used in this publication meets the requirements of the American
National Standard for Information Sciences—Permanence of Paper for Printed
Library Materials, ANSI Z39.48-1992

Printed in the United States of America

9 8 7 6 5 4 3 2 1

For my family

At the time, I was the first player from a small black school drafted in the first round. It said a lot for the Gramblings, the Prairie Views and the other black colleges. It was important for me to be picked in that round, at the very beginning.

—**BUCK BUCHANAN,** during an interview after the creation of the award named after him that honors the defensive player of the year in the Football Championship Subdivision

CONTENTS

Illustrations follow page 106

MAVERICKS, MONEY, AND MEN

INTRODUCTION

The creation of the American Football League (AFL) was the primary source of the unprecedented growth of the National Football League that began during the mid-1960s. The AFL was the brainchild of Lamar Hunt, who decided to start his own professional football league after an attempt to buy the Chicago Cardinals. Characterized as a league made up of NFL castoffs, inferior players, and teams focused more on offense than defense, the AFL was largely perceived as incapable of surviving. But with its innovative and successful use of television and its commitment to finding talented players, particularly those overlooked candidates who played for historically black colleges and universities (HBCUs), the new league not only survived but flourished. In 1960, when the AFL began, all of its teams included African American players and all but one of the original eight teams included an African American from a historically black school. This was in stark contrast to the NFL, which was not at that time fully integrated and would not become so until the 1962 Washington Redskins reluctantly added black players.

The decade of the 1960s has been characterized as one of profound change. As a by-product of this era, the AFL was fundamentally responsible for facilitating the evolution of modern professional football in America. The NFL adopted such aspects of the AFL as the use of on-the-field clocks for keeping official game time, jerseys with players' names on the back, and the two-point conversion. The NFL's willingness to share television revenue and to take a more active and aggressive approach to finding African American players was also vital to the growth of the game.

Several works on the American Football League, primarily by journalists and professional writers, have been published. Ed Gruver's *The American Football League: A Year-by-Year History, 1960–1969*, is a general history of the formation of the league and its subsequent merger with the NFL. Dave Steidel's *Remember the AFL: The Ultimate Fan's Guide to the American Football League* is also a general overview of the AFL, with numerous photos that tell a nostalgic story. In *Going Long: The Wild Ten-Year Saga of the American Football League in the Words of Those Who Lived It*, Jeff Miller interviewed over 170 players, coaches, owners, and league officials to convey the story of the AFL via in-depth interviews and anecdotal quotes.

Biographies of individuals who greatly contributed to the success of the league, such as Michael MacCambridge's *Lamar Hunt: A Life in Sports*, are also enlightening. MacCambridge outlines Hunt's background and family life and his great success in pro football, soccer, and business. *The Cookie That Did Not Crumble*, an autobiography of Cookie Gilchrist, written with the help of Chris Garbarino—the only work that examines the complex and confrontational life of this great African American running back—chronicles Cookie Gilchrist's life off the field and after the end of his career. *The First Black Quarterback: Marlin Briscoe's Journey to Break the Color Barrier and Start in the NFL*, written by Marlin Briscoe with the help of Bob Schaller, describes in detail Briscoe's success in becoming the first African American to start as a quarterback in pro football and chronicles his successful transition to wide receiver and his personal failures in his battle against drug addiction. Mark Kriegel's *Namath: A Biography* is a superb story about the life of the AFL's first superstar, an athlete who symbolized the counterculture movement in America and—more importantly—legitimized the talent in the AFL in Super Bowl III.

Mavericks, Money, and Men examines the AFL and the contributions of African American players to the development of this successful league. The commitment to extend opportunities to black players and the decision of team owners to share television revenue—arguably the two key components of the success of the AFL—profoundly changed pro football. The 1962 championship game and the drafting of Buck Buchanan were the two events that set the wheels in motion. The 1962 championship game, which went to double overtime, provided the kind of drama and excitement that fans had not experienced since the 1958 NFL Championship.

The dominance of the 1963 Chargers—the first team viewed as a legitimate challenge to the NFL champion—caused real debate about the possibility of an AFL/NFL championship game. The foresight of the Kansas City Chiefs in drafting Buck Buchanan as the first overall pick in 1963 was of equal importance. Buchanan—who was the first African American from a historically black school to be selected in the first round—was not chosen by the NFL until the nineteenth round. The signing of Joe Namath and the publicity generated by his contract brought new fans to the league and served as a shot across the bow to the NFL. The merging of every AFL team into the NFL in 1966 was a testament to the respect and acceptance the league had earned from NFL owners in six short years.

Several African American players made significant contributions to the success of the AFL. Early memorable runners such as Abner Haynes, Paul Lowe, and Cookie Gilchrist drew fans as they helped lead their respective teams to championships. Black players were also in the forefront of activism, becoming the first athletes to initiate an organized boycott after they suffered numerous racial indignities at the 1965 AFL All-Star Game in New Orleans. The boycott, which represented black athletes' direct and successful involvement in the civil rights movement, prompted the AFL to move the game to Houston. Although other African American athletes became more vocal and initiated various protests during the 1960s, black AFL players were arguably the first athletes who directly challenged systemic segregation and scored a clear victory. After the merger between the AFL and the NFL, the composition of the victorious Kansas City Chiefs in Super Bowl IV—the first pro football team whose African American players included more than half of its twenty-two starters—was a prelude to the future of the NFL.

In 2014 African American players accounted for 68 percent of the players in the NFL. This shift occurred as the AFL began to extend opportunities to black players in all positions. Marlin Briscoe, the first African American to start as a quarterback in pro football, was offered his opportunity with the Denver Broncos in 1968. James Harris, who started for the Buffalo Bills in 1969, followed. While the NFL manned the most important position on the field with white players only, the AFL started two African Americans in the position. Today fans think nothing of having African Americans play quarterback, but in the late 1960s this was far from the case. The NFL followed the AFL's lead and gradually began to extend opportunities to black quarterbacks, but the process was slow and several players were clear casualties of racism.

A NEW LEAGUE WITH NEW OPPORTUNITIES

The history of African Americans in professional football began when Charles Follis took the field for the Shelby (Ohio) Athletic Club in 1904. Follis was a halfback who played for only two years before injuries forced him out of the game after the 1906 season. Over the next thirteen years in this pre-NFL era Charles "Doc" Baker, Henry McDonald, and Gideon "Charlie" Smith were the only other African Americans to play professionally. In 1920, under the leadership of George Halas—manager, coach, and player of the Staley Starchmakers—the American Professional Football Association was founded. The league, made up of eleven teams, was renamed the National Football League on June 24, 1922. From 1920 until 1933 only thirteen black players played on NFL teams. After the 1933 season a color barrier was established, lasting until 1946. Kenny Washington and Woody Strode of the NFL's Los Angeles Rams began the reintegration of pro football in March 1946; they were joined that same season by Bill Willis and Marion Motley of the Cleveland Browns, in the newly formed All-American Football Conference (AAFC).

The reintegration of the NFL was a slow and meticulous process that was not complete until 1962, when the last all-white team, the Washington Redskins, finally relented and added black players. This did not happen voluntarily; it took pressure from the U.S. secretary of the interior, Stewart Udall, who threatened to withhold access to the newly built RFK Stadium before Redskins owner George Preston Marshall finally integrated his team. This threat forced the Redskins to add Bobby Mitchell, John Nisby, Leroy Jackson, and Ron Hatcher in 1962. During the reintegration process NFL teams added primarily black players who had played on teams at white schools. Of the 173 identified African American players who played in the NFL between 1946 and 1962, only 42 attended historically black schools. What is more interesting is that from 1946 to 1960 no player from a black school was drafted higher than the fourth round. Many were forced to make NFL rosters as undrafted rookies who came out of schools such as Florida A&M University, North Carolina Central University, Virginia State University, and Grambling State University. This despite the fact that Southern University (1949 and 1950), Texas Southern University (1952), Prairie View A&M University (1953), Grambling State University (1955), Tennessee State University (1956), and Florida A&M University (1957) all had undefeated seasons during the 1950s. NFL teams clearly viewed this level of talent as largely inferior and below the competitive standard necessary to justify drafting significant numbers of these players.

The AAFC was the first professional football league to extend opportunities to players from historically black schools. Motley was the first when he joined the AAFC from South Carolina State University, followed by Morgan State University's Elmore Harris, who played for the Chicago Rockets in 1947. John Brown of North Carolina Central University played in 1947 for the Los Angeles Dons, as did Ezzert Anderson from Kentucky State University. Tom Casey joined the New York Yankees in 1948 from Hampton Institute, followed by James Bailey of the Chicago Hornets from West Virginia State University and Ben Whaley of the Dons from Virginia State University in 1949. The AAFC "merged" with the NFL after the 1949 season. Although it was called a merger, only the Browns, San Francisco 49ers, and Baltimore Colts were allowed to join the NFL. The other teams disbanded, and some of their players were added to NFL teams. So although the AAFC was in existence for only four seasons, its teams clearly saw talent at HBCUs that NFL teams in existence since 1920 did not.

The first player to play in the NFL from a historically black school was fullback Paul "Tank" Younger from Grambling. No NFL team drafted Younger when he graduated in 1949, but he was signed by the Los Angeles Rams as a free agent for $6,000. During his collegiate career he scored sixty touchdowns, primarily by running opponents over like a tank. At 6'3" and 230 pounds, Younger played nine seasons with the Rams and one with the Pittsburgh Steelers. He gained 3,640 yards, averaging 4.7 yards per carry, and scored thirty-four touchdowns during his NFL career, but more importantly he opened the door for players from historically black schools to receive the same opportunity. One year later the New York Giants made fullback Bob Jackson from North Carolina A&T University the first player from a historically black school to be drafted in the NFL when they selected him in the sixteenth round. Jackson played two seasons with the Giants; significantly, of the 391 players selected in the 1950 draft, he was the only one from an HBCU. Only five other African American players entered the NFL with Jackson that season, four with the Rams and one selected by the Browns. As difficult as it is to believe, no new black players were added to NFL teams in 1951, although ten were added in 1952, including Ollie Matson (University of San Francisco), who was the first African American to be drafted in the first round when he was chosen by the Rams. Of those ten, only guard Jack Spinks, who joined the Pittsburgh Steelers from Alcorn State University, was from an HBCU. And over the next two years some seventeen black players were added to NFL rosters, but only five of them played at HBCUs.[1]

In 1955 the Green Bay Packers drafted Charlie Brackins from Prairie View A&M University in the sixteenth round. Brackins was a quarterback, the first drafted into the NFL from an HBCU. At 6'2" and 200 pounds he was big for a quarterback; as a three-year starter from 1952 to 1955, Brackins led Prairie View to thirty-three victories in thirty-seven games. On October 16 Green Bay head coach Lisle Blackbourn inserted Brackins in a game against the Browns which the Packers were losing 41–10. With a few minutes left in the fourth quarter he threw two passes, both incompletions, and did not play again. On November 7 the Packers gave Brackins his unconditional release. Arguably Brackins was not given a real opportunity in Green Bay, and much speculation can be offered as to how the history of the NFL might have been vastly different if he had been.

There has been a great deal of debate regarding the opportunities that African American players from black schools received when the American Football League began play in 1960. What cannot be debated is the fact that from 1920 until 1949 no black players from HBCUs played in the NFL, but in the AFL they were allowed to play from the time the league was founded. The AFL has been characterized as extending more opportunities to this population of players than the NFL did, but this characterization is not totally accurate, since both leagues stepped up their efforts to draft these players in the early 1960s. However, the AFL's Kansas City Chiefs were the first team to draft a black player from a historically black school with the first overall draft pick. The selection of defensive end Buck Buchanan in 1963 was historic for this population of players, and his play immediately validated the talent among players at these schools. Buchanan was not selected in the NFL draft until the 265th pick, and this difference epitomized the value the two leagues placed on these players. In essence, AFL teams from their inception had African American players on their rosters from black schools, which helped facilitate a stronger identity with this population of athletes.

The new league began to take shape in March 1959 when Lamar Hunt met Bud Adams at the Charcoal Inn restaurant in Houston, Texas. The two wealthy sons of businessmen talked for a couple of hours about their futile attempts to secure a professional football team. Hunt's father, Haroldson Lafayette Hunt, was the founder and CEO of Hunt Oil and one of the richest people in America; in 1935 he established a trust for his son of more than $500 million, which allowed the younger Hunt to be, as he put it, "self-employed." Adams was the son of K. S. "Boots" Adams, chairman of the Phillips Petroleum Company, and like Hunt had offered to buy a controlling interest in the woeful Chicago Cardinals from owner Walter Wolfner. Arguably Wolfner played a vital role in the formation of the AFL when he provided Hunt with the names of several wealthy businessmen who had approached him about buying the Cardinals. Hunt realized that a new league was possible if he could establish a cornerstone rivalry, which he had decided would be Dallas vs. Houston. While flying on American Airlines to Houston to discuss his plans with Adams, Hunt sketched out on the airline's stationery possible cities for franchises and a potential schedule. When the two men returned to his hotel after dinner, Hunt asked Adams if he would join if Hunt could get four other cities to sponsor teams in a new league. Without hesitation Adams replied, "Hell, yes!"[2]

Born in 1932, Hunt graduated from Southern Methodist University in 1956 with a degree in geology; he was a member of the football team, though his career was not distinguished. He was a third string end, well behind starter Raymond Berry, and saw only twenty minutes of action over his three years on the varsity, not enough to earn a letter. Armed with the financial security of his father's trust fund, Hunt was determined to bring pro football to Texas, and he spent two years after graduation traveling and learning the specifics of financing football and baseball teams. In early 1958 he called NFL Commissioner Bert Bell to inquire about procuring an NFL expansion franchise. Bell told Hunt that expansion was not an option for the league but that he should check with the owners of the Chicago Cardinals, who might be willing to sell the team.[3]

The lowly Cardinals had lost one hundred games and nearly $1 million over the last ten years. The downtrodden club, once owned by the late

Charles Bidwell, now belonged to his widow, Violet, and her new husband, St. Louis businessman Walter Wolfner. Over the course of a year, Hunt talked with Wolfner about buying the Cardinals, but he was willing to sell only a 49 percent share in the team, which Hunt found unacceptable. The 1958 NFL championship game was the defining moment for Hunt and his quest to own a professional football team. Like millions of other Americans, he watched on television as the Baltimore Colts defeated the New York Giants in Yankee Stadium 23–17 in overtime on a touchdown plunge by fullback Alan Ameche. This December game captivated the country, and Hunt was convinced that he had just seen a glimpse of the future, stating in an interview, "This sport really has everything. And it televises well." Buoyed by his insight, in February 1959 Hunt flew to Miami to visit the Wolfners one last time in an effort to buy the Cardinals and move the team to Dallas. Again Wolfner did not budge, but he tried to emphasize to Hunt that his refusal was not personal. He noted that Houston millionaire Bud Adams and several other suitors had approached him about buying the team but he had turned them all down. Hunt headed to the Miami airport and boarded a plane for the long flight to Dallas, but by the time he stepped off the American Airlines plane he had decided to approach several of the people Wolfner had mentioned about starting a new league.[4]

Before Hunt met with Adams, he had mapped out prospective profit and loss statements, provisions for owners, and a rough estimate of the costs of equipment and the revenue from ticket sales. He also had drawn up a tentative schedule for the first season, going so far as to sketch out the likely weekends the regular season would begin and end. With a commitment from Adams, Hunt now began to recruit other perspective owners, among them Bob Howsman, who had tried for years to bring a sports franchise to Denver. Howsman ran the Denver Bears minor league baseball team, which was a member of the Pacific Coast League, and he had overseen the expansion of its downtown stadium from 8,100 seats to 17,500, which routinely sold out. Howsman thought he had positioned Denver to be a part of major league baseball's expansion, but he watched as the Boston Braves relocated to Milwaukee in 1953 and as the Brooklyn Dodgers and New York Giants moved to Los Angeles and San Francisco in 1958. Pro football looked like the only reality for Denver in 1959, so Howsman agreed to join Hunt's proposed league.[5]

Another name Wolfner mentioned was Max Winter, onetime owner of the Minneapolis Lakers of the National Basketball Association. Winter had been part of a group of investors who were unsuccessful in luring the Cardinals to Metropolitan Stadium in Bloomington, a suburb of Minneapolis. When their negotiations with Wolfner broke down, the investors applied for an NFL franchise but were turned down. Winter accepted Hunt's invitation, so the new league now had four cities. Hunt's original plan was to have six teams, and he decided that for the league to have a national image it would need teams in New York and Los Angeles. He contacted William Shea, who was seeking financing for a new stadium project in New York City's Flushing Meadows. Shea put Hunt in contact with Harry Wismer, the director of sports at ABC and one of the nation's leading sportscasters. Wismer owned a 26 percent share of the Redskins in 1959 when Hunt contacted him with the idea of a new league; Wismer now made the fifth commitment.[6]

After meeting with Wismer, Hunt contacted Barron Hilton, son of hotel magnate Conrad Hilton. Hunt had to convince Hilton that his idea could work, which was more of a challenge than his other meetings because Hilton did not follow football at all. "I didn't know a field goal from a three o'clock checkout," Hilton said. But within an hour of meeting with Hunt, Hilton had vowed to join his new league. Now Hunt had to decide how to introduce the new league to the public, and he also wanted to try to get the NFL to consider expansion one last time. He met with George Preston Marshall, owner of the all-white Washington Redskins, in June 1959. Marshall was chairman of the NFL's expansion committee and the owner of the only NFL team with no African American players. A very inflexible man, Marshall met with Hunt for ninety minutes and listed several reasons why expansion was not about to happen in the NFL. Shortly after this meeting Hunt met with Commissioner Bell, who reiterated that the league had no plans for expansion. This was exactly what Hunt wanted to hear, for if NFL owners were firmly against expansion, then his new league would go unchallenged in the majority of their cities. In early July, Hunt asked Davy O'Brien, a former Texas Christian University star who was a friend of Bell's, to tell the commissioner about the new league. The meeting was cordial, but most importantly it set the stage for Bell to break the news about the AFL. Called to testify in Washington, D.C., before a Senate Judiciary Subcommittee as he looked to clinch antitrust legislation for the league, Bell needed ammunition to prove the NFL was no monopoly. On July 28 he told senators that a new league was being formed and would likely field six football teams during the 1960 season, including one in New York, and that none of the twelve NFL owners objected.[7]

The next day, newspapers across the country headlined Bell's bombshell announcement. Bell's testimony brought Hunt's fledgling league to the forefront of the American public's attention, and within a week he and Adams agreed to formally announce the new league at a press conference in Adams's Houston office. During this press conference, on August 2, it was announced that league play would officially begin in the fall of 1960. Twelve days later, on August 14, 1959, the first league meeting took place in Chicago. Each team was required to pay $25,000 to join, and memberships were awarded to Dallas, Houston, Denver, Los Angeles, and Minneapolis–St. Paul. Rival leagues had been created before—in fact, in 1926 the first AFL was started by football star Red Grange's agent C. C. Pyle, but economic challenges caused the league to fold after one year. A second AFL was founded in 1935 and operated for two seasons in 1936 and 1937 before disbanding. Over the course of its two-year existence there were eight teams, but only the Cleveland Rams were allowed to join the NFL in 1937. The third challenge to the NFL was the All-American Football Conference, which was organized by sports editor Arch Ward and began play in 1946. As a league, it too struggled financially, but there were several teams that were individually successful, specifically the Cleveland Browns, who were led by standout African American players Willis and Motley. The AAFC and NFL became bidding enemies over the rights to several players; subsequently a merger was worked out that ended the AAFC but allowed Cleveland, the 49ers, and Colts to join the NFL in 1950.[8]

The four-year experiment that was the AAFC had cost the NFL an estimated $5 million in player signing wars. In 1959 many owners still had bad memories of battling the AAFC and had no desire to see another league begin. Deep pockets had not helped either the first two AFLs or the AAFC, but what Lamar Hunt possessed which the other leagues had lacked was timing. Suburbs were expanding across the country in the 1950s, along with the leisure time of their new residents. Mobility improved as scores of newly built highways let people travel freely, and pro football was growing just as the country was. The NFL started the 1950s with a dozen teams drawing about two million fans. By 1959 those same teams drew nearly three million spectators. The most significant factor in increased fan participation was not the automobile but television. In 1951, for the first time, the NFL championship game was televised coast to coast, by the DuMont Network, which bought the rights to the game for $75,000. This allowed people across America to watch the Los Angeles Rams defeat the Cleveland Browns 24–17. In 1956 CBS began broadcasting regular-season games to select markets, allowing fans to get their first glimpses of NFL stars from other cities. In 1955 NBC was the first network to buy the rights to the NFL championship game, agreeing to pay the league $100,000, and this allowed the 1958 championship game to be seen live in an estimated 10,820,000 homes. Arguably this game facilitated the marriage of major network television and pro football. Hunt clearly recognized the vast possibilities of both pro football and television, and he was determined to make the new league a success.[9]

Hunt's determination would soon be tested by the NFL. Before their August 29 preseason game George Halas, owner of the Chicago Bears, and Art Rooney, owner of the Pittsburgh Steelers, announced their plans for league expansion, which included awarding franchises in January and beginning competition in 1961. When asked about likely cities, they cited Houston and Dallas, a clear message that the NFL intended to have an adversarial relationship with the newly founded AFL. Halas and Rooney exemplified the arrogance of many owners in the NFL. They realized that Hunt and the other AFL owners had deep pockets, but did they have the necessary fortitude for a fight? By placing a team in Dallas, Hunt's home turf, Halas and Rooney clearly intended to intimidate Hunt, perhaps leading to the failure of the AFL itself.

Unfortunately for Hunt and the AFL, this was just the beginning of what would escalate into a full-scale war. NFL owners were committed to causing the collapse of the new league, and their next act was to facilitate dissent among the AFL's owners. In October 1959 Ralph Wilson, a shareholder of the Detroit Lions, signed on to start a team in Buffalo, and Hunt also met with several businessmen in Jacksonville, Florida, who were interested in putting a team together. This never materialized. Instead, William H. Sullivan paid the necessary franchise fee to start a team in Boston. Now the league had eight teams and was ready to initiate its first draft, which only caused NFL owners to try more unscrupulous strategies. First, Halas contacted Hunt and offered him 50 percent of the new Dallas franchise. Hunt would share ownership duties with Clint Murchison Jr., the son of an oil millionaire, but he politely declined the offer. Next Hunt was offered the entire franchise by Murchison, but again he said no, reiterating that he was firmly committed to his fellow AFL owners.[10]

Hunt felt that Commissioner Bell could ultimately help the two leagues to coexist. During one of their early meetings in July, Bell told Hunt, "All of you will enjoy this and all of the owners will get to become good friends down through the years. However, there is one thing that will separate you: when you start to fight over players." Bell was a prophet, but unfortunately he did not live to see his prediction come true: while attending a game in Philadelphia between the Eagles and Steelers in October, he collapsed and died after suffering a massive heart attack. A new commissioner would not be elected until the annual meetings the following January, and Hunt realized that without the leadership of the man who had guided the league over the last fourteen years, NFL owners were surely going to step up their efforts to end the AFL.[11]

NFL owners had an obvious strategy to dissolve the upstart league, force the exodus of two or three teams, and cause the entire AFL to fold. On November 22, as AFL owners met in Minneapolis to begin their first college draft, a story was published that the Minnesota group had been in secret negotiations for an NFL team. As the owners sat in the banquet room of the Cedric Adams Hotel, Harry Wismer came in with a newspaper that had reported the possible move. Someone asked Wismer if he was ready for dinner, and he shouted, "Yes. And this is the last supper!" Pointing to Max Winter of the Minneapolis group, he added, "And he's Judas!" The draft was conducted amid the hangover of the possible Minneapolis defection as teams began with "territorial" selections. Houston took LSU's Billy Cannon, and Dallas selected SMU quarterback George Izo. The thirty-three-round draft that followed was not so much a draft as a lottery. Since some teams had not even begun to hire personnel departments, it was decided that a committee of personnel men would get together and pick a master list of players, which then would be drawn by lot.[12]

Right after the draft, the AFL made two major announcements: first, that the league would have a cooperative television plan that would allow all the teams to share revenue equally and, second, that its new commissioner was Joe Foss. Foss, a U.S. Marine Corps pilot during World War II, and his squadron, who had shot down 135 Japanese planes, were known as "Joe's Flying Circus." Credited with shooting down 26 planes himself, Foss was viewed as a clean-cut hero with leadership qualities. He was given a $30,000-a-year contract for three years and became the squadron leader for the league now known as "The Foolish Club." As commissioner, Foss made several important decisions during his tenure, and one of his best was hiring Milt Woodard as assistant to the commissioner. Woodard was a sportswriter for the *Tacoma News Tribune* and *Chicago Sun Times* and also served as the beat writer for the Chicago White Sox. Memos, letters, and league correspondence were primarily generated by Woodard, who in essence served as the AFL's executive secretary.[13]

When league owners met on January 26, 1960, the first order of business was the election of Lamar Hunt as league president. The next day owners approved the withdrawal of the Minneapolis franchise, and this facilitated an immediate search for a replacement team. Barron Hilton wanted a rival team for his Los Angeles Chargers, and he was adamant that if it did not happen he would withdraw from the league. As a result of his strong stance Oakland was granted a team on January 30. Oakland's franchise, made up of an eight-man syndicate headed by Y. C. "Chet" Soda, inherited the Minneapolis draft list and was given permission to select five players from each of the other teams. With eight teams on board, league owners adopted revolutionary rules. They instituted the first four-teen-game schedule in pro football history (the NFL had a twelve-game schedule), and they adopted college football's two-point conversion rule after touchdowns. Owners Barron Hilton and Robert Howsman recommended that all AFL teams place the names of players on the backs of uniforms, with the idea that it would assist television viewers in becoming acquainted with players. The AFL made the game clock the official timekeeper, while the NFL kept two clocks—one on the field for fans and one kept by officials, a practice that was confusing, particularly at the end of games. Now fans could feel the excitement build during drives at the end of games. The league also gave the media a free hand in game coverage. Cameras would be allowed to show disagreements and fights between players.[14]

The AFL was poised to begin its inaugural season with new rules and with Oakland replacing Minneapolis, but just as the fight with the NFL seemed to slow, it was announced on January 28 that the expansion Dallas franchise planned to play in 1960 rather than 1961, as originally suggested. This news infuriated the AFL brass. Commissioner Foss warned of open warfare and congressional investigations if the NFL moved into Dallas, "the heart of our league." In March, Commissioner Foss asked the Justice Department to file an antitrust suit against the NFL based on the league's placement of a team in Dallas, but the Justice Department refused. Although Foss wanted government intervention to take place between the rival leagues, it did not; competition for players and fans would ultimately lead to the formation of modern football after several years of "open warfare."[15]

The American Football League was now more than an idea on American Airlines stationery. It was an eight-team league made up of the Dallas Texans, Houston Oilers, Denver Broncos, New York Titans, Los Angeles Chargers, Buffalo Bills, Boston Patriots, and Oakland Raiders. The teams were organized into two divisions, the Eastern Division, which comprised the Oilers, Titans, Bills, and Patriots, and the Western Division, which comprised the Chargers, Texans, Raiders, and Broncos. All eight teams had hopes of winning their division and playing for the first championship. With that in mind, AFL owners hired front office personnel and coaches with NFL experience, Canadian Football experience, or college experience. The Texans chose as their coach Hank Stram, a stocky disciplinarian who had served as an assistant coach at the University of Miami (Florida). The Oilers hired Lou Rymkus, a former All-American at Notre Dame who had spent seventeen years in the NFL, first as a player for the Redskins and then as an assistant coach for the Green Bay Packers and Los Angeles Rams. Denver chose Frank Filchock; the former standout quarterback at Indiana University had played for the Redskins and Giants, and after his career was over, he coached the Saskatchewan Rough Riders for ten years until joining the AFL. Harry Wismer wanted a high-profile personality in New York and chose Sammy Baugh, the former All-American quarterback from Texas Christian University who had joined the Redskins in 1937. "Slingin'" Sammy led the NFL in passing six times and took the Redskins to two NFL titles. When Wisner called, Baugh was the head coach of Hardin-Simmons University in Abilene, Texas. The Chargers did not have to look far for their coach—Hilton selected Sid Gillman, who was a graduate of Ohio State University and had played end for the Cleveland Rams in 1936. Gilman, whom many viewed as an offensive innovator, had coached at Miami University (Ohio) and the University of Cincinnati, and was the head coach of the Los Angeles Rams from 1955 until he resigned at the end of the 1959 season. The Bills went with Garrard "Buster" Ramsey, who had been a member of the Chicago Cardinals title teams in the 1940s; by 1959 he was an eight-year veteran of the Detroit Lions defensive staff. In Boston, Billy Sullivan hired Lou Saban, a former All-American at Indiana University and a defensive captain for the Cleveland Browns. In 1959, before joining the Patriots, he led Western Illinois University to an undefeated season as head coach. The Raiders chose Eddie Erdelatz, who had guided the Naval Academy to national prominence with eight successful seasons. In 1955 Navy beat Southeastern Conference champion Mississippi in the Sugar Bowl, and in 1958 it defeated Southwestern Conference champion Rice in the Cotton Bowl.[16]

Although league owners had begun to put organizational infrastructures together that included general managers, head coaches, and assistant coaches, they still needed access to stadiums. The Texans had to share the 75,000-seat Cotton Bowl with the NFL's Dallas Cowboys. The Oilers had trouble finding a suitable stadium. Unable to land Rice University, Bud Adams turned to Jeppesen Stadium, a high school field, for home games. Adams added 14,000 seats to the 22,000-seat venue, and for a mere thirty-eight dollars you could purchase a season ticket to all seven home games; single-game tickets sold for two dollars. The Broncos played in Bears Stadium, which was initially used by the Denver Bears of the Pacific Coast League. It had a seating capacity of only 17,000 for baseball but was expanded to 34,000 to accommodate the Broncos. Harry Wismer's Titans played in the Polo Grounds, which seated 54,500. It had been abandoned since 1957 after the New York Giants moved to San Francisco. The Los Angeles Chargers played in the biggest stadium in the league, the 94,000-seat Los Angeles Coliseum, and the Buffalo Bills played in War Memorial Stadium with a capacity of 46,500. Billy Sullivan was able to secure use of historic Fenway Park for the Patriots, who played for six years in the 38,000-seat stadium, and the Oakland Raiders were forced to play their first season in San Francisco at Kezar Stadium, which was also the home of the NFL's San Francisco 49ers.[17]

With stadiums in place, the AFL now needed television for exposure and revenue. The decision that AFL owners made in terms of how revenue would be distributed helped to change pro football forever. Lamar Hunt pushed the idea of equalizing television revenues as a means of equalizing competitive opportunity. This policy would be adopted by the NFL one year later by newly appointed commissioner Pete Rozelle, who borrowed the idea from the AFL. Rozelle was a compromise selection as commissioner in January 1960; after twenty-three ballots cast over nine days, he was elected with a 7–4 vote. The former general manager of the Rams stated that "borrowing" the television policy of the AFL was "the most important thing I have done as commissioner." The AFL had approached both CBS and NBC, which turned them down, but ABC, which was without a sports division and was a distant third among the major networks, was willing to negotiate. The AFL and ABC eventually hammered out a five-year, $8.5 million deal that would pay each team $1,785,000 for the first year. Included in the deal was a contingent package protecting ABC with sliding scales for ratings and sales slippage. It was estimated that ABC actually paid only $400,000 for first-year rights to AFL games. The deal also contained an explicit provision that each team would get the same amount from an overall league deal, regardless of how many of their games reached "national" audiences. Before the ABC deal was signed, Milt Woodard sent out a memo to the owners addressing potential contracts with radio stations. Woodard indicated that Jay Michaels of the Music Corporation of America had requested that individual teams withhold arranging radio rights for their games until national and regional TV coverage had been assigned. Michaels expected that most of the sponsors for TV would also want to buy time on the radio, and in order to prevent "competitive sponsorship" he suggested waiting until TV commercials were sold first.[18]

In an interview with the *Dallas Morning News* in January 1960, Don Rossi, the general manager of the Texans, predicted that the new league would create 380 new jobs for coaches and players. NFL owners had tried several tactics to finish off the AFL before it could begin its inaugural season. In essence the AFL had been on defense during the first few months of its existence, but that soon changed with the signing of drafted college players. The AFL honored existing NFL contracts with players and lured away no players from the established league. Instead, AFL teams gained player experience by signing NFL rejects and old players who were thought to be at the end of their careers. Most of the AFL quarterbacks, such as George Blanda, Jack Kemp, Babe Parilli, Tom O'Connell, Al Dorow, and Cotton Davidson, had NFL experience. Some players from the Canadian Football League (CFL) seized on the AFL as a chance to play again in the United States. Frank Tripucka, Dave Kocourek, Goose Gonsoulin, Butch Songin, Al Jamison, and Sherrill Headrick had all been playing north of the border before signing with the AFL. But the most spectacular aspect of the player recruiting was the bidding war with NFL teams over well-known college players, particularly Louisiana State University halfback Billy Cannon.[19]

Cannon's experience during the fall of 1959 would foreshadow the chaotic future years of pro football. Though the NFL had for decades lived by the agreement that it would not sign players until their college eligibility had been exhausted, the challenge from the AFL prompted many general managers and personnel directors around the country to jump the gun, secretly negotiating before the draft, and before New Year's bowl games, to sign players to contracts. On November 30, Cannon—traveling under the alias Billy Gunn—checked into the Warwick Hotel in Philadelphia for a secret negotiation with the Rams. GM Rozelle signed the Heisman Trophy running back to a contract with a $10,000 bonus, a $500 check to cover travel expenses, and three one-year contracts at $15,000 per year. They agreed the undated contract would not take effect until after LSU faced the University of Mississippi in the Sugar Bowl on January 1, but even that understanding was confidential, since signing the contract would have made Cannon ineligible for the Sugar Bowl. Bud Adams's Oilers also had the rights to Cannon, and Adams was aware that Cannon had a commitment to the Rams, which Adams intended to substantially increase. Adams talked to Cannon on the phone and offered him a $20,000 bonus and three one-year contracts at $30,000 each year. Cannon came to Houston in December and signed a contract with Adams, but he was skeptical that Adams would really pay him. Adams drove Cannon to his house in his wife Nancy's new white four-door Cadillac. When they arrived, Cannon told Adams that his father had worked in the oil refinery business for years and that if he could give him this car it would mean a lot. Adams, worried about what he would have to tell his wife but more worried about losing Cannon, gave him the keys. After Cannon left, Adams told Nancy, "Billy's gone on and heading back home." She said, "Did he go by cab?" Adams said, "No, he's driving back." Puzzled, she asked, "How's he driving back?" Adams said, "In your car." Then, according to Adams, he received a strong tongue lashing from his wife, who was irate that he had given her new car away.[20]

In order to cause the NFL maximum embarrassment, Adams and the Oilers decided to have Cannon sign immediately after the Sugar Bowl, on the Tulane Stadium field in front of a national television audience. It would come at the earliest possible time that Cannon could sign after his eligibility was up. Then, if the Rams claimed they had already signed him, they would be admitting that they had done so improperly. On New Year's Day, LSU played its rematch with Mississippi in the Sugar Bowl, and when the final gun sounded, the best-known college football player in the nation walked to the end zone. There, under the goal posts, on national television, Cannon signed a contract with the Oilers. Rozelle and the Rams sued the AFL, claiming that they had the rights to Cannon. The case went before a federal judge, who ruled that the contract with the Rams was not binding. Concluding that Rams general manager Rozelle had taken advantage of a "rustic" Cannon, the judge awarded Cannon to the Oilers.[21]

Cannon was not the only player selected by both leagues. Others included his backfield teammate at LSU, running back Johnny Robinson. Both the Detroit Lions and Dallas Texans drafted Robinson, and halfback Charlie Flowers of Mississippi was drafted by both the New York Giants and Los Angeles Chargers. The Texans also drafted running backs Jack Spikes of Texas Christian University and Abner Haynes of North Texas State (the University of North Texas), but the Pittsburgh Steelers had the rights to both players as well. Buffalo signed Penn State quarterback Richie Lucas, the Washington Redskins' first pick, and the Boston Patriots signed Northwestern University running back Ron Burton, the Eagles' first choice. The Los Angeles Chargers scored a real coup when they snatched University of Southern California offensive tackle Ron Mix from the Baltimore Colts. Money was not the only reason that college players signed with AFL teams. For example, Robinson was from the South and thought that Detroit was too far away, so he signed with the Texans for the same amount of money the Lions offered. Arrogance on the part of some NFL teams caused them to lose players, none more so than Carroll Rosenbloom's NFL champion Colts, who did not rush out to sign their draft picks. Subsequently four of their first five selections signed with AFL teams. Upton Bell, son of the late NFL commissioner and a scout for the Colts at the time, stated, "We were NFL champions. We weren't going to fall all over ourselves for a bunch of rookies."[22]

NFL executives became very frustrated with the fact that contract negotiations with players virtually changed overnight. Philadelphia Eagles general manager Vince McNally suggested in an interview that the best strategy would be to put all the players in one room and hold an open auction, "because that's what this thing has become, a rat race." McNally felt that there were now two types of players leaving college, "one who wants to play in the National Football League because they prefer its stability and they don't want to be a pioneer." The other type of player "tells you I want as much dough as I can get, I'm going to sweat you out." McNally also felt that money was not the only factor that helped make the decision for players, and that they were now seeking advice from individuals who were not football people. "These kids have more excuses than you could dream up. You meet their figure and then they say, I'll let you know. I've got to talk it over with my wife, my lawyer, my coach, my minister."[23]

Salaries were not the only contracts that had to be worked out between players and teams; the selection of players to appear on bubble gum cards had to be decided as well. In a memo to AFL general managers Woodard asked that teams identify at least twenty-five players and have them sign releases that would allow bubble gum manufacturers to distribute cards. Woodard wanted releases signed by May 15, virtually two months before training camps were due to open. What was interesting about this agreement was that the revenue from the sale of the cards was to be held in trust for "the player's benefit." This stipulation would be addressed after AFL players formed a Players Association, but during this inaugural season the opportunity to play pro football was simply enough.[24]

The AFL preseason was scheduled to begin on September 11, and owners had agreed that teams would play five preseason games. On July 8, 1960, when the first AFL training camps opened, more than 800 hopefuls vied for 264 roster spots. These camps were made up of former NFL players, CFL players, college rookies, and amateurs who aspired to be pro football players. For example, the Oilers had Heisman Trophy winner Cannon, but they also had former schoolteacher Charlie Hennigan, who kept his teacher's pay stub in his helmet for motivation, and both ended up being great AFL players. The NFL's major criticism of the new league was that it had less-talented players, since the best players purportedly played in the more established league. The idea that the NFL could make numerous mistakes in the evaluation of its former players or college players was virtually never considered, but the AFL would, in fact, prove this over and over again.

NFL owners, general managers, coaches, and scouts overlooked many talented players, especially those who were African American. In 1960 NFL teams were well aware of the black players who were being produced by large, predominantly white schools, but black players at smaller or historically black schools were generally devalued. One year before the creation of the AFL, in the 1958 NFL draft held in December, no player from a historically black school was drafted until the sixth round, when Willie Taylor, center from Florida A&M University, was selected by the Green Bay Packers, but he was cut during training camp. Eleven other players from black schools were selected after Taylor, but only one made an NFL team: Jamie Caleb, who was chosen in the sixteenth round by the Cleveland Browns. Caleb was a halfback out of Grambling State University who played three seasons with the Browns and the Minnesota Vikings.

The AFL actively sought black college talent, and seven players from historically black schools were selected in the inaugural draft. In fact, of the eight AFL teams, only the Los Angeles Chargers appear not to have begun with a black college player. The Oilers began the 1960 season with defensive back Julian "Sus" Spence from tiny Huston-Tillotson College along with receiver John White from Texas Southern University on their roster. The Texans had defensive tackle Walter Napier from Paul Quinn College and defensive back Dave Webster, defensive tackle Rufus Granderson, and running back Clem Daniels, all from Prairie View A&M University. Ernie Barnes of North Carolina Central University played offensive guard for the Titans, and Riley Morris of Florida A&M University played linebacker for the Raiders. The Broncos had three black college players in center: Mike Nichols from Arkansas Pine Bluff (University of Arkansas at Pine Bluff), receiver Jim Greer from Elizabeth City State University, and defensive end Chuck Gavin out of Tennessee State University. The Bills had defensive end Leroy Moore from Fort Valley State University and defensive tackle Jim Sorey out of Texas Southern University. And the Patriots had defensive tackle Jim "Earthquake" Hunt from Prairie View along with offensive tackle George McGee from Southern University.[25]

African American players were on every NFL roster in 1960 except George Preston Marshall's Washington Redskins, who remained all white until 1962. Throughout the 1950s black players had gradually been added to most teams, and several had become the best players on their respective teams. Running back Jim Brown arguably was the best player in the league; he and players such as Emlen Tunnell, Ollie Matson, Dick "Night Train" Lane, Eugene "Big Daddy" Lipscomb, John Henry Johnson, Rosey Grier, Lenny Moore, and Jim Parker were recognized as great players on their teams. Several of these players were nearing the end of their careers, and the AFL provided the opportunity for other black players to make a name for themselves and cause comparisons with their NFL colleagues. In 1960 Abner Haynes was drafted by the Pittsburgh Steelers in the fifth round and the Minneapolis group that was replaced by Oakland; several players were signed by other teams, including Haynes, who was signed by the Texans. This black running back from North Texas State became a star once he arrived in the AFL.

Haynes was born on September 19, 1937, in Denton, Texas; he graduated from North Texas State, where he integrated college football in the state of Texas in 1956 along with teammate Leon King. Haynes walked on at North Texas State after Coach Odus Mitchell got permission from the school's administration to allow him to join the team. Haynes quickly became the offensive and defensive star of the football team but was not allowed to live on campus. He also had several painful encounters with Jim Crow while playing for the Eagles, the worst being when the University of Mississippi, Mississippi State University, and Chattanooga University canceled their games with North Texas State. In 1960 he chose the AFL over the NFL and led the Dallas Texans and the entire league in rushing attempts, yards, and touchdowns. He was the AFL's first Player of the Year and its first Rookie of the Year. He captured the league's rushing crown with 875 yards and also led the Texans in receiving, punt returns, and kickoff returns.[26]

Haynes was not the only black player to make a name for himself on the field that first year. Gene Mingo was the first recognized African American field goal kicker in pro football. Born in Akron, Ohio, as the youngest of five children, Mingo dropped out of school to take care of his sick mother. After she died, he joined the U.S. Navy in 1956 and began playing football for the Oceania Naval Air Station as a very good running back and defensive back. He was honorably discharged in 1959 and initially offered a contract by Coach Weeb Ewbank and the Baltimore Colts for $9,000, but when he arrived in Baltimore the offer had dropped to $5,000 because, according to Mingo, he had not gone to college. Gene declined the Colts' offer, noting, "I can go home and work in the factories and make almost that much. And I don't have to worry about being banged up." The U.S. Department of Commerce, in its 1962 consumer income report, indicated that in 1960 the median family income for two individuals was $5,600. So Mingo's assertion that he could make nearly that much working in a factory was fairly accurate. Luckily for Mingo, the Denver Broncos had signed a fellow serviceman to a contract, so Mingo wrote General Manager Dean Griffing a letter with the help of his sister, asking for a tryout. Griffing had heard of Mingo and sent him a contract for $6,500. He joined the Broncos in training camp, where Coach Frank Filchock was looking for a kicker. Bill Miller, who had been in the Navy with Mingo, said, "Mingo can kick"; Coach Filchock gave him the opportunity, and on his first try he kicked an extra point through the goal posts. This was the beginning of a career that lasted from 1960 to 1972. Mingo played for the Broncos, Raiders, Miami Dolphins, New Orleans Saints, Redskins, and Steelers. He led the AFL in scoring in 1960 with 123 points and again in 1962 with 137 points. He would go on to set several scoring records with the Broncos along with playing several positions, including kicker, running back, defensive back, punt, and kick returner.[27]

Abner Haynes and Gene Mingo were just two of the many African American players who were part of the AFL's inaugural season in 1960. The season officially began on the evening of July 30 in Buffalo, where the Bills took on the Patriots in the first exhibition game. Some 16,474 fans watched in newly renovated and renamed War Memorial Stadium, braving the extremely hot temperatures as the Patriots defeated the hometown Bills 28–7. The Patriots had drafted African American running back Ron Burton in the first round of the inaugural AFL draft out of Northwestern University. Burton had signed with the Patriots despite also being drafted in the first round by the NFL's Philadelphia Eagles. But the unquestioned star of this game was quarterback Butch Songin, who tossed two touchdowns to lead the Pats to victory. Boston head coach Lou Saban was so ecstatic after the game that he shook hands with every member of the team and asked them to sign an official AFL ball.

In Los Angeles, Paul Lowe began his career by setting a record the first time he touched the ball. In the Chargers' first exhibition game against the Titans, the African American halfback returned the opening kickoff 105 yards for a touchdown. Lowe attended Oregon State University and played for the San Francisco 49ers during the 1959 preseason. The 49ers released Lowe before the regular season, so he returned to Los Angeles to help support his wife. He took a job in the mailroom for the Carte Blanche Credit Card Corporation, owned by the Hilton family. Lowe was invited to Chargers camp as a free agent and given an $800 signing bonus. Like every other AFL camp player, Lowe noticed that players came from all walks of life. "When they had tryouts, everybody and their grandmother showed up looking for spots, plumbers, carpenters, shoeshine boys, you name it." Even though Lowe had scored an electrifying touchdown that exhibited his greatest strength—amazing speed—when the exhibition season ended he was the fourth back on Coach Gillman's depth chart. Former NFL backs Ron Waller and Howard Ferguson, along with University of Mississippi rookie Charlie Flowers, were all ahead of Lowe when the regular season began and after the first five games, but that would not be the case when the season ended.[28]

In the early 1960s, segregation was a way of life for African Americans, and this included pro football players. The Oilers and Titans scheduled an exhibition game on August 26 in Mobile, Alabama, and shortly after the Oilers' chartered DC-6 landed, most of the team was bused to a hotel in downtown Mobile. However, the team's two black players, John White and Julian Spence, were discreetly pulled aside by Oiler officials while arrangements were made to house them separately. White was a 6'4", 230-pound tight end from Tampa, Florida, who had come to Houston to play football at Texas Southern University. When his wife gave birth at one of the city's hospitals, he suffered the indignity of being asked to leave because Negroes were not permitted in the visitors' waiting room. Spence was a 5'10" defensive back who weighed 153 pounds, which made him the lightest player in the American Football League. Spence was not drafted after college, but he played two years in the NFL, with the Cardinals in 1956 and the 49ers in 1957. He was out of football for the next two years before he joined the Oilers in 1960. For these two black players, dealing with segregation came with the opportunity, but this did not go unnoticed by their white teammates. When he heard how White and Spence were treated in Mobile, Oilers defensive end Dan Lanphear suggested to Coach Rymkus, "Lou, if that's the way things have to be, let's not play here again."[29]

This was simply a precursor for African American players; throughout the early 1960s they faced numerous challenges off the field, particularly when it came to playing in the South. One of the distinctive characteristics of black AFL players was their willingness to articulate their frustration with this treatment to each other, white players, and coaches. More importantly, this frustration eventually led to their direct action by the middle of the decade.

"WE DON'T TOTE
NO COLOREDS"

Pro football teams had faced racial problems in the South as far back as 1946, when the Cleveland Browns left Marion Motley and Bill Willis behind when they visited the Miami Seahawks, since Florida state law prohibited integrated sports. The following year Coach Paul Brown brought the entire team to Miami but was told by the hotel manager that the black players would have to stay elsewhere. "No, our team stays together," said Brown firmly. After a heated exchange in which the manager intended to stand his ground, Brown said, "I'll tell you what, we'll just get back on the plane and go back home." The hotel capitulated, and the Browns integrated Miami hotels on that evening. In 1952 segregation arguably helped cause the exodus of the NFL's Dallas Texans to Baltimore. When the New York Yankees decided to move to Dallas, they changed their names to the Texans. However, their roster included three black players—Buddy Young, George Taliaferro, and Sherman Howard—immediately causing speculation as to whether they would remain on the team. Howard was traded in a salary dispute, but Young and Taliaferro played in Dallas during the 1952 season, during which the team won one game and lost eleven. The team struggled to attract fans, and the owners reported to NFL commissioner Bert Bell that white Texans' racial prejudice was the reason for the lack of support. The black press agreed with this explanation but also cited treatment of black fans by Dallas State Fairground officials. The *Chicago Defender* described how Monday had been traditionally set aside as "Negro day" each October during the fair. Blacks could eat and enjoy everything except one or two shows that were closed that day, but on all other days of the fair they were segregated or refused service. On Sunday, the day of Texans' home games, there was one open ticket office for blacks, located on the other side of the stadium. When black fans finally got into the stadium, they found that the seats allotted to them were in the end zone directly behind the goal posts. Many black fans demanded their money back and got it, while others swore never to attend another Texans game. In late December, Bell declared that if the city of Baltimore could sell fifteen thousand season tickets in advance, the Texans would become the Baltimore Colts, which is how the team moved out of Texas.[1]

Five years later segregation in Dallas again became a national sports story at the 1957 Cotton Bowl, when the lack of any integrated hotels forced Jim Brown to be separated from his Syracuse University teammates. And in 1959, before the Cowboys franchise had been officially recognized, General Manager Tex Schramm met with the powerful Dallas Citizens Council, the de facto city planners who controlled everything from zoning to racial policies. At the time, the Dallas school system was completely segregated, as were its neighborhoods, restaurants, hotels, and city buses, where blacks were still made to ride in the back. Schramm argued that he could not hope to have a successful pro football team in Dallas if the city persisted in segregating hotels. Schramm's plea brought the case to a head and integration to at least one of Dallas's major hotels: the Ramada Inn next to Dallas Love Field agreed to integrate, provided it would not face opposition from the Citizens Council and other hotels. It was in this context that the American Football League began its first season in 1960.[2]

Racial segregation was a way of life in the Deep South, and although the AFL did not have teams in Alabama, Mississippi, or Georgia, states that were viewed as the most resistant to the civil rights movement, having two teams in Texas would clearly present challenges for the league's black players. The AFL's first game took place when the Boston Patriots hosted the Denver Broncos at Boston University's Nickerson Field on September 9. The Broncos upset the favored Patriots 13–10 in front of some 21,597 curious fans. Unfortunately for black fans and journalists, segregation in Texas did not help to facilitate curiosity but was simply another example of unequal treatment. In Houston, African Americans were forced to sit in segregated seats during the Oilers' first home game on Sunday, September 18, against the Chargers. But the following Sunday the NAACP established a picket line in front of Jeppesen Stadium as fans filed in to see the game against the Oakland Raiders. Black picketers protested the segregated ticket sales policy and carried signs that read, "Don't pay to see the Oilers play segregated games." Black fans were not sold reserved, loge, or bow seats and could sit only in an area that extended from the goal line to the east stands. Regardless of how much a black patron wanted to pay for a ticket, he or she could purchase only a four-dollar segregated seat. The *Houston Informer,* a black newspaper that covered the story, interviewed Jack Scott, who was the publicity director for the Oilers. Scott claimed that the press box in the stadium was not segregated but that "members of the Negro press would not be included." He went on to explain that he was not segregating the press box but that the twenty-seven seats had been allotted to persons the team management deemed "essential." Scott ended the interview by stating that he did not make the policy but was responsible for carrying it out.[3]

The protest by black fans and journalists surely had an impact on the black players for both teams, but not enough to keep them from participating in the game. The Raiders had four black players on their roster in 1960: defensive back John Harris, linebacker Riley Morris, receiver Charley Hardy, and fullback J. D. "Jet Stream" Smith. The Oilers had two: defensive back Julian "Sus" Spence and receiver John White. The game itself was poorly played and featured eight turnovers; the Raiders lost two fumbles and had one interception, while the Oilers also had two fumbles with three interceptions, which helped the Raiders to their first victory of the season, 14–13. The *Informer* estimated that only a handful of black fans watched the game and that only a change in policy to end segregated seating would help attract more than fifty or so African Americans to Oiler games. The newspaper argued that black fans could help the team begin to fill up its thirty-five-thousand-seat stadium, which was averaging around twenty thousand fans.[4]

The Oilers' policy of segregating fans appears to have ended after the 1960 season. Beginning in March 1960 the city of Houston was pressured to change its policy of segregation by black students from Texas Southern University. Unlike other southern cities that had sit-ins, protests, and boycotts, there was very little violence by local whites against black participants. Black businessmen and local leaders met discreetly with white businessmen and political leaders to prevent violence from occurring after black students held a sit-in at Weingarten's lunch counter on March 4 and the following day held a sit-in at Madings Drug Store. The students launched a boycott on Mother's Day, asking African Americans not to spend money in downtown stores, particularly at Foley's, which was Houston's largest department store. This caused Bob Dundas, who was in charge of Foley's advertising and publicity, to come up with a plan to desegregate some seventy lunch counters in the city. Dundas contacted John T. Jones, editor of the *Houston Chronicle,* the city's largest paper, and proposed a news "blackout" that would last for a week as black customers were allowed to sit at lunch counters and be served. This would also help to prevent individual lunch counter operators from being exposed to reprisals by segregationists. Under this policy, lunch counters in Houston were desegregated in August 1960, followed by a pledge from Astros owner Roy Hofheinz not to segregate the Astrodome, which was a newly planned domed stadium that needed a public bond issue for funding. One year later hotels were desegregated, and the following year restaurants and movie theaters were opened to blacks.[5]

Clearly, segregated seating kept black fans from attending Oilers games, but attendance was a challenge for all AFL teams during this first season. The Raiders played in San Francisco and averaged only 9,612 fans per game. The Broncos were slightly better, averaging 13,048 over their seven home games, while the Texans led the league with 24,500 per contest, followed by the Oilers at 20,019. Although the Titans averaged 16,894 per game, the vast Polo Grounds made the crowds seen miniscule. Linebacker Larry Grantham remembered playing before these small crowds the entire season. Grantham, who played football for the University of Mississippi, grew up watching Willie Mays patrol the outfield in this once grand stadium that was literally falling apart. "There were rats in the locker room. What made it worse was Harry Wismer would announce 19,800 over the PA system. We'd look up in the stands and our wives were sitting with their own personal hot dog vendors."[6]

On Sunday, September 25, the AFL illustrated that it had the potential for longevity when the largest crowd of the season filed into the Cotton Bowl to watch the Texans and the Chargers. Many felt these were the two premier teams of the league, and some 42,000 Texans fans were eager to see if their team could rebound from losing the first game of the season in Los Angeles. They were not disappointed: the Texans easily won 17–0, using strong rushing and great coverage in the secondary to shut down Chargers quarterback Jack Kemp, who was leading the league in passing. The Hunt-led Texans used promotions to facilitate fan interest, including the "Huddle Club" for children. It cost one dollar to join, and each child received a team T-shirt and free admission to all games. The Texans put certificates good for free tickets in balloons that were released over the city. They gave away tickets in packages of corn chips and to drivers who had their windshields washed at Sinclair gas stations. Hunt also hired a few dozen young, attractive teachers to sell tickets, offering each one a loaner convertible; the woman who sold the most got to keep her car. Arguably these efforts were successful in helping the Texans draw about 3,000 more fans per contest than their cross-town rivals the Dallas Cowboys, who averaged 21,417 per game.[7]

Segregated seating in Houston kept black fans away, reducing fan attendance, and unfortunately for the AFL, this was not the only racial problem in the city. Visiting teams had to make special arrangements for their black players when they arrived in Texas, and being separated from white teammates was generally accepted. However, when the Buffalo Bills played the Oilers and Texans, one black player openly voiced his displeasure at being treated differently because of his skin color. Willmer Fowler, signed by the Bills in 1960 after playing for Northwestern University, played running back and spoke up vehemently about how he disagreed with the treatment of his fellow black players. "We played Houston the week before we played Dallas, and we stayed in Houston that week after the Houston game. While we were in Houston we stayed on the campus of the University of Houston, we stayed in the dormitories. After our first practice they called all the black players together, and they told us that we would be staying in the dorms, we could eat in the dorms, but we couldn't eat in the main dining room." According to Fowler, they had to go to the faculty dining room to be served. "We couldn't eat out where the students and the other guys were eating—I told all the guys I won't be eating any fucking meals at this place and I didn't have a single meal at that university." Every black player joined Willmer in getting cabs to go to restaurants to eat or to pick up food and bring it back to the dorm.[8]

Several white players on the Bills team recognized that this was wrong, and they too supported the black players. According to Fowler, "when they called us aside in Houston to tell us that we would not be able to eat with the other ball players, Wray Carlton was the first guy to come up and say to the coaches that that was a lot of bullshit. Tom Rychlec was another guy who took a stand for us as well." When the team arrived in Dallas, it was more of the same. Bills announcer Van Miller, who traveled with the team, recalled that "we took the black players over to a black hotel and dropped them off, and then we went over to the Dallas Hilton, and the white players stayed there." After the discrimination in Houston and experiencing the same treatment in Dallas, Fowler was ready to explode. "I wasn't going to play in Dallas because we couldn't stay in the fucking hotel—we could eat there, but we couldn't stay there, and I said that I wasn't going to play."

But the morning of the game Miller talked with Fowler during breakfast and persuaded him to play despite the treatment the black players had received. Fowler and his black teammates decided to play but lost the last game of the season to the Texans in the Cotton Bowl. Whether they were distracted by the week's events or just anxious to have the season over, the Bills' uninspired effort culminated in a 24–7 defeat, which brought their record to 5–8–1 for the season.[9]

During this first season several African American running backs emerged as key players on their respective teams. Fowler finished second on the Bills in rushing, but his career ended the following season after he tore his Achilles. The Boston Patriots featured Alan Miller and Dick Christy in the backfield, but Ron Burton was the first to rush for over 100 yards in a game, when he ran for 127 on sixteen attempts against the Broncos. Burton was drafted in the first round in 1960 by the Philadelphia Eagles, the Ottawa Rough Riders of the Canadian Football League, and the Patriots. He helped to turn Northwestern University into a national power in the late 1950s, which brought recognition to its young unknown coach, Ara Parseghian. However, like Willmer, Burton had several injuries during his time with the Patriots that limited his effectiveness. Both of these African American players were elusive runners who played on bad teams, but in Los Angeles and Dallas two players emerged who were clearly the class of the AFL: Paul Lowe and Abner Haynes.[10]

The Chargers took control of the Western Division after they were shut out in Dallas. They won four straight games with an offense that finished third only to the Titans and Oilers. Quarterback Jack Kemp finished second in the league in passing yards and guided the offense, but it was the running of Paul Lowe that facilitated the necessary balance, which led to the team's success. Former NFL backs Ron Waller and Howard Ferguson, along with rookie All-American fullback Charlie Flowers from Mississippi, initially were the featured backs in Coach Sid Gillman's offense. Lowe was the fourth back until he was inserted into the starting lineup alongside Ferguson in week six against Denver, where he promptly scored touchdowns on runs of 12 and 44 yards. With Lowe starting, the Chargers won eight of their last nine games; he gained 817 yards for the year on 120 carries, finishing second (by just 20 yards) in total rushing yards to Dallas's Abner Haynes, who had twenty more rushing attempts. Lowe led the league in yards per carry with a 6.3 average; twice he gained over 135 yards in a game, and twice he scored on touchdown runs of over 60 yards. Gillman meshed Lowe's running ability with Kemp's precise passing to overwhelm opposing defenses. The Chargers threw the ball 441 times and ran it 437 times. During his five seasons as the head coach of the Los Angeles Rams, Gillman realized that he could not throw frequently in the conservative NFL, but in the AFL he became known as the father of the modern passing game. The Chargers won the Western Division by going 10–4, a surprise because Hunt's Texans were the preseason favorite but were only able to finish second.[11]

In Dallas, Haynes led the league's top rushing attack as he led the AFL in rushing yards and total yards from scrimmage. He was selected Player of the Year by the league's coaches, over Kemp, who finished second in the voting. Haynes commented that he was very happy with his decision to play in the AFL rather than the NFL: "The Pittsburgh Steelers drafted me, but I had a lot of confidence in Dallas and Mr. Hunt. Pittsburgh offered me more money and a lot of friends told me I shouldn't go with the AFL. Now those friends wish they were with me." Haynes indicated that his popularity in the Dallas area had facilitated numerous invitations requesting his appearance at various banquets. "The eating has been real good, so I bought me a set of weights to keep down my stomach. I don't want to play guard next year." Arguably, because of the creation of the Texans in Dallas and Haynes's on-field success, he became the first black professional athlete to gain some level of acceptance in this segregated city of the South.[12]

Unfortunately, Haynes's ability on the field was not enough to draw fans at a level that would enable the team to make a profit. Like all AFL teams, the Texans struggled to draw fans, but Hunt was more alarmed by the growing expenses. The 24,000 fans that the Texans drew each game were much fewer than he had expected, player expenses were far higher than he had originally forecast, and the team's costs—its scouting budget, training supplies, and the numerous items requisitioned by Coach Hank Stram—continued to escalate. In November, Hunt fired General Manager Don Rossi and replaced him with Hunt Oil accountant Jack Steadman, whose attention to detail helped to stabilize the team's losses. Steadman, however, could not prevent the Texans from losing nearly $750,000 during their first season. It was around this time that the legendary quote from Lamar's father, H. L. Hunt, was first reported. Interviewed after getting off a plane in Los Angeles and asked if he was concerned about Lamar, who had reportedly lost a million dollars in his first year in pro football, H. L. replied, "At that rate, he can only last another 150 years."[13]

Unfortunately the Oakland Raiders were not run by a multimillionaire but instead by a group of local businessmen headed by Chet Soda. The Raiders finished their inaugural season 6–8, which was arguably quite an accomplishment. Their ticket office was a converted gas station, and the team's offices were housed in three hotel rooms. The Raiders played their home games in San Francisco's Kezar Stadium, which they shared with the NFL's 49ers. They were fifth in the league in total offense and sixth in total defense. The Raiders were able to win only two consecutive games: they defeated the Texans 20–19 on October 9 and Boston 27–14 on October 16. Rookie quarterback Tom Flores was the AFL's top-rated passer, completing 54 percent of his throws, but the team's defense was next to last in defending the pass. Finally, playing in San Francisco did not help the team's identity with fans in Oakland, and they were the only team whose average attendance was under 10,000. They abandoned Kezar Stadium for Candlestick Park in their last game against Denver, and planned to play all seven home games in 1961 in Candlestick with the hope of moving across the Bay to a new stadium in 1962.[14]

The Broncos were the worst team in the league, finishing 4–9–1, which was disappointing considering they began the year 4–2. Denver had a strong passing attack led by quarterback Frank Tripucka, who led the league in completed passes, pass attempts, passing yards, and passing yards per game. Unfortunately he also led the league in interceptions, with thirty-four while throwing for twenty-four touchdowns. His favorite target was Lionel Taylor, who played one season with the Chicago Bears in 1959 before being cut and joining the Broncos. Like Abner Haynes and Paul Lowe, Taylor was an African American player who took full advantage of the opportunity to play in the AFL after the Bears gave up on him as a defensive back. The Broncos made Taylor a receiver, where he flourished; he led the league in receptions with ninety-two, was second in receiving yards per game, and was third in receiving yards for the season. They also had the first full-time African American field goal kicker in pro football in Gene Mingo, who led the league in field goals made with eighteen. Mingo led the league in field goal percentage, and he and Johnny Robinson of the Texans were the only two players to return punts for touchdowns. The 1960 Broncos had bad uniforms (they wore mustard gold jerseys, mud brown pants, brown helmets with white numbers, and vertically striped gold and brown socks), but with eight black players on their roster, they extended more opportunities to African American players than any other team in the league. Taylor and Mingo were joined by Mike Nichols, a center from Arkansas Pine Bluff (University of Arkansas at Pine Bluff); Chuck Gavin, a defensive end from Tennessee State University; Willie Smith, a guard from the University of Michigan; Jim Greer, a receiver from Elizabeth City State University; Henry Bell, a halfback who did not attend college; and Al Day, a linebacker from Eastern Michigan University.[15]

Like every other team in the league, the Broncos had one major problem—low attendance—which forced its first ownership group, led by Bob Howsman, to sell the team at the end of the season. Howsman said, "We weren't prepared to lose that kind of money, because we didn't have it." The team was sold to a consortium that included Cal Kunz and Alan and Gerry Phipps, and it remained in Denver. Finances were dire throughout the league, particularly in Oakland, Boston, and New York. The Los Angeles Chargers were drawing so poorly at the Los Angeles Coliseum that the AFL Championship game was scheduled for Houston's Jeppesen Stadium. Barron Hilton's Chargers had lost nearly $900,000, and at the 1960 World Series between the New York Yankees and Pittsburgh Pirates, *San Diego Union* sports editor Jack Murphy heard that Hilton was considering moving the team from Los Angeles. After the Series, Murphy talked local civic leaders into inviting the Chargers to San Diego, where the mayor and city council embraced the idea. Plans were drawn up to add a second deck to San Diego's Balboa Stadium, increasing seating capacity from 20,000 to 34,500. After the AFL Championship game the Chargers moved to San Diego, helping to transform the city from a sleepy little naval town to a large metropolitan area.[16]

On January 1, 1961, the AFL's first championship was decided by the Oilers and Chargers. Both teams had high-scoring offenses, but the defensive units turned in surprisingly strong performances. Houston boasted one of the league's best running tandems in Billy Cannon and Dave Smith, who finished third and fourth in total rushing yards. The Chargers had Paul Lowe, the league's second-leading rusher. The Oilers quarterback was NFL veteran George Blanda, who guided the league's best passing attack, while quarterback Kemp led the Chargers. The defenses on paper were similar: Houston finished second in total defense while Los Angeles finished fourth. Charger kicker Ben Agajanian scored the first championship points for the rookie league with two first-quarter field goals of 38 and 22 yards. Then George Blanda threw eight straight passes to drive Houston over the goal line. The last pass covered 17 yards to fullback Dave Smith, giving the Oilers a 7–6 lead. Blanda's 18-yard field goal later in the quarter boosted Houston's lead to 10–6. Behind the running of Lowe, who averaged just under 8 yards per carry on the afternoon, the Chargers rallied late in the quarter. With five seconds to go, Agajanian's 27-yard field goal cut the Oilers' lead to 10–9 at the half.[17]

The offenses moved better in the second half, when the Oilers relied on Blanda's passing and the Chargers on Lowe's running. Houston upped its lead to eight points with a 7-yard Blanda-to-Bill-Groman touchdown pass, but the Chargers came right back on a long drive culminating in Lowe's 2-yard dash into the end zone. The game turned for good in the fourth quarter when on third down from his own 12, Blanda called, "Pass Z, Slant Four, Swing and Go." The play was designed to isolate running back Billy Cannon on a fly pattern against strong safety Jim Sears, who kept creeping up to the line of scrimmage. At the snap Cannon slanted for the sideline, but as Sears closed he broke off the pattern and headed upfield. Cannon pulled in Blanda's pass at the Houston 35 and went in for the touchdown. The Houston defense secured the 24–16 win by stopping the Chargers on downs at the Oilers 35- and 22-yard lines.[18]

Billy Cannon, riding the crest of his touchdown reception, was the game's MVP. For their AFL Championship, each triumphant Oiler walked away with a winner's share of $1,016.42. George Blanda, who threw for three touchdowns and 301 yards, had some biting comments for his old employers. "I've waited eleven years for this moment," he said. "I've waited eleven lousy years. This is my first championship. The damn Chicago Bears never won one during my ten years. Maybe if Halas had let me play, they might have. How about that?" The Oilers' victory was also a win for the league in terms of television ratings. Jay Michaels of MCA, in a telegram written to Milt Woodard, assistant to the commissioner, on January 30, 1961, indicated that the AFL Championship game was aired in 15,383,000 homes, which equated to a 48.3 share of the audience. Michaels wrote that this was the third-best share of any football game of the year and placed the game in the top fifteen audience for the period. He concluded by stating that the Sinclair Oil Corporation, which was a primary sponsor of AFL games in 1960, showed a 70 percent increase in sales for the last quarter of the year compared with the corresponding quarter in 1959.[19]

After the television cameras were turned off, the reality of playing in segregated Houston was felt by black players. This was eloquently articulated by Chargers backup fullback Blanche Martin. He had been the starting fullback for Michigan State University as a junior in 1957 when the team went 8–1. He had a severe knee injury during the 1958 spring game that took a year to recover from, but he graduated as a three-time Academic All-American and was signed by the Titans in 1960. He hurt his knee in the second game of the season and was cut, then re-signed with the Chargers for the rest of the season. After the AFL Championship game Martin had to catch a plane back to Michigan to interview for graduate school. He had about two hours to shower, say good-bye to his teammates, and get to the Houston airport. With little time to spare, Martin stood in front of the hotel as one empty cab after another passed him by. Finally a sympathetic white cab driver stopped and asked what his problem was. When Martin explained that he needed to get to the airport quickly, the driver said, "You don't understand, do you?" "Understand what?" Martin asked. "We don't tote no coloreds," the man replied. Martin offered to pay twenty dollars, and the driver stared at the bill in Martin's hand and mentally weighed his role as a southern white man sworn to uphold segregation against the prospect of earning more than a day's pay for one run. He looked around to see if anyone was watching and growled, "Get in and get down!" Martin jumped into the cab and lay on the floor for the entire ride to the airport. He would go on to practice dentistry for more than forty years in Detroit and never played pro football again.[20]

Although AFL teams lost significant amounts of revenue during this first season, the reality of a championship game provided some solace that the new league had the potential to survive. For AFL owners, that potential was predicated on being successful in the upcoming draft. In a memo dated October 14, addressed to members of the Executive Committee, the league's plan to get a jump on college players was proposed. There is no name on the document, but it probably came from the commissioner's office. The memo referenced a territorial "Negotiation List," with a stipulation that the information remain "very, very confidential." Ground rules and a map for the negotiation list were established: Oakland's territory was designated as Northern California and Oregon; Los Angeles's territory was to be Southern California and Arizona; Denver's territory was Colorado, New Mexico, Wyoming, Utah, Kansas, and Nebraska; Dallas was given northern Texas; Houston was assigned southern Texas; Buffalo's territory was upstate New York, Massachusetts, and the rest of New England; and New York was given Maryland, Virginia, eastern Pennsylvania, West Virginia, New Jersey, southern New York State, Delaware, and Washington, D.C. All other sectors were regarded as "open," and AFL clubs could choose players from their own territory or go into open territory for their choices. The memo ended by stating, "Two players shall be selected on or before November 14, 1960, to be submitted to the league office in order of preference."[21]

On November 23 the AFL began its second draft. The first six rounds were done by telephone, and the process was completed December 5–6, when selections were made for rounds seven through thirty. The Broncos held the first pick and selected Bob Gaiters, a halfback from New Mexico State University. Next Boston selected Tommy Mason, a running back from Tulane University. The Bills then took Ken Rice, a tackle from Auburn University; Oakland selected Joe Rutgens, a defensive tackle from the University of Illinois; the Titans took Tom Brown, a guard from the University of Minnesota; Dallas took E. J. Holub, a linebacker from Texas Tech University; and for the last two picks, the Chargers selected Earl Faison, a defensive end from Indiana University, and the Oilers picked Mike Ditka, a tight end from the University of Pittsburgh. This draft included future pro football stars such as Herb Adderley, Bob Lilly, and Fran Tarkenton, who all opted to play in the NFL. But Billy Shaw, Ernie Ladd, and Faison turned the NFL down and went on to have stellar careers in the AFL.[22]

The AFL continued to present opportunities for African American players from historically black schools to play pro football. In this draft eight players were selected from these schools, but the NFL also began to step up its efforts in drafting black players from black schools. In the 1960 draft, twelve players from black schools were selected by NFL teams, and one year later eleven players were chosen, three more than were selected by the AFL. The competition between the two leagues for college players clearly was beginning to go beyond the boundaries of large, predominantly white institutions, and during the decade of the 1960s black players from black schools would help to shape the history of both the AFL and NFL.

Several white players from schools in the South were selected along with African American players from historically black colleges. The rigidly segregated University of Mississippi had five players picked by AFL teams, while Grambling State University had two players selected, as did Florida A&M University. In May 1961, as black and white Freedom Riders directly challenged segregation in the South, pro football was beginning to extend more opportunities for African American players on the field. Some thirty black players were on the eight AFL teams during the inaugural 1960 season, and some nineteen new players would be added to rosters in 1961. The NFL extended opportunities to twenty-seven new black players as well in 1961, which brought its total number to well over sixty.

This first season was played against the backdrop of racial and political change that swept across America in 1960. On February 1 four students from North Carolina A&T University started the sit-in movement in Greensboro, N.C., at a Woolworth five-and-dime-store lunch counter. By February 10 the movement had spread to fifteen southern cities in five states. Then on April 15–17 delegates representing over fifty colleges and high schools from thirty-seven communities in thirteen states met at Shaw University and formed the Student Nonviolent Coordinating Committee. This student-led organization adhered to the ideology of nonviolence, but it also embraced the possible need for increased militancy and confrontation. In May, President Dwight D. Eisenhower signed the Civil Rights Act of 1960, which established federal inspection of local voter registration polls and introduced penalties for anyone who obstructed a person's attempt to register to vote. The new federal law extended the life of the Civil Rights Commission and was designed to deal with discriminatory laws and practices in the segregated South that effectively disenfranchised African Americans. However, because it was narrowly focused on voting rights and provided limited power for enforcement against state registrars, many deemed the legislation ineffective.

The status of African Americans was a central issue in the presidential election as Senator John F. Kennedy and Vice President Richard Nixon faced each other in the hard-fought campaign. Kennedy outmaneuvered his Republican opponent by criticizing the Eisenhower administration for not ending discrimination in federally supported housing and declared that it could be done "with the stroke of a pen." He also seized the opportunity to telephone Coretta Scott King in October when Martin Luther King Jr. was arrested and sentenced to jail in Georgia after leading a sit-in. After King's release the following day, African Americans clearly identified with the young senator, who won the election with a margin of little more than 100,000 popular votes.

African Americans had high expectations that the new president would be more receptive and concerned about racial discrimination in America. In his first few months in office President Kennedy appointed more than fifty African Americans to important positions. Yet he also named some white supremacists to the federal bench. During the campaign he stated that federal housing discrimination could be ended "with the stroke of a pen," but he did not take that step until November 1962. The president was also very concerned about the mounting violence occasioned by the civil rights movement. His brother Robert, the newly appointed U.S. attorney general, met with student leaders in June 1961 and urged them to redirect their energies to voter registration projects and lessen their concentration on direct-action activities.

Although the newly elected president and his younger brother were worried about the strategies of various civil rights organizations, they decided to use direct action to take on the all-white Washington Redskins. Owner George Preston Marshall was vehemently against integrating his team, which finished the 1960 season with one win, nine losses, and one tie. This earned the Redskins the number-one overall pick, which they used on Wake Forest University quarterback Norm Snead. They also selected nineteen other white players during the draft. This was the last straw—Marshall's racism had become a public embarrassment. Stewart Udall, the new secretary of the interior, was made aware by department lawyers that the city's new stadium, slated to open in October 1961, was built on federal land. It was part of the National Capital Parks System, which, as with all government buildings, had clear rules forbidding discrimination in hiring. Udall checked with Robert Kennedy, who said, "Go get him! Make him do it!" Udall called a press conference and sent a warning letter to Marshall stating that as the "residential landlord" of the parks area, the Interior Department could deny use of the stadium to any party practicing discriminatory hiring practices. NFL commissioner Pete Rozelle privately prodded Marshall as well, and he finally capitulated in late August by agreeing to bring on black players in 1962 in exchange for use of the stadium beginning in 1961. So while the NFL was trying to fully integrate its league, the AFL was ready to begin its second season as a fully integrated operation.[23]

Although the NFL felt that its brand of football was superior to that played in the AFL, its commissioner clearly recognized that the policy of sharing television revenue in the new league was a model worth borrowing. In 1960 CBS held the contracts for nine of the twelve NFL teams, each individually negotiated, ranging from a high of $175,000 for the New York Giants down to $75,000 for the Green Bay Packers. NBC had a separate deal with the Baltimore Colts and Pittsburgh Steelers which gave them the rights to broadcast one national game a week. The Cleveland Browns had their own far-flung independent network, sponsored by Carling Beer, which stretched from Texas to the East Coast and competed with CBS in numerous markets. In comparison, the AFL's deal with ABC was for five years and produced roughly $400,000 for each team in the first year. Bill MacPhail, who was in charge of sports programming at CBS, did not want two or three games broadcast at the same time, since this would dilute the audience and frustrate advertisers. He made an informal presentation to NFL owners, offering to pay $3 million a year for the exclusive rights to the league's regular-season broadcasts, to be divided by the NFL in any way it saw fit. It took Commissioner Rozelle until January 1961 to persuade the teams to allow him to negotiate a contract on behalf of the entire league.[24]

On April 26, 1961, the NFL announced an agreement with CBS that would pay the league $4,650,000 a year for the rights to games in 1961 and 1962. The fourteen teams would share equally in the proceeds, which averaged $332,000 a year. League games played away from home by each team would be telecast back to the home area. CBS got the rights to playoff games, but the championship games between division winners had already been sold to NBC under a two-year agreement for $615,000 per year. Rozelle also indicated that on-field fights between players would be shown from a distance, with no close-ups. "That's the wrong kind of example for youngsters," he proclaimed. This was clearly in reference to the way AFL games were being broadcast, which included close-ups of on-field fights and confrontations on team sidelines. Initially the agreement with CBS was rejected as a violation of antitrust law by U.S. District Court Judge Allan K. Grim. But Baltimore Colts owner Carroll Rosenbloom used his close relationship with the Kennedy family to get Congress to grant an antitrust exemption for the NFL. Subsequently, on September 30, 1961, President Kennedy signed the Sports Broadcasting bill into law, giving pro football an exemption from antitrust statutes. On January 10, 1962, CBS signed the first national TV contract with the NFL at the same terms that had been agreed on a year earlier—$4,650,000 per season for two years.[25]

The AFL's second season began with the influx of new college players along with a player who had played out his option in the NFL. Willard Dewveall, an offensive end with the Chicago Bears, played through 1960 without signing a new contract and agreed to terms with the Houston Oilers for the 1961 season. This made him the first player to jump to the AFL from the active ranks of the NFL. Also during this second season, owners realized that fan support was their biggest challenge, and in 1961 they came up with a creative innovation. League owners decided to schedule an All-Star Game after the season to showcase the AFL's talent. Many NFL supporters snickered at the idea of such a contest, but it provided one more television date for the league to win new fans.[26]

The Oilers and Chargers were clearly the best two teams once again in 1961. Houston finished with a record of 10–3–1 while San Diego went 12–2. The Chargers added two rookie African American players who instantly improved the team's defense. Ernie Ladd was a 6'9", 317-pound tackle from Grambling State University who was joined on the defensive line by 6'5", 262-pound end Earl "Tree" Faison from Indiana University. They helped the Chargers' defense give up the fewest total yards in the AFL while also allowing the fewest passing yards and setting a pro football record with forty-nine interceptions. The Oilers were a stark contrast to the defensive-oriented Chargers, scoring 513 points on the season, which set a pro football record. Once again they met to decide the AFL Championship, this time in San Diego on Christmas Eve.[27]

The 29,556 fans who filled Balboa Stadium and those watching on television at home anticipated a high-scoring game. Instead, fans and viewers watched the defenses for both teams control the game. Played on a sunny 59-degree day, the game settled into a bruising defensive battle, and some thirteen players had to be helped off the field. The only score of the first half was a 46-yard field goal by George Blanda late in the second quarter. In the third quarter the Oilers increased their lead to 10–0 when Blanda threw a touchdown pass to Billy Cannon. The Chargers got a field goal early in the fourth quarter, but on their final drive Oilers safety Julian "Sus" Spence intercepted a pass that sealed the win for Houston. The 5'9" Spence was one of three African American players on the 1961 Oilers, where he was joined by receiver John White and offensive lineman Bob Kelly. Spence came into the NFL out of tiny Huston-Tillotson in 1956, when he played for the Chicago Cardinals; he played for the San Francisco 49ers in 1957 before joining the Oilers in 1960. In mid-September the Oilers had released Spence, and now his heroic interception brought not only personal redemption but also the 1961 AFL Championship to Houston.[28]

An argument can be made that this was one of the most physically punishing football games ever played. The gridiron casualties mounted with each change of possession. Brutal tackles and vicious blocks rendered a half-dozen players unconscious. Two players sustained knee injuries requiring surgery. A total of nineteen teeth were knocked out. A dozen players were assisted off the field, with the casualties evenly divided between the teams. Interviewed years later about the game, Oilers cornerback Tony Banfield, an All-AFL selection from 1961 to 1963, said, "It was a grudge match from the previous season. The cool climate kept guys fresh and as a result people were connecting at high velocity. The hitting was fierce. More guys were seriously hurt in that game than in any other I could ever remember." At times, sideline scenes resembled the triage area of a MASH unit. Dr. James Whitehurst, the Oilers' team physician, had worked high school, college, and pro games for over a decade: "I never witnessed a more brutal or punishing game than that one," he recalled. Millions of television viewers enjoyed this grueling struggle, which enhanced the American Football League's credibility. It was certainly a more thrilling spectacle than that year's NFL Championship game, in which the Green Bay Packers blanked the New York Giants 37–0.[29]

Very few people felt that the AFL Champion Oilers could compete with the NFL's finest team, and this was arguably true. The Green Bay Packers won their fourth NFL Championship in 1961, led by head coach Vince Lombardi, who took over the team in 1959. Lombardi's teams ran the ball efficiently, tackled well on defense, and committed very few turnovers. After finishing 11–3 and winning the Western Conference, the

Packers annihilated the New York Giants in the championship game. AFL owners recognized that the signing of college players was crucial in helping to change the competitive landscape in professional football and, more importantly, in attracting fans to games. The urgency to sign top college players was felt more in the upstart AFL than the NFL, and in late 1961 the new league was embarrassed by its mishandling of its draft.

In order to protect their athletes from overzealous general managers, universities obtained an agreement that neither league would hold its draft before December 2, a full month before the bowl games. On November 19 the *Dallas Morning News* revealed that the AFL had already conducted a secret telephone draft of college seniors. Two days later NFL commissioner Pete Rozelle unleased a blast of righteous indignation. He declared that the AFL "has brought discredit upon professional football as a whole in the eyes of the colleges and the public. The National Football League joins college leaders, who are shocked by the AFL sneak draft." Rozelle hinted that the AFL's action was precipitated by desperation, and speculated that they might soon begin drafting sophomores and juniors. AFL commissioner Joe Foss was greatly embarrassed and claimed not to have known of the entire proceeding, which was "organized and conducted by the owners without the participation of the league office." Titans owner Harry Wismer publicly contradicted Foss by stating, "If he didn't know about it then he is a very poor commissioner. I told Milt [Woodard, the assistant commissioner] we were happy about our draft selections, and he told me not to say it too loud because Foss doesn't want people to know what we're doing."[30]

Foss tried to take the high road and minimize the damage, pledging not to recognize any contract signed before the official draft. However, he was put in a more compromised position when Wismer revealed the Titans' choices. Although the selections were ostensibly secret, Wismer stated that his first pick was halfback Ernie Davis of Syracuse University, who had broken most of Jim Brown's rushing records. Several weeks later Davis would become the first African American player to win the Heisman Trophy, and he was the star Wismer felt his team desperately needed to compete with the Giants and draw spectators to the Polo Grounds. But three days later Foss issued a memo to the presidents and general managers of the AFL teams concerning the cancelation of what was termed the "negotiation list." Foss stated that "after investigating and considering more fully the various ramifications of the negotiation poll conducted secretly by presidents of the AFL without my knowledge I feel it has the aspects of a premature draft and I hereby declare it null and void." Foss went on to say that only the draft on December 2 conducted by the commissioner would be the authentic and official one. Wismer was livid and charged that Houston owner Bud Adams had organized the draft but that Foss had known all along what was happening. Ralph Wilson, owner of the Bills, came to Foss's defense, saying that he, Hunt, and Adams had planned the draft without the commissioner's knowledge.[31]

The official draft was held on December 2; the Titans, selecting in the fifth position, were still hoping to secure the rights to Davis. Wismer said he was prepared to offer the Syracuse halfback $100,000 for three years plus a $15,000 bonus. "If anybody wants to top that," he added, "I'll top what they want to offer." How Wismer was going to come up with such a large amount of money when he could barely meet his team's weekly payroll demands was open for debate. The Raiders, with the worst record in the league, had the first choice and selected quarterback Roman Gabriel of North Carolina State University. Denver next picked tackle Merlin Olsen of Utah State University. With the third pick Dallas selected halfback Ronnie Bull of Baylor, leaving only the Buffalo Bills between Wismer and Davis. Ralph Wilson thwarted Wismer's ambitions by selecting Davis with the fourth pick. It took forty-five minutes for the Titans to make the next pick, and they finally selected quarterback Sandy Stephens of the University of Minnesota. Davis was also selected by the Washington Redskins on December 4 during the NFL's draft, as a result of the pressure mounted by Secretary of the Interior Stewart Udall, who had warned Redskins owner George Preston Marshall to integrate his team in order to have access to the newly built stadium in Washington, D.C.[32]

Davis, an economics major, said during an interview that he was just looking for the best deal, including an off-season job to prepare him for a career after football. He had no particular preference for any team and indicated that Marshall's well-known racial attitudes would not prevent him from signing with the Redskins. In mid-December, Marshall traded Davis's rights to the Cleveland Browns. Cleveland wanted Davis to join the league's leading rusher, Jim Brown, in their backfield, and in exchange the Redskins received two black players: Bobby Mitchell, an established running back, and Leroy Jackson, a running back from Western Illinois University who was picked in the first round by the Browns. Wismer hoped to broker a trade for Davis with Buffalo, but those hopes were dashed when Cleveland signed Davis to a three-year contract valued at $65,000 plus a $15,000 bonus. Interviewed in late December, Bills general manager Dick Gallagher reported that the team had offered Davis a three-year deal worth well over $100,000. If this was accurate, then clearly this economics major did not base his decision solely on money. Browns owner Art Modell was also interviewed, and his comments imply that the Bills' offer was more than Cleveland's: "It's certainly gratifying to know that young athletes like Davis consider their long range future rather than immediate financial gain." Sadly, Davis, the object of such a bitter struggle, never played a game for the Browns or any other pro team. In July 1962 he was diagnosed with leukemia, and he died on May 18, 1963, at age twenty-three. On the eve of the AFL's third season, the internal struggle over Davis and subsequent loss to the NFL of his potential ability indicated that the young league had much work to do before it could legitimately challenge the established NFL.[33]

"WE WILL KICK
TO THE CLOCK"

The AFL's third season began with much optimism, particularly from ABC television. On August 1, 1962, the network issued a press release for prospective sponsors in which it stated that thirty-seven regular-season games would be telecast on eighteen dates in addition to the championship game. ABC added that the eighteen dates represented an increase of two from the 1961 season, and that those additional dates would be Saturday afternoons in December along with fifteen Sunday afternoons and Thanksgiving Day. The first televised game was set for Sunday, September 9, when the Titans traveled to Oakland to take on the Raiders, followed by the AFL Champion Oilers taking on the Bills in Buffalo. With the help of television the AFL during this third season continued to establish itself among fans all across America. The Oilers and Texans played the first double-overtime game in pro football to decide the AFL Championship, capturing a large television audience. Although his team would be crowned champions after winning this dramatic game, Lamar Hunt realized that he could no longer compete with the Dallas Cowboys, and for the greater good of the league he moved his AFL Champion Texans to Kansas City. And it was during this season that a dominant African American player entered the AFL and quickly drew comparisons to Jim Brown because of his running style. Cookie Gilchrist set several records on the field, and like Brown, he was seen as a challenge off it.[1]

The Bills went 7–6–1 in 1962, winning one more game than the previous season, but they laid a foundation for the future with the acquisition of two key players who brought a championship to the city of Buffalo. On August 4 the Bills signed fullback Cookie Gilchrist, formerly with the Toronto Argonauts of the CFL, to a free agent contract. Gilchrist was a black player with a tremendous amount of pride and a reputation for being contentious. He also challenged the societal taboo of interracial relationships early in his career when as a high school star he was placed in jail for dating Betty Ann Richards, who was white. Gilchrist never played college football. As an eighteen-year-old junior at Har-Brack High School in Breckenridge, Pennsylvania, Gilchrist was projected as one of the top college prospects in the country. Because he was too old to play football his senior year, he dropped out of high school and enrolled in Cheshire Academy to improve his grades for Michigan State University. But when the Cleveland Browns offered him a contract for $5,500, Gilchrist opted to head to Cleveland. "That money was more than my father made in a year. The Browns teased me when I joined the club. They told me they had seen all-Army, all-pro, and all-world players, but this was the first time they had seen all-schoolyard."[2]

According to Gilchrist in his autobiography written with Chris Garbarino, what Paul Brown did was unethical and cost him any opportunity to go to college. Brown knew full well that the NFL had a rule stipulating that players could not be signed until their college class had graduated. Art Rooney, owner of the Pittsburgh Steelers, filed a grievance with NFL commissioner Bert Bell, who voided the contract with the Browns. By signing a professional contract, Gilchrist was now unable to qualify for college scholarships, so he could not be classified as a student athlete by the NCAA. Gilchrist decided that he would not accept the Browns' offer because, as he said, "they never paid me one cent of the promised $5,500 and they also destroyed my chance to get my college education. Coach Brown was not really looking for me to get more seasoning in Canada; this would just be his way to keep me under his control until I became old enough to play in the NFL. I decided to pursue football in Canada, but on my own terms, with no help from Coach Brown or his associates." Gilchrist became a star, first playing for Ontario-based Sarnia in 1954 and then Kitchener, and in 1956 he joined the Hamilton Tiger-Cats, whom he led to the Grey Cup in 1957. After Hamilton, Gilchrist migrated to Regina, Saskatchewan, and finally to the Toronto Argonauts, where he was eventually suspended for breaking curfew. His career in Canada came to an end after near-fights with coaches, protracted holdouts, and refusal to adhere to team curfews.[3]

While playing in Canada, Gilchrist married a white Canadian named Gwen, whom he met in Hamilton, and by 1962 they had two children. At the same time as Gilchrist was being placed on waivers by Toronto and not being claimed by a single CFL team, the Los Angeles Rams were trying to find a replacement for their leading rusher, Ollie Matson, who they felt was coming to the end of his career. According to Gilchrist, once the Rams discovered that he was married to a white woman, the team's management decided not to pursue his services, but the Buffalo Bills needed a running back and needed to put a winning product on the field if they hoped to change their financial future. Harvey Johnson, the Bills' director of player personnel, in the spring of 1962 signed Gilchrist to a $20,000 contract with a $5,000 signing bonus. Gilchrist felt the Bills badly needed to turn their franchise around and "the issue of whom I was married to, became a non-factor. What mattered to the Bills was how well I played football and whether I could help the franchise survive." At 6'3" and 251 pounds, with a 52-inch chest and a 31-inch waist, Gilchrist had the physique of a bodybuilder and a bruising running style that quickly made him the AFL's equivalent to Jim Brown. His debut with the Bills in an August exhibition game against the Titans was remembered more for what he did in the locker room than on the field. Guard George Flint recalled, "At halftime, Cookie stripped down and took a shower, we all wondered what the hell he was doing." Coach Saban panicked and went around to several players asking whether he was quitting. But "Cookie had this routine—he would change his T-shirt, his jock and his socks at halftime of every game. Sometimes he would shower too. He would change his stuff and make it dry." Added Flint, "He just wanted to be fresh for the second half."[4]

Although Gilchrist helped the Bills' running game, they started the season 0–5 largely because of inconsistent quarterback play. Starting quarterback Al Dorow was replaced by backup Warren Rabb in game four, but an injury in San Diego changed the fortunes of the Bills at this most important position. On September 16, Jack Kemp, the starting quarterback for the Chargers, injured the middle finger on his throwing hand in a game against the Titans. "I threw a pass to Lance Alworth, who scored a touchdown, but I hit the helmet of a blitzing linebacker and dislocated my right middle finger, but I stayed in the game because I didn't want John Hadl to play." The Chargers placed Kemp on the waiver list on Friday the 21st in order to make space for another player for their upcoming game and planned to recall him after the game. The Bills, Broncos, and Patriots all claimed Kemp, and Coach Sid Gillman of the Chargers initiated a protest, claiming he made a mistake and wanted to recall Kemp.

Commissioner Foss upheld the Bills' claim, and on September 25, after they paid the $100 waiver fee, the rights to Jack Kemp belonged to the Bills. Although he now had a new team, Kemp did not want to relocate to Buffalo and threatened not to report unless he had a no-cut contract, which owner Ralph Wilson refused to provide. Kemp eventually relented and joined the team on October 7. In three games with the Bills, Kemp threw five touchdowns and six interceptions, but he was a much better passer than Dorow or Rabb. Nevertheless, it was clearly the running ability of Gilchrist that fueled any success the 1962 Bills had. He was named co-AFL-MVP after becoming the first player to rush for over 1,000 yards (1,096) in a season. He also set the record for touchdowns with thirteen, while averaging 5.1 yards per carry.[5]

As Gilchrist and Kemp fueled optimism for fans in Buffalo, for fans following the other team in New York there was nothing but pessimism. The Titans finished the season with a record of 5–9, but their problems on the field paled in comparison to what was going on off the field. Harry Wismer was scrambling to raise enough cash to start the year for what he believed would be his final season in the Polo Grounds. He managed to get a $200,000 loan from Howard McCullough, sales manager for Brunswick Corporation, who received an assignment of the Titans' share of proceeds from the league's ABC television contract. By November that money was gone, and Wismer, who owned 80 percent of the team's stock, was asking for $1.25 million for half ownership as players' checks bounced regularly. On November 8 the commissioner's office took over the team's payroll and management by assessing the other seven teams $40,000, which was loaned to the Titans. Wismer was given an ultimatum by Commissioner Foss to sell the team quickly, which was going to be difficult considering his obligations were just over $2 million. On February 6, 1963, the Titans of New York filed for bankruptcy protection. The list of creditors in the bankruptcy court's docket stretched twenty-six pages with debts large and small; it included 227 claims that involved everyone from the taxman to the barman. The court ruled that Foss was free to find a buyer for the franchise, and on March 28 the sale was consummated to Sonny Werblin, president of Music Corporation of America. Leon Hess, Phil Iselin, Donald Lillis, and Townsend Martin were also investors and called themselves the Gotham Football Club, Inc. Werblin and his investors bought the Titans for $1 million; at the closing Wismer was given a check for $1 million, which he promptly endorsed and handed over to the bankruptcy trustee.[6]

Wismer had reached out to Lamar Hunt and Bud Adams for loans, but they both refused, arguably because they realized that the Titans needed an owner with more capital. Of course for Hunt, money was not a problem, but he badly wanted his team to be more successful on the field, and they became so when they took control of the Western Division by going 11–3, putting them in the championship game for the first time. The Texans had not been able to win more than eight games during the two previous seasons, but the acquisition of quarterback Len Dawson immediately changed the team's fortunes. Dawson had played for Coach Hank Stram at Purdue; in 1957 he was drafted with the first overall pick by the Pittsburgh Steelers, where he spent three years backing up Bobby Layne. Then he was traded to the Browns, spending two years as their backup. After the 1961 season Paul Brown released him, at Dawson's request, and no NFL team claimed him. He signed with the Texans and with Stram's patience and coaching eventually regained his confidence and pinpoint passing ability. Stram restored Dawson's belief in himself, and by the time the Texans began the season, Dawson had supplanted Cotton Davidson as the team's starter. Dawson set a new league record by completing 60.9 percent of his passes, while throwing for 2,759 yards and twenty-nine touchdowns. He was named co-AFL-MVP with Cookie Gilchrist; more importantly, however, he became the Texans' team leader.[7]

With the emergence of Dawson and the running of Abner Haynes, the Texans averaged nearly 28 points a game and started the season 6–1. Unfortunately, because the Cowboys caused a split in the Dallas fan base, the Texans were averaging only 10,100 fans per game. Hunt and GM Jack Steadman began to discuss cities in which they could relocate, and during the fall the initial choice was New Orleans. Hunt had engaged in preliminary talks with a well-connected insurance salesman named David Dixon, who wanted 25 percent of the team in exchange for arranging access to a stadium. Dixon indicated that he could possibly get access to Tulane Stadium, but he was unable to get provisional approval. Segregation in New Orleans was also being criticized by local African American leaders, who spoke out when black fans were relegated to one section in City Park Stadium during an exhibition game between the Oilers and Patriots. These factors weighed heavily on Hunt as he spent most of the season agonizing over where to move his young, dominating team. This changed dramatically on Christmas Eve morning, when Hunt arrived at his office and found a message on his desk. It was classified as confidential and extremely urgent: "Please call mayor H. Roe Bartle in Kansas City."[8]

As the Texans prepared to meet the Oilers for the championship, the Raiders were in the process of changing coaches. After three seasons the Raiders had an AFL record of 9–33 and had won only three of their last thirty-eight games. But owners Wayne Valley and Ed McGah had a plan to turn the team around, and it centered on recruiting a young assistant coach from the San Diego Chargers. On January 18, 1963, thirty-three-year-old Al Davis became head coach and general manager of the Oakland Raiders. Few recognized it at the time, but the future of the Raiders—and pro football—was heading in a new direction.[9]

Two final issues were addressed in early December. The first was a proposal from the Denver Broncos to change the penalty for an offensive lineman downfield on a pass play from fifteen yards and loss of down to fifteen yards without loss of down; Denver felt the rule was too punitive to the offense. The proposal was approved and adopted for the 1963 season. Also, Milt Woodard had early returns on television revenue from ABC, and he informed owners that the total net income for seventeen telecasts that season was $1,599,700. Woodard estimated that each club would receive $188,200 in income and that the championship game would generate $94,000 for the league.[10]

For the AFL, the 1962 championship game provided exposure that could not be quantified by television revenue. The game between the Houston Oilers and Dallas Texans was a watershed moment for the upstart league and professional football, all because of a confluence of well-timed events. The game was scheduled to be played at the site of the Eastern Conference champion, which meant that Houston's cozy Jeppesen Stadium would be packed. The AFL had successfully gambled that the game would not be challenged by a divisional playoff in the NFL (the NFL allowed for a week in the schedule between the end of the season and the championship game to make room for any tie-breaking playoffs), so there were no other pro football games being played that weekend. For writers covering the title game, there was a bonus, the fourth annual Bluebonnet Bowl, played in Houston's Rice Stadium the day before, featuring Missouri against Georgia Tech. This matchup brought in more writers from the Midwest and Southeast, who could piggyback the two games in a single weekend. Finally the weather up and down the East Coast was bad, so many people were at home on December 23, 1962, but the television networks were mainly showing holiday-themed programs. So for the most part the choice was between watching the Oilers and Texans or watching the NBC Opera presentation of Menotti's *Amahl and the Night Visitors, Ted Mack's Amateur Hour,* reruns of *Ozzie and Harriet,* and game shows.[11]

Houston was favored by almost a touchdown when the division winners met at Jeppesen Stadium beneath an ominous cloud cover. The showdown battle pitted teams that were evenly matched. Each had regular-season records of eleven wins and three losses. Dallas had beaten Houston 31–7 in Houston, but the Oilers won 14–6 just one week later in Dallas. The Texans' offense during the season featured one wide receiver, Chris Burford, and his twelve touchdown catches. But Burford was hurt late in the season and was out for the game, so Hank Stram decided to move versatile running back Abner Haynes out to flanker. Behind Dawson at quarterback he inserted Jack Spikes and Curtis McClinton, two full-backs. The visitors stunned the Houston crowd by racing out to a 17–0 lead at the half with Stram's makeshift offense working like a charm. Tommy Brooker got the scoring started by kicking a 16-yard field goal in the first quarter. In the second quarter Spikes rambled 33 yards, setting up a catch by Haynes near the sideline and allowing him to run untouched for a 28-yard touchdown. With the quarter coming to an end, Haynes scored his second touchdown on a 2-yard rush heading into halftime.[12]

The weather changed as the third quarter began: it became colder and the wind was stronger, blowing up to twenty-five miles an hour. Veteran quarterback George Blanda had been cold in the first half as well, throwing two interceptions, including one at the Texans' 9-yard line. After halftime he came out more focused, and receiver Willard Dewveall decided to help Blanda concentrate by expressing his opinion in language that his quarterback could fully appreciate. Dewveall grabbed Blanda's jersey and said, "Listen you SOB, you better throw to me this half. I've been wide open all day." It worked. Early in the third quarter Blanda hit Dewveall with a 15-yard touchdown. The Oilers' defense also figured out what the Texans were doing and shut down their offense with several sacks of Dawson. But still trying to force passes to covered receivers, Blanda threw his third interception of the day when the Texans' Johnny Robinson picked off a pass in the end zone at the end of the third quarter. In the fourth quarter Blanda kicked a 31-yard field goal, and with 5:58 left, Charley Tolar tied the score on a 1-yard run. The overflow home crowd sensed the happy comple-tion of a magnificent comeback and a third straight Oilers championship when Houston reached the Dallas 35 with time running out. Blanda lined up at the Texan 41-yard line with less than three minutes left for what many thought would be the game-winning field goal. As the kick lifted off his toe, all-league middle linebacker Sherrill Headrick found a gap in the Houston line and got a hand on the ball, tipping it away. As regulation play ended, the two teams prepared to make history by playing only the second championship sudden-death overtime period in pro football history.[13]

Houston's captains, Al Jamison and Ed Husmann, were waiting at midfield when referee Red Bourne was ready to conduct the overtime coin toss. ABC's sideline reporter for the telecast, Jack Buck, was also there with mike in hand to help bring the proceedings to the television audience. Abner Haynes was the first Dallas captain to reach midfield, well before E. J. Holub, and they had been given instructions from Stram that if they won the toss, he wanted to kick. Stram had decided that the wind was so strong that it would affect not only punting but the kickoff game as well. He reasoned that if Houston were to kick off, they would have the wind and Blanda would likely kick the ball out of the end zone for a touchback, thus giving Dallas the ball on its own 20. The Texans had a weak kicking game, and if they were forced to punt a poor kick into the wind, they might give the Oilers great field position for a game-winning field goal. The Texans, as the visiting team, made the call, and Bourne explained that if no one scored after fifteen minutes the teams would continue playing until someone scored. He then directed his attention toward the Dallas captains, and as he made the coin toss, he told them to "call it." Standing next to Buck, Haynes called "Heads!" The coin came up heads, and Bourne said, "You have the choice of receiving or kicking." Haynes leaned into Buck's microphone and said, "We will kick to the clock." The clock was at the north end of the field, the same direction the wind was coming in from. With his answer Haynes had given the ball and the wind to the Oilers; he should have elected instead to defend the goal in front of the clock, which would have given the Texans the favorable wind position. Houston then most likely would have elected to receive, and Stram's desires would have been fulfilled.[14]

According to Stram, this historic mix-up happened because "the official never gave Abner all the choices. That's what screwed it all up. The normal procedure is to ask if you want to kick, receive, or defend the goal. But the official asked what are you going to do, kick or receive? Poor Abner's been taking the heat all these years, but that's really what took place." Although defended by his coach, Haynes took responsibility for what he said: "I was thinking running game. The field was slanted. So when I said kick to the clock, I was simply pointing downhill. It was a stupid statement because you're supposed to be checking the wind. I didn't want to give them the wind. That was my mistake." Luckily for the Texans, their defense made several big plays in overtime, including when Johnny Robinson picked off Blanda around midfield for his second interception of the game and the fourth for the Oilers veteran quarterback. Houston got the ball back, and Blanda meticulously drove the Oilers to the Dallas 36, where they could almost taste the victory champagne. But Blanda decided to try to get one more first down. On second down from the 35 he looked for Charley Hennigan, but the ball fluttered in the wind and was intercepted by defensive end Bill Hull, who dropped into coverage and returned Blanda's fifth pick of the day to midfield. Thus the first overtime ended with the Texans at the Houston 48, and now Hunt's team had the ball and the wind to their backs.[15]

Dawson brought the Texans to the Houston 18, where Dallas prepared to kick the winning field goal from the 25-yard line. Kicker Tommy Brooker remembered, "It was very quiet in the huddle, sort of like you were in church. As Lenny Dawson was cleaning one of my cleats, I was leaning on Curtis McClinton our fullback, one of the rookies we had. He was hardly even taking a breath, but I could feel his eyes on me. To me, it was just another play in the game 'cause I had been playing end. I told them not to worry. I think E. J. Holub was my snapper, he got the ball back real fast. The objective is to kick in 1.3 or 1.4 seconds. Lenny held the ball and everything looked like it went pretty smooth." With Brooker's successful kick, pro football's longest game was over, 77 minutes and 54 seconds after it had begun. Fans who had been crowding the end zones poured onto the field. Brooker was carried off the field on the shoulders of his teammates. "I've never seen a team fight for a win like this one did today," said a proud, champagne-drenched Stram in the locker room. "None of us will ever forget it." Of course for Abner Haynes the win meant more to him than to any other player on the Texans team: "My mother and dad were in tears the way the TV guys had dogged me and how stupid I was. If the Oilers had taken the kick and scored, I'd have to leave the country." The game became an instant classic, watched by 56 million Americans on ABC. In the *Washington Post*, columnist Shirley Povich wrote, "The AFL was born at the age of three, so magnificent was this game."[16]

Lamar Hunt was very proud of his team. He gave each player a gold championship ring with the player's name engraved on the side, along with the score of the game, the date, and playing time. Hunt was determined to provide his players with not only beautiful rings but also a new city that would embrace his football team with enough fans to allow it to survive financially. On December 26, 1962, he flew to Kansas City, and after checking into the Muchlebach Hotel, he was picked up by Mayor Bartle's blue limousine. When Hunt stepped inside the vehicle, the 320-pound cigar-smoking mayor shook his hand and welcomed him to the city. Bartle and Hunt had several highly secretive meetings until the major points of a deal were worked out. Kansas City offered the Texans a seven-year lease at Municipal Stadium for the rental fee of $1 per year for the first two seasons. (The Texans had been paying $10,000 per game to rent the Cotton Bowl.) After two years the city would get 5 percent of gross receipts after ticket sales topped $1,100,000, but if they did not reach that mark, the $1-per-year lease rate would remain in place. The team and the city would share equally in profits from concessions. The city also agreed to install 3,000 more permanent seats—and the option of 11,000 more temporary seats in the stadium—as well as to construct an office building and practice field for the team. A good negotiator, Hunt had GM Jack Steadman contact the Cowboys' Tex Schramm to see if they would be willing to buy the temporary locker facility on the team's practice field. The Cowboys not only bought the facility but also quietly agreed to pay for the Texans' expenses to move out of town.[17]

On February 8, Lamar Hunt called a press conference in Kansas City, announcing that he had entered an agreement with the city to move the franchise, provided the city could sell 25,000 season tickets by May 15. Hunt kept his word even though Kansas City sold only 15,182 season tickets by May 15, and one week later it was made official that the Texans were headed north. Hunt had to change the team name, and a team-sponsored contest received 4,866 entries, including the "Royals," "Monarchs," "Meat Packers," "Steers," and "Mavericks." As a way of paying homage to the area's Native American heritage, Hunt announced on May 26 that the team's new name would be the "Chiefs."[18]

Three weeks before Lamar Hunt began to make plans to move his team to Kansas City, he and his fellow owners conducted the AFL's draft. The league held its annual draft on December 3, 1962, and Hunt's Texans drafted first as a result of trading quarterback Cotton Davidson to the Raiders for their first-round pick. They selected Junious "Buck" Buchanan, Grambling State University's giant defensive tackle, making him the first African American number-one draft choice in professional football. Buchanan was not chosen by an NFL team until the nineteenth round, when the New York Giants selected him with the 265th pick. Buchanan, 6'7" and weighing 287 pounds, was a standout football and basketball player who grew up in Birmingham, Alabama, where he attended Parker High School. Several other outstanding players from historically black schools were selected after Buchanan. Receiver Willie Richardson from Jackson State University was picked in the third round by the Titans, and receiver Homer Jones from Texas Southern University was chosen in the fifth round by Houston. Running back Hewritt Dixon of Florida A&M University was selected in the eighth round by Denver; Stone Johnson, a halfback from Grambling, was chosen in the fourteenth round by the

Texans; and the Broncos selected halfback Bob Paremore in the seventeenth round from Florida A&M. The last two players drafted from historically black schools were tackle Bob Burton from Grambling by Houston in the twenty-fourth round and halfback Jim Tullis from Florida A&M by Boston in the twenty-sixth round. Although the NFL doubled the number of black players drafted from black schools—their teams chose sixteen players, including Buchanan, Paremore, Richardson, and Hewritt—NFL teams did not place the same value on these players: Paremore was the first to be drafted, and he was not chosen until the sixth round by the St. Louis Cardinals. Only once since the NFL draft began in 1936 has a player from a historically black school been drafted with the first overall selection, and that was defensive end Ed "Too Tall" Jones from Tennessee State University in 1974 by the Dallas Cowboys.[19]

For African Americans living in the South, historically black schools were the only option for attaining a higher education until the *Brown* decision in 1954. Arguably no other institution of higher education better symbolized the region's commitment to segregation than the University of Mississippi. James Meredith integrated the university in October 1962 after he was provided legal support from the NAACP. This was facilitated by Medgar Evers, the organization's first full-time field secretary, who was appointed in December 1954 after he applied and was denied admission to the university's law school. Ironically the University of Mississippi's last great football team was its 1962 team, which went undefeated and untied. Although undefeated, the University of Mississippi was still ranked behind the University of Wisconsin, which had one loss and played undefeated University of Southern California for the national championship. As champions of the Southeastern Conference (SEC), the University of Mississippi headed to the Sugar Bowl, where it defeated the University of Arkansas 17–13. The opportunity to play for the national title could not happen because of Mississippi's staunch commitment to segregation—both USC and Wisconsin had African American players. USC played Wisconsin in the Rose Bowl, where the Trojans defeated the Badgers 42–37. During this time final polls were voted on before bowl games, and in both the AP and UPI, USC was number one, followed by Wisconsin and then Mississippi. When Meredith decided to challenge the University of Mississippi, no other SEC member more fully embodied the cultural heritage of the Old South. Through extensive use of such evocative symbols as the song "Dixie," the Confederate battle flag, the mascot "Colonel Rebel," and the team nickname of Rebels, the university created a remarkable fusion of school traditions and Deep South imagery. Even the school's informal name of Ole Miss, a term that referred to the mistress of a plantation, recalled the antebellum era.[20]

With the help of Evers and counsel from the NAACP's legal defense team, headed by Constance Baker Motley and Derrick Bell, Meredith was forcibly integrated into the University of Mississippi. This did not happen without vicious resistance, however. On Saturday, September 29, just before Meredith's impending registration, Governor Ross Barnett delivered an emotional address at halftime of the Mississippi-Kentucky football game in Jackson. Surrounded by a sea of Confederate flags, Barnett raised a clenched fist and proclaimed, "I love Mississippi! I love her people! I love her customs! I love and respect our heritage!" On Sunday evening, after federal marshals escorted Meredith to campus, a full-fledged riot broke out, led by students and people from surrounding southern communities. President Kennedy had to use federal troops to restore order on the campus, but during the riot two people were killed and some one hundred more were wounded or injured. This did not stop Meredith from registering on October 1 and attending his first class, in American history. Football seemed to help calm down the university's students and its supporters. Although the federal government had forced the university to accept integration in the classroom, the football field remained a protected space where white Mississippians could demonstrate their athletic prowess and celebrate cultural pride. Football thus became an important symbol of an unchanging white Mississippi and its southern white heritage.[21]

Interest in the AFL was on the rise in 1963. Fan attendance at AFL stadiums was improving: in 1960 the league's average attendance was 16,538, and in 1962 it was 20,487. The NFL averaged 40,106 fans in 1960 and 40,851 per game in 1962, but thanks to the NFL's "blackout" rule, which prohibited games from being televised in host NFL cities, the AFL was gaining much-needed TV exposure. According to announcer Curt Gowdy, who broadcast AFL games for ABC beginning in 1962, "The NFL had a blackout routine where, if the New York Giants were at home, there were no games on TV in that area. They opened the door for us. On Sundays, we were the only pro football game on TV in those areas where NFL teams were playing at home." This greatly helped ratings for AFL games, along with the exciting finish of the 1962 championship game, which caused people to talk about the new league. The NFL rescinded its blackout rule after the 1962 season, but by then the popularity of the AFL was growing each day. ABC picked up the option for the 1963 season, which stipulated that if it could get 100 percent sponsorship, each AFL team would receive $240,140. If sponsorship reached 75 percent, teams would receive $206,000. ABC estimated that AFL teams would probably receive around $225,000 for the 1963 season. Feeling that exposure from television was fueling fan interest, AFL owners decided that the league offices needed to be relocated to a city that could provide better exposure as well. In May the AFL offices were moved from Dallas to 609 Fifth Avenue in New York, at the KLM building. The NFL had won the battle over Dallas, pushing both the Texans and the league offices out of the city, but the war between these two entities of pro football was far from over.[22]

In a series of memos sent to potential sponsors beginning on June 18, 1963, Thomas Moore, president of ABC, listed those sponsors that had already bought television time, including the Lincoln-Mercury division of Ford, the Goodyear Tire and Rubber Company, Union Carbide Corporation, the Gillette Company, and Liberty Mutual Insurance Company. Three days later Moore circulated another memo to possible sponsors, announcing that a new weekly show would premier in the fall called "AFL Highlights." It was going to be a live studio report of all the AFL games played the previous weekend, hosted by Curt Gowdy and Paul Christman. The show was slated to air on Saturdays, beginning September 7, from 4:30 to 5:00 P.M. Eastern Standard Time. Gowdy and Christman would preview upcoming games, show special features, and have occasional guests live on location or in the studios in New York. Moore emphasized that every game played would be filmed, including night games, and the most important action would be presented on the show. This was the first show of its kind and arguably the precursor for today's pregame/postgame shows, such as "Inside the NFL," which aired weekly on HBO beginning in 1977, and even sports networks such as ESPN and the NFL Network.[23]

Before the 1963 season began, the Kansas City Chiefs experienced the ultimate setback when rookie Stone Johnson was fatally injured in a preseason game in Wichita, Kansas, on August 30. The Chiefs were playing the Oilers when Johnson, a running back from Grambling State University, fractured his fifth cervical vertebra and suffered damage to his spinal cord while blocking on a punt return. He was paralyzed from the chest down and hospitalized, but he died ten days later. Johnson had been an Olympic sprinter at the 1960 U.S. Olympic trials, where he equaled the world record in the 200-yard dash, running it in 20.5 seconds, but finished fifth in the finals when he ran a 20.8. He had endeared himself to the squad through not only his talent but also his demeanor and approach to the game. The sudden death of their teammate devastated many of the Chiefs, particularly Abner Haynes, who grew up with Johnson in Dallas. "He was our quarterback at Lincoln High School and on the track team. We were close partners. We walked up Malcolm X Boulevard every day, maybe twenty blocks, to get to Lincoln. There were fights, prostitutes, graveyards. You develop relationships in that walk." Haynes seemed to be distracted all year, and Chris Burford felt that Johnson's death "had a tremendous effect on our whole team. I don't think Abner was ever quite the same."[24]

The 1963 San Diego Chargers were definitely not the same team that won only four games the previous season. Injuries to key players forced the Chargers to watch the Texans dominate the Western Division on their way to the 1962 championship. The Chargers made two major off-season moves that greatly changed their fortunes. First they consummated one of the biggest trades in AFL history when they dealt second-year guard-tackle Richard Hudson and their top two draft choices, Florida tackle Frank Lasky and Penn State guard Harrison Rosdahl, to the Buffalo Bills for the rights to veteran quarterback Tobin Rote. The former 1957 championship quarterback for the Detroit Lions was signed after playing for the CFL's Toronto Argonauts. The second major change occurred when Coach Gillman moved the Chargers' training camp from the University of San Diego to Boulevard, California, some sixty miles east of San Diego. In this isolated site, at a dilapidated facility called Rough Acres Ranch, the players could concentrate on football. The "field" was a barren patch of dirt where grass would not grow, so each morning the ball boys spread sawdust to try to cover it. Rough Acres was also home for a host of snakes and spiders, and in the evening the players fell asleep to the sound of bats screeching in the rafters.[25]

The camp toughened Gillman's players, arguably helping the Chargers post an 11–3 regular-season record. In some ways playing football was easy compared with surviving camp. Receiver Dave Kocourek recalled that "Ernie Ladd was a great Ping-Pong player. He would go over and pick up the ball in a tree well, and in the tree well would be a snake. We killed about 20 rattlesnakes in the course of training camp." This was the final element to the Chargers' success—not snakes but team togetherness. At a time when racial tension was rife around the country, Gillman encouraged his players to mix off the field. Paul Lowe, Ron Mix, Ladd, Earl Faison, and John Hadl engaged in daily card games, while Sam DeLuca and Bert Coan held what Mix described as "world problem solving sessions." Keith Lincoln and Ladd dueled daily at noon for the World Ping-Pong Championship, and Mix and receiver Don Norton got together for guitar sessions.[26]

Ladd helped anchor the AFL's best team defense, while Lance Alworth, Lowe, and Kocourek anchored the league's top offense. Tobin Rote's passing led the Chargers to finish third in passing offense, and Lowe eclipsed a 1,000-yard rushing for the first time in his career. The Chargers dominated both sides of the ball, but two of their three losses came from the Oakland Raiders, led by former assistant Al Davis. Before Davis left for the Raiders, he helped sign receiver Alworth, who was perhaps the Chargers' best player in 1963. Alworth's uncanny leaping ability caused him to be a seven-time AFL All-Star, and Davis was dispatched to try to keep him from signing with the San Francisco 49ers after the 1962 draft. Davis met Alworth and his parents in a coffee shop in Little Rock before his college team, the Arkansas Razorbacks, took on the University of Alabama in the Sugar Bowl. Davis marked up the tablecloth as if it were a coaching chalkboard and made a presentation that has become football—and dining— lore: "That X is where the flanker lines up, Lance, as soon as you sign with us, you're my X and nobody can take that position away from you."[27]

Davis left the Chargers and signed a three-year $60,000 contract to become the Raiders' new general manager and head coach in early January. He immediately made sweeping changes in the Raiders' front office and coaching staff. He also remade the Raider image, throwing away the nondescript black, gold, and white uniforms in favor of a simple but sophisticated look modeled on the army's black and gold. His silver and black colors became the backdrop of the franchise and the basis for his motto, "A commitment to excellence." But the team Davis took over was anything but excellent; in winning just three games in two years the Raiders had lost both an estimated million dollars in operating costs and most of their modest following. When the Raiders put up signs urging fans to follow the team, someone scrawled, "Who are the Oakland Raiders? And where are they going?" On the *Captain Satellite* children's television program, the following question was asked: "What has 22 legs and lives in the cellar?" The answer, "The Oakland Raiders." But Davis and his staff began to overhaul the team, and by opening day they had made eighteen trades. The biggest addition was the signing of free agent Art Powell, a classic deep receiver perfect for the vertical passing game Davis was installing. After signing Powell, Davis said: "He is the answer to all our problems. He's the kind of performer you must have to win in this league." Powell was not re-signed by New York, and with quarterback Tom Flores now recovered from an infected lung, Powell led the league in receiving yards and finished second in receptions. Clem Daniels also contributed mightily to the Raiders' offense, leading the league in rushing yards with 1,099 and averaging 5.1 yards per carry. The defense had few recognizable names but terrorized opponents with a dazzling array of blitzes. After starting out the season with two wins, the Raiders lost four straight games, but then the miracle began. Oakland started winning and never stopped, taking its last eight contests to finish 10–4, one game behind the Chargers.[28]

The signing of Powell by Davis was his first major decision in Oakland and exemplified the kind of leader he was and would be for this team. Davis made decisions based on who could help his team win, and throughout his tenure players were brought to the Raiders who were castoffs from other teams. Powell was a Canadian Football League star who, like Gilchrist in Buffalo, was married to a white Canadian woman but was released by the Titans after the 1962 season. Like Gilchrist, Powell had a reputation as a malcontent, and his mixed marriage did not sit well with many owners in 1963. But Davis had no qualms with who Powell was married to as long as he caught the ball. On December 22, in a game against the Houston Oilers, Powell set Raider single-game records for most points scored with 24, most touchdowns with four, and most receiving yards with 247. According to defensive end Ben Davidson, who joined the Raiders in 1964, "Davis looked at Powell and his wife and saw while the skin didn't match, Art could catch the ball, so his thinking was that maybe we can forget about his wife's skin not matching. That was Al's first project." The city of Oakland had experienced some profound changes since its economic boom during World War II, and one of them was a dramatic rise in its black population. In 1950 there were 47,562 African Americans in Oakland; by 1970 that number had increased to 124,789. During the early 1960s, as African Americans competed for jobs and housing, racial tension in the city increased, and on many occasions violence was sparked as the predominantly white police force patrolled black neighborhoods. It was against this backdrop that the Raiders began to gain fans in what by 1966 would be one of America's most racially charged cities.[29]

In the Eastern Division, Coach Mike Holovak's Patriots finished on top but tied with the Buffalo Bills at 7–6–1, and both teams had games that ended in ties against Kansas City. The Patriots had a solid defense led by defensive linemen Larry "Wild Man" Eisenhauer, Jim "Earthquake" Hunt, Bob Dee, Jesse Richardson, and Houston Antwine. Richardson was one of the last pro football players to play without a face mask: "I could see better without it, I didn't wear tape either, and no pads." He suffered no fewer than five broken noses during his career, and he reset each one himself. Middle linebacker Nick Buoniconti, though undersized, added a strategic dimension with his frequent blitzes. After finishing tied with the Bills, Boston played a one-game playoff in Buffalo on December 28. Bulldozers had to move snow from the field, and frigid winds dropped the temperature to 10 degrees. Some 33,044 fans plus television viewers watched as the Patriots defeated Buffalo 26–8: the Bills had six turnovers and were held to seven total rushing yards. The highlight of the game for Boston took place when Eisenhauer decided to sink his teeth into the left ankle of running back Cookie Gilchrist underneath a pile of players. "I wanted to see if he was frozen," Eisenhauer explained. "He wasn't, and he screamed and then got real mad. He jumped up and tried to kick me in the face. But he missed, slipped on the ice and fell right on his head. It was a very memorable play in my career."[30]

For Gilchrist and the Bills, the game and season were a disappointment; favored to win the division, the team lost three of their first four games. But they then won four of their next five and finished the season 7–6–1, tied with the Patriots. Gilchrist led the AFL in rushing touchdowns with twelve, and on December 8 in a game against the Jets he did something no one had ever done in the history of professional football: he rushed for 243 yards on thirty-six carries, breaking Jim Brown's record of 237 yards, set in 1957 and equaled in 1961. Gilchrist scored five touchdowns in the game, and two holding penalties against receiver Glenn Bass actually negated 50 additional yards. This was the highlight of the season for Gilchrist, since he was totally shut down by the Patriots' defense in the playoff game. This made for a long off-season for him and the Bills to reflect on what could have been.[31]

The 1963 AFL season was played as several major historical events unfolded. The year marked the centennial of the Emancipation Proclamation, and in April, Dr. Martin Luther King Jr. launched a desegregation campaign in Birmingham, Alabama, that resulted in the arrest of more than 2,000 protesters, including numerous children. The police and fire departments also used attack dogs and powerful water hoses on these African American citizens. In May an agreement was reached by white businessmen and black leaders to integrate downtown establishments and to hire African Americans. On June 11 two African American students were forcibly integrated into the University of Alabama despite the opposition of Governor George C. Wallace, and the next day Medgar Evers was assassinated at his home in Jackson, Mississippi, in front of his wife and children, by segregationist Byron de la Beckwith. In August, to support President Kennedy's civil rights legislation, Dr. King, along with other civil rights leaders, held the March on Washington, in which some 250,000 people participated. This was the largest civil rights demonstration in history, and many people felt a real sense of optimism after the march, but on September 15 in Birmingham, Alabama, a bomb exploded in the Sixteenth Street Baptist Church, killing four black girls. Then, on Friday, November 22, President John F. Kennedy was assassinated in Dallas, Texas. With the death of the president, both the AFL and NFL had to make the crucial decision to cancel or play games as the cloud of this tragedy hovered over the country.

Despite the chaos, NFL commissioner Pete Rozelle was able to talk with Pierre Salinger, Kennedy's press secretary, for two to three minutes. During the conversation the two men agreed that the president would have wanted the games to go on and that the country would be reassured by the presence of football games on Sunday. This was solidified by the fact that no games were scheduled in either Dallas or Washington that weekend. Rozelle's statement on behalf of the league took the long view: "It has been traditional in sports for athletes to perform in times of great personal tragedy. Football was Mr. Kennedy's game. He thrived on competition." In retrospect the decision to go ahead with the games would seem crass and misguided, especially after Lee Harvey Oswald was killed by Jack Ruby on national television less than two hours before the first kickoff that Sunday. In contrast, Assistant Commissioner Milt Woodard, who could not contact Commissioner Joe Foss, went back and forth about playing and not playing. He called NFL officials, who informed him that they planned to play, and he never received word from Foss, who was flying. While sitting in his office with director of publicity Jack Horrigan, Woodard decided to cancel the games. While the AFL was lauded for its restraint, Rozelle took a series of critical hits: "Rozelle's decision was probably the cheapest move ever made in the history of a sport not noted for good taste, or the grand gesture," wrote Charles McCade in the *San Francisco Chronicle*.[32]

At least two elements of that weekend's fallout could not have been foreseen. Rozelle could not have known that Oswald would be shot on the morning of Sunday's games, heightening the sense of chaos within the country. More importantly, he could not have anticipated the role that television would play during the long weekend. The previous cataclysmic events that had been the touchstones for most American lives—the attack on Pearl Harbor, FDR's death, or the dropping of atomic bombs on Hiroshima and Nagasaki—had been experienced through radio reports. But on that weekend of November 22–24 a nation sat in front of the television, watching itself mourn and gaining a sense of itself in a way it never had before. In that heightened context, Rozelle's decision seemed like a rash one. In contrast, the AFL clearly recognized the sensitivity of this historic, country-changing event. Three days after the president's assassination Milt Woodard issued a memo to league executives concerning preparations for future games. In the game that followed the president's funeral, he advised that the "best of taste be used in half-time presentations." He also felt that all halftime arrangements for the rest of the season be scrutinized to be sure they were in no way insensitive. He instructed teams to have an appropriate period of silence before the start or at halftime of the games that were to be played on Thanksgiving and on Sunday, December 1. His final instructions addressed the type of entertainment used during games: "If bands are presented, the music should be dignified and any strutting or hula-hipped drum majorettes should be eliminated."[33]

The AFL gained respect in the eyes of the national media for rescheduling its games, and the championship game played in San Diego on January 5, 1964, between the Chargers and Patriots was again watched by millions and well attended. Some 30,127 filed into Balboa Stadium on a Sunday afternoon with the temperature a cool 57 degrees. Coach Sid Gillman had decided to change the Chargers' offense, and he designed a game plan called "Feast or Famine." This featured wholesale changes that the Chargers had not previously shown all year. To counter the Patriots' blitzes, he had running back Paul Lowe go into motion, and this kept Boston off balance all day by disorganizing its usually precise defense. Gillman also designed formations to draw Boston's linebackers up to the line of scrimmage; they were good cover men but were too light to play defensive end. On the second play of the game, running back Keith Lincoln took a handoff and burst through the middle of the Boston defense for a 56-yard gain. Tobin Rote's quarterback sneak seven plays later gave San Diego a 7–0 lead. After stopping the Patriots on the Chargers' next series, Lincoln headed around the end for a 67-yard touchdown, making the score 14–0. This was only the tip of the iceberg for Boston: Lincoln ran wild with 206 yards rushing and 123 yards receiving, and completed one 20-yard pass. The Chargers crushed the Patriots 51–10 for their first AFL Championship and the city of San Diego's first professional title of any kind. The champagne flowed freely in the Chargers' locker room, and the players celebrated and shouted "bring on the Bears," who had recently won the NFL Championship over the New York Giants by a score of 14–10. Gillman proclaimed, "We're champions of the world. If anyone wants to debate it, let them play us." After the game Gillman sent a telegram to Rozelle which read: "PETE—EVEN POPE JOHN RECOGNIZED THE OTHER LEAGUE." Gillman received Rozelle's reply the next day: "SID—YES BUT IT TOOK HIM TWO THOUSAND YEARS."[34]

The Chargers set AFL records by gaining 610 yards of total offense and averaging 10.2 yards per play. Their performance sparked the inevitable comparisons between the NFL champions and the AFL champions. For the first time, an AFL team was able to inspire significant talk among followers and leaders of pro football. According to Mike Ditka, who played tight end on this Bear team, "If the Chargers would have played us, they would have gone up against one of the best defenses that ever played in the league. They talk about the '85 Bears defense; the '63 defense was awfully good. The Chargers had a lot of firepower. It would have been a hell of a game." Lincoln felt that the 1963 Chargers also helped to change the way pro football was played: "A person could put up a good argument that Sid Gillman is the father of the West Coast offense. His thing was to stretch the field. That was the big complaint about the AFL back then. . . . Well, everything that's been done has copied that. . . . They're throwing the Goddamn ball. They're doing everything that they criticized Sid for."[35]

4

BOYCOTT IN NEW ORLEANS

In 1965 the AFL All-Star game scheduled for New Orleans was boycotted by African American players after they experienced wholesale segregation in the city. Their boycott caused the game to be moved to Houston, and this organized protest served as a clear example that black athletes could challenge institutional racism in America and be successful. Arguably this thought-out public stand by the AFL's black athletes paved the way for Muhammad Ali, Tommie Smith, John Carlos, Arthur Ashe, and others to also defy racism. Clearly the organized activities of the larger civil rights movement resonated with these pro football players when they arrived in the "Big Easy." Along with the fact that the federal government had responded to the movement's organized push for equality by passing the 1954 *Brown* decision and 1964 Civil Rights Act, New Orleans itself was beginning to slowly change racially. In 1960 six-year-old first-grader Ruby Bridges became the first African American to integrate a school when she was forcibly admitted into William J. Franz Elementary. In 1963 Tulane University, the city's most prestigious institution of higher education, which had remained all white for 129 years, was integrated by eleven black students. And beginning in 1960, local blacks had organized boycotts of stores on Dryades Street, where the majority of blacks shopped. Over the next three years some stores gradually removed "colored" and "white" signs from toilets and drinking fountains and slowly increased black employment. These factors provided the context for the boycott initiated by fed-up black players, an action that caused white AFL owners to capitulate and move the game. Before the season began, the owners had landed a new television contract that provided much-needed financial stability to each team, and the new league had finally turned the corner after hemorrhaging money during its first four seasons. Owners were not about to allow the boycott to stop the support garnered by fans and the media; it was simply more practical to move the game.[1]

Ironically the future of the AFL dramatically improved in 1964 because of the NFL. As the leagues competed against each other for players and fans, the NFL in early January was negotiating a new television contract led by Commissioner Pete Rozelle. The three networks were instructed to submit sealed bids to the NFL offices on Friday, January 24, by 11:00 A.M. Bill MacPhail showed up for CBS, Carl Lindemann for NBC, and Roone Arledge for ABC. NBC's bid, which was opened first, was $10.3 million per season and $20.6 over two years. ABC's bid was next, and it called for $13.2 million per season, virtually tripling the annual value of the previous CBS deal, $26.4 million in all. The final bid belonged to CBS, and it was for $14.1 million per season and $28.2 over two years. This was the winning bid, and CBS also included a plan to, for the first time, broadcast doubleheader games the last five weeks of the regular season. The fourteen NFL teams had been making $365,000 per season in television revenue; with the new contract each club would now bring in $1 million per season. NFL owners, who anticipated that the bids would improve revenue for their teams but did not know by how much, met on Clint Murchison's island in Spanish Key while the negotiations took place. Art Modell called Rozelle and asked how it had gone. "Fourteen point one million," said Rozelle. After a pause Modell said, "Well, it could be worse. I had been hoping for a little more, but, hell Pete, seven million a year isn't half bad. We can make it—" "No, Art," said Rozelle, interrupting. "Fourteen million per year. Twenty-eight million for two years." There was a longer pause, and Modell's next words were, "Pete, you gotta stop drinking at breakfast."[2]

Ignorant of the possibilities of doubleheaders, NBC came in a distant and humiliating third in the televised bidding. Embarrassed, Lindemann, NBC's head of sports, left the press conference and returned to his office. Waiting for him was a note to return a phone call. When Lindemann read the words, "Call Joe Foss," his spirits soared. Right away Lindemann met with Foss and Sonny Werblin, and they rapidly came to terms on a massive $36 million, five-year pact that would commence with the 1965 season. ABC's contract had called for each AFL team to be paid $261,000 in TV revenue; under NBC's new contract each club was to receive $900,000. With expenditures running about $800,000 per team, NBC helped legitimize the AFL. On January 29, 1964, Joe Foss signed the AFL's TV rights over to NBC. Billy Sullivan called January 29, 1964, "the greatest day in our history." Foss called it a turning point. "After I signed the contract, people stopped asking me if we were going to make it. Everyone knew we were." When news of the deal reached NFL owners, it caused many to pause and realize that although their revenue would substantially increase, the AFL had actually gained ground on the established league. "Well," said the Steelers' Art Rooney, "they don't have to call us Mister anymore."[3]

What began to transpire early in 1964 and continued at a fevered, ruinous pace over the next thirty months was the most tempestuous period in the history of professional football. The irony is that even as the battle critically wounded several teams and owners in both leagues, and cost both the NFL and AFL millions of dollars, the epic war *helped* pro football. Arguably Sonny Werblin was most responsible for helping to bring this dramatic increase in revenue to the AFL because of his relationship with NBC. For nearly twenty years, Werblin had worked for the Music Corporation of America, where he was the manager of musical, movie, and television stars. He had negotiated numerous contracts with executives at NBC during this time. Werblin decided that publicity was one of the best ways to attract fans, and with the Jets poised to move into Shea Stadium in the fall of 1964 he was determined to generate fan interest in New York. Werblin immediately began to utilize his team's added revenue by signing the Jets' number-one draft pick, bruising running back Matt Snell from Ohio State University. Snell was an African American player who was born in Georgia but moved to New York, where he went to Carle Pace High School. His high school team lost only two games that he started, and after graduation he attended Ohio State University, where he was a three-year starter at fullback, defensive end, and halfback. He was the featured back in the Buckeyes' offense his senior year and was named the team's Most Valuable Player. For Werblin, the signing of Snell was crucial because he was also selected by the New York Giants in the fourth round; in order to begin to gain ground on the Jets' cross-town rivals, Werblin felt it was imperative that Snell was signed.[4]

According to Snell, Coach Woody Hayes summoned him to his office, where the Giants' Tim Mara awaited and offered a $12,000 contract with a $5,000 bonus. Snell was ready to sign, but Hayes instructed him to wait and see what the Jets were willing to offer. Two weeks later Weeb Ewbank offered Snell $15,000 and a $10,000 bonus. When the Giants found out about this offer, Mara returned with Emlen Tunnell, the outstanding African American defensive back who had played for the Giants in the late 1940s and 1950s and was now an assistant coach. Mara and Tunnell made a counteroffer to Snell but indicated that it was their final offer—a $20,000 contract and a $20,000 bonus—but Hayes said, "That sounds like a very good offer. Let me talk to Matt about it, and we'll get back to you." Werblin flew into Columbus the next day, and when Snell approached the football office, there was a long black stretch limousine in front. Werblin offered Snell a $20,000 contract and a $30,000 bonus, and asked if there was anything else he wanted. Snell smiled and said, "I always wanted a new Thunderbird." Werblin said, "You got it." Snell asked, "You're taking it out of my bonus, right?" Werblin said no, and that it was a gift from the Jets. Snell was still somewhat apprehensive and said, "I'm not looking for you to make a down payment on the car." Werblin responded that the car was his and would be delivered. "I can't put it in writing because it would have to be part of your contract and we'd have to give you a 1099." Coach Hayes said, "Don't hit him with the taxes." Snell added he did not want a lease, and Werblin said, "No, we'll find a way to do it." The car was delivered to Snell at school, and he never heard from the Giants again.[5]

Snell helped the Jets improve during 1964, but the class of the AFL was the Buffalo Bills, led by the running of Cookie Gilchrist, the passing of Jack Kemp, Daryle Lamonica, and a strong defense. They opened the season by crushing the Chiefs, 34–13 and did not lose until the tenth game of the season, when Boston beat them 36–28. The Bills won the Eastern Division with a record of 12–2, the two losses coming from the Patriots and Raiders. Buffalo's defense led the league in fewest points allowed, fewest rushing yards, and fewest touchdowns with twenty-eight over a fourteen-game schedule. The Bills allowed only four rushing touchdowns, while the Chiefs' defense was second, allowing nine rushing touchdowns. Gilchrist provided very physical running; he led the league in rushing yards with 981, rushing touchdowns with six, rushing yards per game at 70.1, and rushing attempts per game with 16.4. He also set the tone in the last game of the season against Boston, which entered the game with a record of 10–2–1, and with a win at home in Fenway Park the Patriots would win the division. The start of the game was delayed because of snow, but on the Bills' first play from scrimmage Gilchrist began by thoroughly intimidating the Patriots' defense on a 9-yard run. "I hit Patriots defensive back Chuck Shonta with all I had. I didn't try to go around him because I wanted them to know we were going to run right through them. Shonta lay on the ground, knocked unconscious by my blow. While the rest of the Patriots defense huddled around their unconscious teammate, I stood nearby taunting them. I made sure they heard me when I said, which one of you motherfuckers is next?" Needless to say, there were no takers, and the Bills won the game 24–14. The running of Gilchrist was balanced by the passing of Kemp and Lamonica, who complemented each other—Kemp was the precision passer and Lamonica threw long passes, or "bombs." The final piece in the Bills' success was the addition of the first soccer-style kicker in professional football, Pete Gogolak, a Hungarian refugee who had played at Cornell and kicked the ball sideways accurately enough to score 102 points. Gogolak finished second to Gino Cappellitti of Boston in field goals made—Cappellitti kicked twenty-five and Gogolak nineteen—but his style was revolutionary and changed kicking at all levels of football forever.[6]

Both the San Diego Chargers and the Kansas City Chiefs had changed locations to increase fan attendance by moving to existing stadiums in those cities. The Chargers and Chiefs changed their team names after moving, and so did the New York Titans, who became the Jets after moving into a new stadium that was close to LaGuardia Airport. The Jets moved into newly built Shea Stadium and immediately began to attract huge crowds. In their first game of the season in the new stadium on Saturday, September 12, they defeated the Denver Broncos 30–6. The game drew an AFL record crowd of 45,665, and ticket takers, ushers, and grounds crew were suitably attired in the Jets' kelly green and white. Jets souvenirs were everywhere, and the Jetliners, a 110-piece band, entertained the fans. Werblin's investment in Snell paid off right away: the rookie finished second in rushing yards with 948, and he caught fifty-six passes for 393 yards. Interestingly the star of the first game and this inaugural season in Shea was not the Jets' African American running back but a Native American middle linebacker named Wahoo McDaniel, who had played the previous two seasons with the Oilers and Broncos. This Choctaw and Chickasaw player was an off-season wrestler who made the Jets' first tackle of the season, and the public address announcer proclaimed to the crowd, "Tackle by Wahoo McDaniel." As McDaniel began to dominate the game against his former Broncos teammates, the P.A. announcer shortened the description to "Tackle by Wahoo." In the second half, as the Jets took control and the crowd began to relax, the announcer would wait for a McDaniel tackle and ask the crowd, "Tackle by who?" to which Jets fans would clap and shout back, "Wahoo!" New York, led by McDaniel and Snell, played hard, but as the season wore on, teams focused on stopping the run, causing slow-footed quarterback Dick Wood to struggle as defenses blitzed and pressured him. But clearly the fans of New York were attracted to the Jets. In 1963 the team drew 103,550 fans to their seven home games in the dismal Polo Grounds. At the end of the season they led the league in attendance, drawing 298,972 fans for an average of 42,710 per game. Arguably, for those New York fans who could not get Giants tickets but refused to sit in the drafty, dirty Polo Grounds, the Jets became a very popular alternative.[7]

The popularity of the Jets caused the Giants to be creative in attracting fans. In September the Giants put on pro football's first known closed-circuit television game. On September 25 the Giants aired the game against the Washington Redskins in six area theaters, charging six dollars for tickets, the same as for a box seat at Yankee Stadium. It was estimated that between 6,000 and 9,000 people viewed the telecast with a total of approximately 23,000 seats sold. Milt Woodard visited the theaters to observe the audience and ascertain if this was something the AFL should implement. The experiment provided him with much-needed data about pro football fans and the economic opportunities presented by pro football games. Woodard noted that theaters had restrictions that stadiums did not, such as no smoking allowed except in the balconies. No beer and no other vending items were sold. There were no commercials, and he estimated that 90 percent of those in attendance were men between the ages of twenty-seven and forty. There were very few teenagers and only a few women. He thought that perhaps 10 percent of the patrons were African American and 80 percent did not wear a necktie. Woodard indicated that his no-tie observation was the most important of the report because it verified a theory he had had for several years: "The professional football fan is basically a blue collar worker who finds that professional football is his best sports outlet." The Giants had two more games scheduled for closed-circuit television, and Woodard felt that attendance would be based on how well the team was playing at the time. Pro football on closed-circuit television in theaters did not exist on a long-term basis, and the AFL did not participate, but clearly it paved the way for the sport to be viewed in homes. Cable television, which facilitated the creation of ESPN, Fox Sports, and the NFL Network, helped lead to DirecTV, which now allows subscribers to pay a fee to view every NFL game in the comfort of their own homes.[8]

Although Lamar Hunt and Bud Adams were the principal founders of the AFL, and their respective teams won the first three championships, they clearly had different philosophies when it came to African American players. The Oilers failed to sign the top African American players, and the perception was that black players were not extended the same opportunities on the field as their white counterparts in Houston. While successful AFL teams featured African American running backs with lateral moves such as Abner Haynes, Paul Lowe, and Cookie Gilchrist, Houston stuck with its original all-white backfield from 1960 of Bob White, Billy Cannon, Charley Tolar, and Dave Smith. The same went for its defensive backfield, which was mostly white, mostly slow, and mostly costing the team games. The Oilers finished last in passing defense, and teams averaged a league-high 53 percent pass completion rate against Houston's secondary. The Oilers struggled to draft quality players in general; in 1964 they had seven picks in the first five rounds. However, they passed on several future great players, including Mel Renfro, Leroy Kelly, Roger Staubach, Bob Brown, Paul Warfield, Paul Krause, Bob Hayes, Jethro Pugh, Matt Snell, and Gerry Philbin. Their top draft choice was All-American defensive lineman Scott Appleton from the University of Texas, who had just won the national championship. Unfortunately his career with the Oilers was a major disappointment; he played for only three years and battled alcoholism and drug addiction before being traded to the Chargers. The Chiefs fared much better with their number-one draft pick, defensive lineman Buck Buchanan.[9]

Born on September 10, 1940, in Gainesville, Alabama, Buchanan attended all-black Parker High School in Birmingham. He played football and basketball in high school and was offered a scholarship by legendary Grambling State University coach Eddie Robinson to play both offense and defense. Buchanan entered Grambling as a 6'6", 225-pound freshman but left as a 6'7", 245-pound senior. He was clocked at 4.9 in the 40-yard dash and 10.2 in the 100-yard dash. Buchanan had long arms, was quick and strong, and was particularly effective at intimidating quarterbacks by batting down passes. The Chiefs made him the number-one selection in the 1963 draft, and Buchanan recognized this historical achievement. "I signed with them because I considered it an honor to be the first player chosen by the league. I thought it was very significant to have that honor, since I had played for a small black school. I was determined to prove that players from small black schools could play in the big leagues." During his rookie season the Chiefs played him at defensive end, but in 1964 he was moved to tackle, where he flourished. Twice chosen as the Chiefs' MVP, Buchanan missed only one game due to injury during his thirteen-year career. After his second season Buchanan began a streak of eight years in which he was named to either the AFL All-Star Team or the NFL Pro Bowl. The Chiefs started to build their defensive unit around this athletically gifted, dominating player, and the team's fortunes began to change quickly.[10]

The Buffalo Bills and San Diego Chargers met at War Memorial Stadium, which was nicknamed the "Rockpile," for the AFL Championship. The game was played on Saturday, December 26, and the temperature was a reasonable 43 degrees, which was unusually warm. The defending champion Chargers were favored, led by an offense that could score by running and passing, but star receiver Lance Alworth was out and this limited their big-play ability. Their defense was intimidating and overly confident, and while the Bills were on their sideline getting last-minute instructions from Coach Lou Saban, Earl Faison walked over to their huddle and said they had better play all out "because I just might kill somebody today." Defensive back Butch Byrd said, "I just looked at him. Everyone looked at him. He was just wide-eyed." San Diego won the coin toss and took just two minutes and eleven seconds to score the game's first touchdown on a 26-yard pass from Tobin Rote to tight end Dave Kocourek. Since Alworth was out, the Chargers used a draw and several short passes to running back Keith Lincoln to set up the game's first score. The Bills were unable to move the ball on the ensuing possession and were forced to punt. During their second drive linebacker Mike Stratton made what many consider the most famous tackle in AFL history. Rote floated a pass to Lincoln in the flat, and as he extended his arms to make the catch, Stratton came up on the dead run and buried his helmet in Lincoln's midsection. Lincoln was helped from the field and done for the day with broken ribs. Lincoln's backfield mate, Paul Lowe, vividly remembered the details of the hit. "I was pretty close to that play, and I just said Oooh. I could hear the ribs breaking and I remember thinking, I'm glad it was him and not me."[11]

The hit changed the momentum of the game; from this point on, the Bills' defense controlled and bottled up the Chargers' offense. Lincoln remembered that Rote had been indecisive on the play, looking down the field for an open receiver before turning to throw to him. Passing to Lincoln late did not help to cause the hit—more importantly, Rote floated the ball: "He threw the Goddamn ball to me like you'd throw a snowball down a chimney. And just as the ball got to me, Stratton hit me. He separated my sternum and rib cage. It was a good hit, a clean hit." On the Bills' next possession Gogolak kicked a 12-yard field goal, and the first quarter ended with the Chargers leading 7–3. In the second quarter fullback Wray Carlton scored a touchdown on a 4-yard run and Gogolak kicked a 17-yard field goal, which put the Bills up at halftime 13–7. Neither team scored in the third quarter, but in the fourth quarter Bills quarterback Jack Kemp scored from one yard out and the game ended 20–7. The Buffalo Bills were AFL Champions as a result of strong defense and a ball-controlled offense, outgaining the Chargers 387 yards to 259.[12]

The AFL All-Star Game was scheduled to be played in New Orleans on January 16, 1965, at Tulane Stadium. Local businessman Dave Dixon had tried to persuade Lamar Hunt to move the Texans two years earlier to New Orleans, and he had been lobbying the NFL for an expansion franchise in the city. The NFL had not been very receptive to Dixon, so he set his sights on bringing an AFL team, and the All-Star Game would be a great way to show fan support. But from the time black players arrived in New Orleans, they faced racial discrimination, starting with trying to hail cabs to get from the airport to their hotels. Several black players found this very difficult. According to Bobby Bell of the Chiefs, white players were being picked up and taken to their hotel, but when black players approached a white cab driver, the cabbie would say, "No. Can't go." Bell said that finally one of the porters told them that "you guys have to call a colored cab. They have to come from the city to get you." Cookie Gilchrist had a similar experience. He tried to hail a cab, and the driver told him, "You need a colored taxi." Gilchrist replied, "I don't care what color the taxi is, I just want to go to my hotel." Then, according to Gilchrist, the driver noticed Jack Kemp exit the terminal and wave at him; at that point the cabbie told Gilchrist that if Kemp allowed him to ride in the cab, he would take both players to the Fontainebleau Hotel. Gilchrist then did a mock step-and-fetch-it shuffle and said to Kemp, "Mr. Kemp, the nice white taxi man said that I could ride in his taxi if you allow it, Sir." Kemp responded by saying, "Quit kidding, Cookie," but he talked with the driver, who took them to their hotel. The treatment of black players by white cab drivers clearly varied. Ernie Ladd, who was 6'9" and weighed over 300 pounds, remembered having a different experience than Gilchrist or Bell. After arriving, Ladd said he "got a cab with Dick Westmoreland and Earl Faison, two of my teammates from the Chargers. A white cab. No problem." All three African American players were taken to the Roosevelt Hotel, where the West All-Stars were staying. The three players checked in and then decided to go to the French Quarter, so they asked the same cab driver to take them, but this time he refused. After being taken there by a black cab driver, the players became very frustrated as white driver after driver refused to take them back to the hotel. Westmoreland proclaimed, "I don't need to take this crap. I'm taking my black ass home. I'm not playing." Faison said, "If you're not playing, I'm not playing."[13]

The next morning Art Powell called Gilchrist, and a meeting was set in the Roosevelt Hotel. All the black players on the East All-Stars came over, along with a couple of white players, Ron Mix and Kemp. Mix initially tried to persuade the black players to play the game and make statements about how they disagreed with the treatment they had received. But the black players were adamant that their displeasure could best be illustrated by not playing. They talked about how they were treated and what should be done next, and they also pointed to the recently passed 1964 Civil Rights Act, which they felt should not have allowed this blatant discrimination. Gilchrist eventually called for a vote to boycott the game. Before asking players to decide, he said, "You all know I will kick the ass of whoever votes to stay and play." The vote was unanimous, 21–0, to leave New Orleans. Ernie Ladd was elected to make the official statement to the press, and the players quickly left the room before he had a chance to decline. Chuck Burr, the publicity director for the Bills; Dixon; and Ernest Morial, president of the New Orleans NAACP, held another meeting with players later in the day but could not persuade them to play. A contingency plan was quickly put together when the news reached the owners and commissioner, and the game was moved to Jeppesen Stadium in Houston. Commissioner Foss issued a statement to the press explaining why the game was moved and placing the blame squarely on how the league's African American players had been treated. "Negro players run into problems in nearly every city. But I guess what went on in New Orleans was more than they could be expected to take. I can't say that I blame them." The game was held in Houston on January 16 and the West All-Stars won 38–14, but in many ways the outcome was inconsequential. The boycott was the first organized action by black professional athletes which caused a professional league to move a game. These brave individuals organized a successful boycott that pressured white AFL owners to move the game to Houston and caused businesses in New Orleans to lose revenue. Two years later the NFL granted the city its franchise, but when the Saints began play in 1967 the treatment of black citizens at restaurants and by cab drivers had improved.[14]

The African American sports writer Sam Lacy wrote about the boycott in an editorial for the black newspaper *Afro-American*. Lacy had championed integration in baseball for several years. He had covered Jackie Robinson's journey to the major leagues and witnessed the racism and discrimination Robinson faced when he joined the Brooklyn Dodgers in 1947. Lacy himself was barred from press boxes, forced to dine at segregated restaurants, and forced to stay in black hotels and boarding houses.

By 1965 he had witnessed a great deal of change in sports and in America, but he also recognized that there was much still to do. In his editorial he criticized comments made by Mayor Victor Schiro of New Orleans, who felt the black players had unfairly focused on his city: "If these men only played football in cities where everybody loved them, they'd all be out of a job today. They should have rolled with the punch and played." Lacy wrote that the expectation that African Americans should tolerate discrimination is a part of the American fabric that must change. "Why is it that colored people are destined to be the only ones in this country showing the Christian attitude of turning the other cheek? Why is it that we must content ourselves with being first class citizens only when the bugle blows for war and at income tax time?" Lacy felt that his grandfather had to "roll with the punches" and that a new mentality by this generation of African Americans could be seen in the actions of the players: "When these young football players packed their gear and quit New Orleans in protest against local bigotry, the action was so totally unexpected that it rocked the entire sports world. And I for one, just loved it."[15]

This boycott is arguably one of the most important in the history of African Americans in sports. For the first time since black players integrated the three major sports in America, a concerted, organized, successful boycott against racial discrimination took place. Black players such as Jackie Robinson, Larry Doby, Earl Lloyd, Kenny Washington, Bill Willis, and numerous others had to accept racist behavior from white opponents and discrimination while traveling on their respective teams. By taking the uncompromising stance not to play in New Orleans, black players in the AFL served as a legitimate example of what the power of organized protest can accomplish. Although black athletes had initiated past protests—for example, Robinson and his Negro League teammates refused to buy gas at stations that did not allow them to use the bathroom, and Bill Russell and his black Celtics teammates refused to play an exhibition game in Lexington, Kentucky, because of racial discrimination in 1961—black players for the first time pressured an entire league to move a game from one city to another. Two years later Muhammad Ali refused to be inducted into the U.S. armed forces, and three years later, in 1968, black athletes boycotted the Olympic Games, citing continued discrimination in America. These two events have overshadowed what happened in New Orleans in 1965. Before Ali refused to step forward, before Tommie Smith and John Carlos raised their fists in the air, black AFL players checked out of their hotel rooms and forced the league to move its All-Star Game to Houston. Citing the recently passed 1964 Civil Rights Act as justification for their actions, these players had had enough and felt it was time to challenge southern segregation head on, as united black men.

Although the boycott was successful, Cookie Gilchrist and Abner Haynes felt they were identified as the leaders and because of this traded to the worst team in the league—Denver. Gilchrist and Haynes believed the owners blamed them for the actions taken in New Orleans, and having to toil for the Broncos was their punishment. Buffalo traded Gilchrist to Denver in February, less than one month after the boycott, for running back Billy Joe. Haynes was dealt days after the All-Star Game in January for linebacker Jim Fraser and cash. Gilchrist felt that his involvement in the boycott was a factor in the Bills' decision: "The Broncos were having a hard time drawing fans; the infusion of Abner Haynes, who was acquired through a trade with the Chiefs, and I would hopefully give Denver the drawing power they sought. But I sometimes wondered, if Abner and I had not taken a stand against racial discrimination in New Orleans, would we have finished our careers in Kansas City and Buffalo, respectively." Gilchrist felt that he and Haynes were the most outspoken players during the boycott, which effectively destroyed the AFL's chance to add a new franchise in the Crescent City and obtain more financing for the league. Of course there is no written correspondence by league owners to validate Gilchrist's theory, but Denver was last in average attendance in 1964, drawing only 16,894 per game. After the Broncos acquired Haynes and Gilchrist, their season ticket sales jumped from 8,000 to just over 22,000, and they finished the 1965 season fourth in league attendance, drawing 31,398 per contest. Perhaps league owners were punishing Gilchrist and Haynes for their roles in the boycott, but clearly they had to recognize that these two marquee players could help the league's worst team draw fans.[16]

The 1965 draft helped to forever change professional football in America. The seeds of the future were sown with the anticipated future revenue the teams in both leagues would get from the historic television deals. Realizing that the cost to sign players was going to increase, during the summer of 1964 owner Dan Reeves of the Los Angeles Rams wanted to devise a way to contact college players earlier. During the summer, in a conversation with Commissioner Rozelle, Reeves said, "We need to get an earlier start on relationships, it should be like rushing someone in a college fraternity." Reeves devised a plan in which Los Angeles businessmen, salesmen, and advertising executives would make contact with players the Rams were interested in several weeks before the draft. This would give his team a jump start over AFL teams that might be interested in the same players. Rozelle loved the idea and decided to implement it league wide; it was called "Operation Hand-Holding" but was commonly known as the NFL's babysitting program. On November 28, 1964, when both drafts were held, more than one hundred NFL "field men" left teams with instructions for wooing prospective players.[17]

Invariably some players found themselves caught in the middle between aggressive AFL and NFL teams, such as Gale Sayers, an African American running back from the University of Kansas. Called the "Kansas Comet," Sayers was a two-time All-American who gained nearly 4,000 all-purpose yards. He was a threat as a rusher, pass catcher, and kick returner; during his sophomore year he averaged a jaw-dropping 7.1 yards per carry, and his exciting running style was unique. The Chiefs drafted Sayers with their top pick while the Chicago Bears chose University of Illinois linebacker Dick Butkus first with the third overall NFL pick and Sayers second with the fourth overall choice. The Bears dispatched former NFL player Buddy Young to babysit Sayers, and George Halas offered him $25,000 a year for four years. The Chiefs offered $27,500 a year for four years, which was lower than Sayers expected. "I really felt that if Lamar and the Chiefs had offered me $50,000 a year for three years, I probably would have gone to Kansas City." The Chiefs lost Sayers to the NFL, but they were determined not to let the same thing happen with Otis Taylor.[18]

The pursuit of Taylor by the Chiefs and the Dallas Cowboys has become a legendary tale of intrigue. At 6'3", 220 pounds, and fast, strong, and able to block, Taylor was a marvelous athlete. By now the NFL was well aware of the talent many athletes had at small black schools. Taylor, who played at Prairie View A&M University, ran with long strides that allowed pro football a glimpse into its future at the wide receiver position. The Cowboys invited Taylor and teammate Seth Cartwright to spend Thanksgiving in Dallas and then proceeded to switch the players between three hotels over the next few days. Lloyd Wells, who was the first black scout in pro football, had known Taylor since he was in junior high school. From 1953 to 1963 Wells served as sports editor of the *Houston Informer*, where he helped promote black college and high school football games. It was at one of these games that he met Lamar Hunt, who made him a Chiefs full-time scout in January 1966. Wells was responsible for Taylor, and once he found out that the Cowboys were holding him, he started checking hotels and motels. The Cowboys had convinced Taylor that he would be paired with Olympic gold medalist Bob Hayes as the team's receivers. When Wells finally discovered which motel Taylor had been checked into, he gave the porter twenty dollars to help find the room and then posed as a reporter from *Ebony* magazine to gain entrance. Wells returned sometime around

3:00 A.M. and had Taylor sneak out his bathroom window. Three days after Thanksgiving, when the draft took place, the Chiefs selected Taylor in the fourth round, but the Cowboys gave up on him. Taylor was not drafted by an NFL team until the Philadelphia Eagles chose him in the fifteenth round. Right after the draft, Taylor signed with Kansas City for $15,000 per year with a $15,000 bonus along with a new red Thunderbird.[19]

The signings of Sayers and Taylor paled in comparison to the impact the signing of Joe Namath had on both the AFL and NFL. The Jets selected the quarterback from the University of Alabama with the first overall pick, and the St. Louis Cardinals chose him with the twelfth pick in the first round. Namath, from Beaver Falls, Pennsylvania, was blessed with a strong arm and one of the quickest releases in the history of the sport. Sonny Werblin, who realized that Namath had not only talent but also charisma and glamour, had to have him regardless of the cost. The Giants tried to get the Cardinals to trade the pick, but St. Louis was confident they could sign the young player; however, it became clear very quickly that the Cardinals were no match for Werblin. Al Davis had made a scouting trip to watch an Alabama game in 1962, and when he returned to give Sid Gillman a report, he did it using his distinct language. "What'd you see?" asked Gillman. "I saw a guy who tips the field," said Davis. "What do you mean?" "This sonofabitch plays like he's going downhill," said Davis. To Davis, Namath played as if the game was easy and represented few challenges that his superior physical abilities could not overcome. Namath signed a record-breaking contract with the Jets. It was the largest contract in American team sports, worth $427,000, and it sent shock waves throughout pro football. Namath's salary called for him to be paid $25,000 a year from 1965 to 1967 with an option for 1968 at the same amount. This fell in line with the average salary of NFL players during that time of $35,000 per year. But the contract also called for a $200,000 deferred bonus along with payments to family members.[20]

"The $400,000 did a great harm to the sport," proclaimed Art Modell, owner of the NFL Champion Cleveland Browns. "Utterly ridiculous," complained the *New York Times*' Arthur Daley. "No untested collegian is worth half that much." "I guess I'll have to ask for a raise of about $980,000," said the Browns' Frank Ryan, who threw a league-leading twenty-five touchdowns on his way to the NFL championship. "If a fellow who hasn't even pulled on his cleats in pro ball is worth $400,000, then I must be worth a million dollars." Ryan's teammate Jim Brown reportedly was paid $60,000 a year, which was the highest in the league. Not everyone agreed that Namath was overpaid; at the Senior Bowl in Mobile, Alabama, he threw for 246 yards, including a 53-yard bomb to gold-medal Olympic sprinter Bob Hayes. "Best passer I have ever seen," said Hayes. "He's worth every penny." Werblin's investment on the surface looked as though he had overpaid for an untested, inexperienced football player, but what he was paying for was publicity. Werblin realized that Namath would be the face of the franchise, attracting younger fans who were a part of America's counterculture. Werblin wanted the Jets to be seen as the opposite of the Giants, and when asked about Namath's interests, he would say, "Girls and golf, girls and golf." In comparison the Giants' Wellington Mara had drafted University of Michigan's Bob Timberlake to replace Y. A. Tittle as quarterback. To the delight of Mara, Timberlake was considering enrolling at Princeton Theological Seminary to study for the ministry. The signing of Namath generated publicity for not only the Jets but also the entire league; fans wanted to watch out of sheer curiosity. Jets fans were the most curious, and they responded at the box office, where season-ticket sales increased by 25,000.[21]

Namath was the talk of the 1965 draft, and African American players Taylor and Sayers were fought over by AFL and NFL teams, but they were not the only players the leagues competed for. Several players from historically black colleges were drafted by both AFL and NFL teams. Thirteen players from HBCUs were drafted by AFL teams and twenty-one by NFL teams; of these, eight were drafted by both leagues. Taylor signed with the Chiefs, and he was joined by linebacker Gene Jeter of Texas Southern University, who signed with the Broncos over the Packers, along with running back Doug Goodwin of University of Maryland Eastern Shore, who signed with the Bills instead of the Packers. But defensive tackle Frank Molden from Jackson State University signed with the Steelers as opposed to the Oilers; halfback Smith Reed of Alcorn State University chose the Giants over the Chiefs; defensive end Roy Hilton from Jackson State picked the Colts over the Oilers; running back Bobby Felts of Florida A&M University likewise went with the Colts instead of the Oilers; and defensive back Mike Howell joined the Browns instead of the Chargers. Once again, more black players from black schools were drafted by NFL teams, but again the NFL draft consisted of twenty rounds with fourteen picks per round, while the AFL also had twenty rounds but only eight picks per round. By now the NFL clearly was aware of the talent at historically black schools. For example, Jethro Pugh, a defensive tackle from Elizabeth City State University, was drafted by the Cowboys and became a cornerstone of their defensive line, which turned this once-expansion team into NFL champions. Cannonball Butler was a running back out of Edward Waters College who played with the Steelers, Falcons, and Cardinals for eight seasons. He still is the only player out of this small black school in Jacksonville, Florida, to play in the NFL.[22]

Events in mainstream America clearly had in impact on African American players in the AFL; they used the passage of the 1964 Civil Rights Act as justification for their boycott in New Orleans. President Lyndon B. Johnson was finally able to get the act passed in the summer despite a marathon filibuster by its opponents. The act banned discrimination in places of public accommodation, including restaurants, hotels, gas stations, and entertainment facilities as well as schools, parks, playgrounds, libraries, and swimming pools. The desegregation of public accommodations irrevocably changed the face of American society. The act also banned discrimination by employers and labor unions on the basis of race, color, religion, national origin, and sex in regard to hiring, promoting, dismissing, or making job referrals. Most important, it allowed government agencies to withhold federal money from any program permitting or practicing discrimination. And it created the Equal Employment Opportunity Commission to monitor discrimination in employment.

In an effort to take on voter registration, civil rights activists descended on Mississippi in a project called "Freedom Summer." Black and white participants helped to recruit African Americans in the most oppressive state in America to register and cast votes in mock elections. Shortly after this project began, three volunteers went missing. Two were white New Yorkers, Michael Schwerner and Andrew Goodman, and the third was African American James Chaney of Meridian, Mississippi. They were killed in an ambush by Klansmen outside Philadelphia, Mississippi, and their bodies were discovered on August 4. Later in the month, at the Democratic National Convention in Atlantic City, New Jersey, the Mississippi Freedom Democratic Party challenged the state's regular Democratic delegation for their seats. A compromise was worked out that seated all the white Mississippi regular delegates and gave the MFDP two at-large seats. It was during this convention that America was introduced to Fannie Lou Hamer, a native Mississippian who was a sharecropper and had been beaten savagely by police one year earlier because of her activism. Hamer coined the phrase "I'm sick and tired of being sick and tired." During televised hearings before the credentials committee that were viewed by millions of Americans, Hamer testified about the conditions endured by many African Americans in Mississippi. In a voice filled with emotion, Hamer asked, "Is this America, the land of the free and the home of the brave, where we have to sleep with our telephones off the hooks because our lives be threatened daily, because we want to live as decent human beings, in America?" President Johnson called a press conference during her speech in an effort to get the networks to cut away, but the speech was played back that night and viewed by a prime-time audience.[23]

Although it was clear that the AFL was not going to fold, the NFL was still the league with profitable franchises. Every team made money in 1964 except the Cardinals and the Cowboys, and two teams were sold: William Clay Ford bought the Lions, and a group headed by Jerry Wolman bought the Eagles. The NFL Championship was played before a prime-time audience in Cleveland as some 79,544 fans were on hand to watch the Browns defeat the heavily favored Colts 27–0. Millions more watched on television as Cleveland used the passing attack of quarterback Frank Ryan and receiver Gary Collins to win their first championship since 1953. Blanton Collier had replaced legendary head coach Paul Brown in 1963, and Collier made several changes after his first season, one of which was letting his team leaders know that racial divisions had to stop. Collier realized that his team lacked cohesion and that over the course of the last decade the Browns had become more racially divided than ever. The problem had been simmering over slights as large as salary inequity to a lingering resentment among black players that they were excluded from certain club-sponsored cocktail parties. In essence the team lacked camaraderie; they simply played together. Black player sentiments were summed up by Jim Brown: "If we can't go to all the stuff, the fun stuff, then we won't do the fake stuff. They room us together, we'll stay together. We'll play hard, dress right, carry ourselves with class, and be team people. But we don't have to kiss any ass, or take any attitude, to pacify some redneck from Mississippi." Collier confronted the problem openly by relying on team leaders such as Brown to solve it, which they did. This championship team became a tight-knit group of players that had something that is difficult to measure—chemistry.[24]

FROM MERGER
TO SUPER BOWL

alled the eighth wonder of the world, the Houston Astrodome opened on April 9, 1965. Major league baseball had granted Houston and New York expansion teams that began play in 1960. Roy Hofheinz, owner of the Houston Colt 45s, changed the team's name to the Astros after America's first fully domed stadium constructed for baseball and football opened. Critics said it housed the ninth wonder of the world—the ninth-place Astros. Cynics called the one-million-plus fans who paid to see them the tenth wonder of the world for being the largest crowd to watch a loser in baseball history. Nevertheless, together with NASA it put the city of Houston on the international map. Bud Adams thought he had a lease agreement with Hofheinz in late 1964 for the Oilers to play in the dome beginning in 1965, but Hofheinz tried to squeeze Adams over parking, program concessions, and exhibition game promotions. The AFL planned to kick off the new season by unveiling its newest stadium and newest star; the New York Jets were scheduled to play the Oilers week one in the Astrodome. Unfortunately negotiations completely broke down, and Adams had to work out a deal with Rice University to use Rice Stadium. The Jets planned to bring their star quarterback along slowly, and the many curious fans faced disappointment there as well. The largest Oilers crowd to date, some 52,680, watched on September 12 in 100-degree heat as Mike Taliaferro led the Jets to a 21–27 defeat, instead of Joe Namath, who never left the bench.[1]

The signing of Namath was a clear victory for the AFL over the NFL, and this achievement, along with the new television revenue, caused AFL owners to explore expanding the league. In June, at the owners' meeting, expansion was discussed and agreed on. AFL owners declared that they intended to add two new teams for the 1966 season, and on July 21, 1965, the expansion committee decided to award the city of Miami the next franchise. Two groups were in line to own the new team, one led by the Gulf American Land Corporation, headed by Leonard Rosen and represented by Connie Mack Jr. The other group was headed by Danny Thomas Jr. and represented by Joe Robbie. On August 16 it was announced that the Thomas-Robbie group would be the new partners of the team. Robbie had been a classmate of Joe Foss at the University of South Dakota, and he had received assurances from Mayor Robert King High that his team could use the Orange Bowl Stadium. In what clearly indicated how far the AFL had come, the initial fee of $25,000 paid by the founding members of the "Foolish Club" was now $7.5 million.[2]

With the addition of Miami the league needed another team to keep balance, and on June 8, one day after agreeing to award Miami a franchise, the owners voted to grant approval to the city of Atlanta as well. Although Pete Rozelle had publicly stated that the NFL would not expand until 1967, he was infuriated by what he considered the AFL's aggressive behavior. Rozelle sent public opinion pollster Lou Harris to Atlanta to conduct a poll among its citizens. The question he asked was, "Which would you prefer to have in Atlanta, an AFL or NFL team?" The Harris poll concluded that an overwhelming number of Atlanta's football fans preferred the NFL. On June 30, Rankin M. Smith, a forty-one-year-old executive vice president of the Life of Georgia Insurance Company, was granted an NFL franchise for $8.5 million. This caused AFL owners to criticize Joe Foss, who they felt was not aggressive enough as commissioner in dealing with the NFL, which eventually led to his demise as the first leader of the AFL.[3]

Without question Jets quarterback Joe Namath was the superstar who helped propel the growth of the AFL. Arguably people tuned in or attended Jets games out of curiosity just so they could see the "$400,000 player." His teammates were just as curious and anxious to see their new high-priced quarterback. Namath kept everybody waiting as he arrived at training camp at Peekskill Military Academy at 5:55 P.M. on July 14, a full five minutes before the deadline for players to report. "Don't see why he's so early," groused one of the veterans. Like most of America, the Jets were a team in transition; the civil rights movement had peaked, and a growing militancy had begun to replace it, the civil unrest in the Watts section of Los Angeles being one indication of this change. The Jets were divided along the same lines that separated the rest of the country: young and old, haves and have-nots, black and white. According to tackle Winston Hill, a black Texan, the team "reflected the racial tone of the country." Hill recalled how a couple of black rookies made the mistake of walking into a place where linebacker Larry Grantham was getting hammered, something he did quite often. "Go find your own bar," he snapped. "You have to look at my history," explains Grantham. "When you're raised like I was in Mississippi, you don't come to New York and all of a sudden make a one-hundred-and-eighty-degree turn. It wasn't until I was in the pros that I even played against blacks. It took a while."[4]

Jets fans had to wait as head coach Weeb Ewbank brought his prized rookie along slowly. Ewbank finally turned the team over to Namath on November 7, and he led the Jets to a 13–10 comeback against the Chiefs on the road. He would start the remainder of the season and finished with solid stats, throwing eighteen touchdowns and fifteen interceptions while being named to his first Pro Bowl. His play on the field began to win respect from his teammates as well as his opponents. Bills defensive end Ron McDole remembers that Namath also had a sense of humor: "One time we were playing in New York, I hit Namath and Tom Sestak hit him and Jim Dunaway hit him, all three at the same time. Joe used to back-pedal all the time instead of turning and running. He was lying down and looking up at us and said, did you happen to pass anybody up there in a green-and-white uniform? Didn't you even fall over anybody? Did you jump over anybody?" In addition to being humorous, Namath was a maverick. After Namath requested that the Jets' equipment man tape his shoes so that they looked white, Bill Hampton decided to have several pairs of white shoes specially ordered. At a time when all football players wore black shoes, this went directly against the game's military aesthetic. The new color did not go over well initially with fans, including those at home games, who called him a "fag." The shoes made him more of a target of fans and opposing players, but Namath seemed to relish the notoriety.[5]

Although the Jets finished with a losing record, going 5–8–1, the team had a cornerstone quarterback and also began to put together its defense. Along with Namath, the Jets drafted defensive end Verlon Biggs in the third round out of Jackson State University. Listed at 6'4" and 275 pounds (which was mostly muscle), Biggs was a prototype for a new athletic defensive end. Arguably Biggs would have been voted AFL Rookie of the Year if not for Namath, who became the first quarterback in either league to win the award. Biggs and Gerry Philbin, the Jets' other defensive end, anchored their line. Blessed with natural strength and speed, Biggs contrasted with Philbin, who relied on sheer drive and ferocity. According to Ewbank, Biggs was a pass rusher with a penchant for making the big play: "He was a great team player who was always where he was supposed to be." And although it did not happen right away, Biggs was responsible for helping to change Grantham's racial outlook; as native Mississippians, both men had grown up under segregation. But Grantham began to realize that he benefited immensely as an undersized linebacker playing behind the giant African American defensive end. "Big and strong as Verlon was, we got to be real good friends," recalls Grantham. "I could just lay back and hide behind his big ass."[6]

In Boston a rookie fullback emerged who had a very physical running style but struggled to keep his weight down. Jim Nance was drafted out of Syracuse University and came to the Patriots after playing behind Heisman Trophy winner Ernie Davis. As a sophomore this African American player led the Orangemen in rushing, and during his senior season in 1964 he scored thirteen touchdowns, which tied Jim Brown. Nance was the first African American to win an NCAA heavyweight wrestling title. His first came in 1963 as a sophomore, and he won again in 1965 during his senior year; both garnered him All-America honors. Nance gained a modest 321 rushing yards on 111 attempts, largely because his weight ballooned during the season, and he found himself on the bench after weighing 280 pounds, some fifty over his ideal playing weight. Joining Nance in the Patriots' backfield was veteran Larry Garron, who had toiled at fullback since the team's inception in 1960. Initially he blocked for Ron Burton and Billy Lott, but he led the Patriots in rushing in 1963 and 1964 by amassing rushing totals of 750 and 585 yards, respectively. Garron was an African American player from Marks, Mississippi, who had played for Lou Saban at Western Illinois University. Saban received death threats from racist fans who did not want him to bring his black players to Jonesboro, Arkansas, when they played Arkansas State University. The atmosphere surrounding the game was tense, so Saban made Garron the team captain for this game because he felt Garron was very level-headed. Garron recalled how Arkansas State's opposing players would "try to ride you off to the sidelines and people would come out of the stands and try to trample you." However, neither Nance nor Garron could help the Patriots during this terrible season, which they finished 4–8–2.[7]

In the Western Division the Chargers once again repeated as champs, going 9–2–3 by featuring both a strong offense and defense. They led the

AFL in team offense by leading in both passing and rushing. Running back Paul Lowe, who rushed for more yards than any back in league history with 1,121, was named UPI Player of the Year. Quarterback John Hadl finished fourth in the AFL in passing, and receiver Lance Alworth had his best season as a pro, finishing first in receiving yards with 1,602, the second most in league history. The success of the team and its exciting style of play translated into the Chargers drawing an average of 25,593 fans from 1962 through the 1965 season. Owner Barron Hilton felt that the team had outgrown Balboa Stadium, which was built in 1915. It had no seats, and spectators sat on long concrete rows. The locker rooms were far from satisfactory, and the toilets often overflowed. On April 27, 1965, with help from the mayor, the San Diego City Council endorsed the construction of a multipurpose stadium in the Mission Valley area of San Diego. On November 2 the citizens of San Diego approved the construction of a $27 million stadium with a 73 percent vote. And on December 24 groundbreaking ceremonies were held and the construction of San Diego Stadium was under way.[8]

The Denver Broncos were a stark contrast to the Chargers. Once again they finished last in the Western Division after winning just two games in 1963 and 1964. They improved to 4–10 in 1965. The acquisition of Cookie Gilchrist and Abner Haynes helped increase season-ticket sales, but neither player played defense, and the team finished next to last in total defense. They were particularly bad against the pass, yielding the second-most yards and giving up the second-most passing touchdowns in the AFL. The Broncos' first game epitomized their season: in San Diego on September 11 quarterback Mickey Slaughter threw three touchdown passes, while Gilchrist and Haynes scored touchdowns in a 34–31 loss to the Chargers. Gilchrist finished behind Paul Lowe in rushing yards, but he led the league in rushing attempts with 252, some 30 more than Lowe. Gilchrist was now thirty years old, and his 928 total rushing attempts over the past four seasons were more than any other player in the league. The wear and tear of professional football was taking a toll on his body, as he stated: "My knees were starting to swell and ache following each game, and I was finding it more and more difficult for my body to recover from the constant abuse it was facing on the gridiron. The 1965 campaign would be my last full and productive season in professional football." As Gilchrist and Haynes led the first real rushing attack by the Broncos, Coach Mac Speedie tried Slaughter, John McCormick, and Jacky Lee at quarterback and never settled on one. Despite the revolving door at quarterback, receiver Lionel Taylor still led the AFL in receiving, his fifth pass-catching title in the league's six years of play.[9]

The Buffalo Bills and San Diego Chargers met on December 26 to once again determine the AFL Champion. The rematch was played in San Diego before 30,361 fans in very comfortable 54-degree weather. Just as they had going into the previous year's game, the Chargers appeared to be overly confident. Jack Kemp felt that the overconfidence was based on the absence of Cookie Gilchrist—in essence the Chargers thought the Bills were not the same team without their dominating, physical running back. The Chargers were heavy favorites, and many felt their offense would control the game, but once again the Bills' defense was the deciding factor. Through the first quarter and the first ten minutes of the second, both defenses kept the scoreboard at zeros, but Buffalo broke through first when Kemp hit Ernie Warlick on an 18-yard touchdown pass. After forcing the Chargers to punt, Butch Byrd fielded the kick on his own 26-yard line and, after key blocks by Paul Maquire and Dave Kocourek, took it the distance for a touchdown. At the end of the second quarter Pete Gogolak's 24-yard field goal attempt was blocked, which made the score at halftime 14–0 Bills. The lead was extended early in the third quarter on an 11-yard Gogolak field goal, and the Bills' kicker added a 39-yard field goal with seconds left in the quarter. Buffalo's domination continued when a 32-yard field goal was added early in the fourth quarter, which made the score 23–0 and put the game out of reach. This was the final score as the Bills were crowned AFL Champions for the second straight year. "Before the game, everybody predicted that the Chargers would win by four or five touchdowns," recalled Mike Stratton. "It was very satisfying when they didn't even score. Coming to a place where you're playing on their turf with all of their sports writers, and everyone is predicting that they'll score X number of points, averaged X number of points per game the whole season, and it's going to be a blowout, and they didn't even generate one score."[10]

The Bills' ability to repeat as AFL Champions in some ways was secondary compared with the battle over college players between the rival leagues. On October 21, 1965, AFL commissioner Joe Foss circulated a memo to league owners indicating that according to "a reliable source" the NFL had set up a network of engagements for eligible college players in preparation for the draft. These engagements, according to Foss, were to take place during the weekend of November 27, when both drafts were occurring in New York. According to the informant, the NFL was going to get the jump on players by "babysitting" in numerous hotels and motels, just as in the previous year. Foss suggested that the AFL's draft date be moved up several days, and he also emphasized that teams not try to sign players until their seasons were over, including bowl games. Both drafts were held on November 27, and both leagues allowed their expansion teams to pick first. The Miami Dolphins were given the first two picks; they selected running back Jim Grabowski from the University of Illinois and quarterback Rick Norton from the University of Kentucky. The NFL's Atlanta Falcons selected linebacker Tommy Nobis of the University of Texas with the first pick, and then they selected quarterback Randy Johnson from Texas A&M University at Kingsville with the last pick in the first round. Arguably this draft helped to profoundly change professional football: the two leagues spent a combined total of $7 million to sign their 1966 draft choices.[11]

The Oilers' Bud Adams wrote $850,000 in bonus checks alone, and would have written more if All-American Nobis had chosen to sign with them. Nobis was on the cover of *Life* magazine and the subject of a national—in fact, interstellar—bidding war. Astronaut Frank Borman, a Houston resident and Oilers' fan, spent two weeks in orbit with James Lovell on the historic Gemini 7 mission in December 1965. During one broadcast that the astronauts beamed back on national television, Borman said, "Tell Nobis to sign with the Oilers." Despite this plea from thousands of miles above the earth, Nobis decided to sign a reported $600,000 deal with the Falcons. The NFL's babysitting system, employing some 100 individuals responsible for compiling information on various players, was effective. The NFL had info on more than 300 players, including what AFL teams had offered the player, whether that player would be difficult to sign, and his personal preferences. The NFL bragged that it had signed 140 of its draft choices while losing only 28 to the AFL, but that number was deceptive because many of the players taken in the early rounds did not have high-caliber talent. "During those years," said the Cowboys' Gil Brandt, "for a lot of teams, it wasn't about drafting the best player available so much as the best signable player available."[12]

By the end of 1965 it was clear that money was an issue for both leagues despite the increase in revenue from television. The Cowboys wanted running back Grabowski badly, and General Manager Tex Schramm spent several days before the draft negotiating a potential contract with Grabowski's agent, Arthur Morse. Schramm was instructed by Cowboys owner Clint Murchison to drop out after learning that Green Bay had offered a package of more than $500,000. So instead of selecting Grabowski, whom they really wanted, the Cowboys chose Iowa guard John Niland; Grabowski went to the Packers, where he signed an $850,000 contract. The unique nature of the publicly owned Packers dictated that all profits went back into the team rather than to shareholders, meaning that when teams were spending money, Green Bay had the most money to spend. This ate at Schramm, who hated losing players for any reason, and the fact that the Cowboys could not afford Grabowski left him very angry. "That was the first time we couldn't get a player because of money," he said. Financial limitations did not just affect NFL teams; in the AFL the Chargers had two blackboards going into the draft, the first with names of players who would be very costly to draft and the second with players who were more affordable. According to Coach Sid Gillman, "we always drafted from the second board." Schramm decided that he did not like the implications of the draft and what it meant regarding parity in the NFL. The Packers had defeated the Cleveland Browns in the NFL Championship game, winning their third title in five seasons. Schramm feared that if the situation persisted, the present environment would empower the league's strongest team and perhaps lead to the death of some of the weaker ones. As difficult as it was to swallow, Schramm came to the conclusion that the battle had gone on long enough and that it was time for a truce.[13]

The word "truce" was not often used in America in 1965 as the civil rights movement continued to push for the end of racial discrimination. In January, Dr. Martin Luther King, Jr., kicked off a voter registration drive in Selma, Alabama, and was arrested in February along with hundreds of demonstrators. On February 21, Malcolm X was assassinated; this former member of the Nation of Islam had attracted young people with his defiant message of self-protection. Malcolm criticized the goal of racial integration and King's message of redemption through brotherly love, and Malcolm's ideology began to be embraced by many young civil rights activists, who were becoming increasingly disillusioned by white violence. On Sunday, March 7, violence once again was used on peaceful protesters as the Southern Christian Leadership Conference led a march that set out from Selma to Montgomery. As they approached the Edmund Pettus Bridge, the marchers were severely beaten by state troopers and county police led by Sheriff Jim Clark, an event captured in graphic detail by television cameras. In the aftermath the federal government decided to act and passed the Voting Rights Act in August, outlawing literacy tests and empowering the U.S. attorney general to send federal examiners into the South. Within months approximately 80,000 new voters had been registered. In Mississippi, black registered voters soared from 28,500 in 1964 to 251,000 in 1968. But the optimism that came with the passage of the Voting Rights Act was quickly replaced with the reality of civil unrest in Watts. Its residents, who were 98 percent black, faced high unemployment, overcrowding, inadequate public transportation, inaccessible health-care facilities, and increasing crime and drug addiction, and the police were viewed as an occupying force. The arrest of a black motorist sparked a level of unrest that required the National Guard to quell. The violence reduced the Watts community to rubble and ashes and left 34 people killed, 1,032 injured, and 4,000 arrested and more than $35 million in property damage.[14]

The ideals of desegregation were not confined to lunch counters, movie theaters, water fountains, restrooms, and schools. In sports, although many schools in the South had reluctantly admitted African Americans as students, their football teams remained all white. By the mid-1960s these recently integrated schools began to relax their policy of not playing schools with black players. At the end of the 1964 season the University of Mississippi placed opportunism ahead of ideological purity and made the momentous decision to accept an invitation to play in the Bluebonnet Bowl in Houston. The opposing team, from the University of Tulsa, included several African Americans, among them star defensive lineman Willie Townes, who ironically was a Mississippi native from Hattiesburg. The results of the historic contest proved disappointing to Mississippi fans when Tulsa pulled off a 14–7 upset. Sportswriters selected Townes, who on several occasions tackled Mississippi running backs behind the line of scrimmage, as the most valuable lineman in the game. Townes's outstanding performance inspired a widely circulated joke spoofing Mississippi's switch to integrated competition. The joke came in the form of a question: "Who was the first Negro to integrate the Mississippi backfield?" The answer: "Willie Townes!" For Townes, it was not personal; he dominated teams in 1964 and 1965 as a two time All-Missouri Valley Conference first team player, and Tex Schramm selected Townes in the second round right after the Cowboys picked Niland.[15]

The AFL and NFL drafts once again brought on several players from historically black schools. The AFL drafted twelve players, of whom eight made rosters, while the NFL drafted twenty-two players, fifteen of whom made teams. Running back Emerson Boozer from the University of Maryland Eastern Shore was the highest-drafted player from a black school; he was picked in the sixth round by the Jets but was not selected until the seventh round by the Pittsburgh Steelers. Defensive back Ken Reeves from Norfolk State University was the first player selected from a black school in the NFL draft when the Atlanta Falcons picked him in the fourth round. Boozer was an elusive back who at 5'11" and 190 pounds was an outstanding open field runner who possessed strength and intensity. He ran for over 2,500 yards in college, thanks in part to great linemen such as Clarence Clemons. Clemons played with Boozer for two years, attending college on a football and music scholarship. After graduating from the University of Maryland Eastern Shore, Clemons played saxophone in several bands before joining Bruce Springsteen's E Street Band in the 1970s. Boozer was drafted so that he could team with Matt Snell in the Jets' backfield as they continued to add talent that would translate into victories on the field.[16]

After this draft it became very clear to Schramm that something had to be done. The negotiations toward a league merger in 1966 were so complex and secretive, so multilayered and fragmented, that even after the dust had settled, many of the participants still clung to differing accounts of the entire process. In 1965 there were extensive negotiations between Carroll Rosenbloom and Ralph Wilson, and later in the year Art Modell joined Rosenbloom and Schramm for a meeting with Wilson in Miami. But when the indemnity price of joining the league was named—Wilson recalled the asking price as $50 million—the Bills' owner announced that the meeting and negotiations were over and walked out. In virtually every one of these negotiations the NFL position had been that while it would consider a merger under certain circumstances, it was not interested in taking all the teams, and the two AFL clubs in NFL markets—the Jets and Raiders—would have to move. But by the spring Schramm wanted a deal and contacted Rozelle. They then called Hamilton Carothers, the NFL's general counsel, who explained that in order for the two leagues to come together, they would need congressional approval. Carothers pointed out that if some AFL teams were not included or forced to move, this would surely prompt legislators in that state to oppose the merger. His final instructions were that any negotiations needed to be kept confidential—the merger talks could not afford leaks. They decided that Schramm would represent the NFL and that he needed to reach out to someone who was discreet and influential in the AFL. "I suppose," Schramm said, an expression of mocking distaste curling his lips, "it's got to be Luh-*maahr*."[17]

On April 4, 1966, in the Chiefs' offices on Sixty-Third Street in Kansas City's Swope Park, Lamar Hunt was working on the wording of a newspaper advertisement when he received a phone call from Schramm. The Cowboys' president had never cared for Hunt, viewing him as obstructing their growth in Dallas. But on this day Schramm seemed unusually polite and asked if Hunt "might be able to come to Dallas to discuss a matter of mutual importance." Hunt was headed to Texas in two days for an AFL owners' meeting in Houston, so he adjusted his schedule to include a layover in Dallas before continuing to Houston. On the evening of Wednesday, April 6, he got off his plane at Love Field in Dallas and walked to the statue of the Texas Ranger in the terminal's lobby. There, waiting next to the statue and reading a paper, was Schramm. They shook hands and quietly moved to the door, walking into the vast Love Field parking lot, where they sat in Schramm's Oldsmobile in the twilight and spoke for forty-five minutes. Once inside, Schramm delivered his message. "I think the time has come to talk about a merger, if you'd be interested in that." "Fine," said Hunt, evenly. "I'm interested." Schramm then made a few things clear: the NFL would want Pete Rozelle to be the commissioner of a merged league and further discussions would have to be confidential, but the NFL was finally willing to consider a merger in which it would accept all existing AFL franchises.[18]

Hunt continued his trip, heading down to Houston for the owners' meeting. He did not tell any of his colleagues because there had been negotiations before and nothing had happened, plus there was a more pressing issue at the meetings. On April 8, Commissioner Joe Foss resigned when it became clear that he would be fired by the AFL owners. Criticism of Foss had grown steadily over the years, and the success of the NFL's babysitting program, along with the older league's eleventh-hour landing of Atlanta as an expansion franchise after the AFL had announced it planned to move to the city, only weakened his position. For its new commissioner, the AFL selected Al Davis. This was an alarming choice for leaders in both leagues. For starters, Davis was hardly beloved within the AFL. Writing a year earlier in *Sports Illustrated*, Bud Shrake noted that outside the city of Oakland, "and maybe the block in Brooklyn where he used to play stickball as a kid, it is not certain where Al Davis would finish in a popularity contest among sharks, the mumps, the income tax, and himself. If the voters were the other American Football League coaches, Davis probably would be third, edging out income tax in a thriller." But still chastened over the results of the 1966 draft, and on the recommendation of Raiders owner Wayne Valley, the majority (by a mere one vote) of the AFL owners decided Davis would be the perfect man to run the league in the event the war escalated. He was given a five-year contract at $60,000 annually, a private limousine, and an expanded budget to operate the league.[19]

On May 3, Schramm visited Hunt at his home on Armstrong Parkway. They sat down together, and Schramm outlined a more detailed framework of a deal. The NFL would ask for an $18 million indemnity from the AFL but would take all eight teams from the league and would consent to let all the teams remain in their present markets. In essence the New

York Giants and San Francisco 49ers expected financial competition in their markets from the Jets and Raiders and wanted compensation for the expected loss of revenue. Later that week, at a meeting in Sonny Werblin's apartment, Hunt first mentioned the proposal to his fellow owners. They had all decided not to include Davis at this meeting. Werblin and Valley were less than enthusiastic about sharing markets in New York and the Bay Area with established NFL franchises, but Hunt was able to change the AFL bylaws so that a merger required only a two-thirds majority instead of a unanimous vote. Hunt then contacted Schramm on May 10 and expressed optimism that any problems separating them could be solved and told Schramm to continue talks with the NFL.[20]

Everything seemed to be progressing until May 17, when Giants owner Wellington Mara announced the signing of Buffalo placekicker Pete Gogolak at a league meeting. This broke a verbal agreement between both leagues that neither would recruit a player from the other league. Gogolak had been frustrated with his salary, particularly when he saw unproven college players being given higher contracts: "I asked for $20,000 and they offered me $13,000, which I thought was a slap in the face because they were drafting guys out of college and giving them $20,000 bonuses and big salaries, and I was the second leading scorer in the league." Gogolak became a free agent on May 1, and the Giants were the only team to contact him, offering him a three-year $96,000 contract, which he signed right away. Several individuals at the meeting became livid with Mara. "This is a disgrace!" announced Vince Lombardi. "Wellington, I can't believe that you would do something like this to put us all into jeopardy!" "Goddamnit," said Carroll Rosenbloom to Mara, "if you'd wanted a kicker, why didn't you just ask me? I'd have given you one."[21]

This was arguably the single most provocative act of the war between the leagues. And it did not take much to provoke Al Davis; the next day he had compiled a list of ten players in the NFL who had played out their options. The AFL's response to Gogolak's signing came very quickly: on May 23 quarterback Roman Gabriel of the Los Angeles Rams signed a four-year $400,000 contract with the Oakland Raiders. San Francisco's quarterback, John Brodie, agreed to a three-year contract with the Houston Oilers at $250,000 per season. The Oilers also reached a contract agreement with the Chicago Bears' All-Pro tight end Mike Ditka, offering to pay him a $50,000 signing bonus. The Jets sought out Packers halfback Paul Hornung, and Davis, acting on behalf of the Jets, contacted Green Bay stars Willie Davis and Herb Adderley. Schramm realized that at this rate a merger would be difficult to achieve. After talking with Rozelle, he met with Hunt on May 31, and they worked out the major points of the merger. Hunt flew to New York later that day and presented the deal to the other AFL owners, many of whom balked at the figure of $18 million. But Hunt knew this was a very good deal for the AFL: they had twenty years to pay off the total, which amounted to $2 million per team over this period. This paled in comparison to the instantly increased value and revenues for each team in the league, as well as the reduced costs of a stabilized environment with a common draft. The NFL had absorbed teams from other leagues since its existence in 1920, but this would be the first and only time an entire league would be merged into America's preeminent professional football league.[22]

Over the next few days several details were worked out, including letting Davis know about the merger and the fact that he was about to be out of a job. Davis was angry that he had been left out of the negotiations and the particulars of the merger. He thought the merger would set up pro football like major league baseball, in which the American and National Leagues maintained separate regular-season schedules, league presidents, and identities that operated under one commissioner. Davis believed he would be president of the AFL while Rozelle headed the NFL. He accused the AFL owners of "selling out" and called the merger football's version of Yalta. For the first time, on Wednesday, June 8—despite Davis's bitterness—a press release spelled out publicly the details of the merger, which included the following stipulations:

- Pete Rozelle as commissioner
- A world championship game that season
- All existing franchises retained
- No franchises transferred from present locations
- Two new franchises no later than 1968
- Two more teams as soon after 1968 as practical
- Interleague preseason games in 1967
- Single league schedule in 1970
- A common draft the following January
- Continued two-network coverage[23]

The two most pressing issues were getting congressional approval of the merger and the setting up the championship game that was to be played after the upcoming season. There was also the matter of informing the networks, which were not happy after committing millions to the NFL and AFL championship games, now in effect semifinal contests. Rozelle struck a compromise by allowing both CBS and NBC to broadcast the final game, which Hunt decided to call the Super Bowl, the idea coming from a toy his kids played with called the "super ball." Naming the game was easy compared to getting the House Judiciary Committee to approve the merger. Rozelle had to reach out to David Dixon, who had been trying to get a pro team in New Orleans for years. Dixon contacted House Majority Leader Hale Boggs from Louisiana, who attached approval of the merger to a budget bill that was sure to pass in both houses. The final approval came on October 21, and as Rozelle was walking up the stairs of the Rotunda right before the vote, he said, "Congressman Boggs, I don't know how I can ever thank you enough for this. This is a terrific thing you've done." Boggs was a veteran of Louisiana politics and savvy enough not to let such transparent politesse go unremarked. "What do you mean you don't know how to thank me? New Orleans gets an immediate franchise in the NFL." "I'm going to do everything I can to make that happen," Rozelle assured him. At that Boggs turned and was prepared to leave, stating that the vote would not happen. Rozelle caught Boggs and said, "It's a deal, Congressman. You'll get your franchise." Boggs immediately replied, "If this doesn't work out, you will regret this for the rest of your fucking life!"[24]

Arguably the merger of 1966 worked out not only for the city of New Orleans, which finally got its franchise the following year, but also—more importantly—for pro football as a whole. That the timing of the merger was perfect was validated in November 1965 by a poll and report commissioned by the NFL. Louis Harris and Associates conducted a poll of three thousand households across America to survey the attitude of sports fans and found that as of October 1965 football had become America's number-one sport. According to Harris, a poll taken the previous April had reported that baseball was the nation's favorite pastime. The report concluded with an observation that was profoundly prophetic: "It is quite clear that the full potential of NFL football has hardly been tapped." Pro football would not look back. The AFL had opened entirely new markets for the sport, and in some ways the competition between the leagues had helped to fuel fan curiosity. Discussions around who was better, the yearly NFL champion or AFL champion, helped generate fan loyalty; the war over college players and rising salaries gave the media plenty to cover; and now the opportunity to have a yearly championship game facilitated dialogue about the potential outcome. Barron Hilton could not wait, however, although the merger surely meant that the value of his team would dramatically increase in the coming years; his Chargers had been hemorrhaging money since losing around $900,000 in 1960. They lost on average

$645,000 a year through 1964, and his father, Conrad, was ready to name him president and chief executive officer of the Hilton Hotel empire, provided he was free of pro football. On August 25 millionaire Eugene Klein and Sam Schulman headed a group of twenty-one investors who put up $10 million to buy the Chargers.[25]

The merger, money from television, and the increased value of AFL franchises did not go unnoticed by the players. On January 14, 1964, the AFL Players Association was organized by Tom Addison, linebacker from the Boston Patriots. Addison was elected the first president, and he submitted proposals for a players' pension fund and medical plan. The Players Association was endorsed by 264 eligible players. The representatives from the other eleven teams were Jack Kemp (Buffalo), vice president; Jim Tyrer (Kansas City), secretary-treasurer; Fred Glick (Houston); Wayne Hawkins (Oakland); Larry Gratham (New York); Bud McFadin (Denver); and Ron Mix (San Diego). All the player representatives were white, and this did not change when Kemp was elected president in 1966. Although he immediately gave the organization more structure and a broader agenda, its all-white makeup stayed the same.[26]

The Players Association proposed that there be more investigation of players involved in fines, that fined players have the right to petition the commissioner through a written letter, and that players thrown out of games be automatically fined. It also requested that television revenue from the AFL Championship and All-Star games be divided between the players and owners, with 25 percent going to players in 1966 and with that amount increasing to 40 percent in 1969. The final major issue addressed in the association's minutes was a recommendation that the owners of Denver and Buffalo modernize their dressing-room facilities. For the owners, the major issue was player compensation from the championship game and All-Star Game, and this was addressed by paying each individual player a set amount for each game. The association gradually began to get various concessions from league owners, and within two years contracts between the association and owners were being hammered out to deal with numerous issues affecting players.[27]

For the AFL, the 1966 season represented a new beginning, but more importantly it presented the first opportunity to compete directly against the NFL. At the end of the season the AFL Champion would take on the best the NFL had to offer in the Super Bowl. For Al Davis, who felt he was pushed out as commissioner of the AFL, this offered the chance to get even with Pete Rozelle and the NFL in general. Davis had worked hard all his life to be involved with football. Although he did not have the necessary skills to play at the high school or collegiate level, he was determined to carve out a niche for himself in the game he loved. After attending several colleges, Davis eventually graduated in 1950 from Syracuse University, where he took courses in football strategy while majoring in English. In 1952 he was inducted into the army and coached the Fort Belvoir football team to a record of eight wins and two losses. After leaving the army, he served as a volunteer coach with the Baltimore Colts before landing a job as an assistant coach for the Citadel for two seasons in 1955 and 1956. Davis next landed at the University of Southern California, where he was assistant coach and recruiter for the Trojans. During his three seasons at USC the team was placed on probation for illegal payments to players and other benefits; they were also sanctioned for inducing recruits signed by other schools to break their letter of intent. After the 1959 season, head coach Don Clark was fired, and Davis met Sid Gillman at a coaching clinic. Gillman hired Davis to coach the backfield of the 1960 Chargers before Wayne Valley called and made him head coach and general manager of the Raiders after the 1962 season. Davis immediately turned the team around and planned to do the same as AFL commissioner when he was hired in April, but the merger prevented him from putting into place his vision for the league. He was unwilling to serve as AFL president under Pete Rozelle and returned to the Raiders after his two-month tenure. Davis never forgot this slight and held a significant amount of resentment toward Rozelle and the new NFL. He returned to the Raiders as not only general manager but also one of three general partners after having bought 10 percent of the team. As soon as he got back to Oakland, he made several key moves: he hired John Rauch as head coach, he traded for cornerback Willie Brown, and when veteran quarterback George Blanda was released by the Oilers after the season, he took a chance that Blanda could still play.[28]

The Raiders finished second to the Chiefs with a record of 8–5–1. They played in the new Oakland–Alameda County Stadium, which was built at a cost of $25 million and was second to none. The new stadium had a football capacity of 53,000 and could be reconfigured for baseball as well. The 1966 Raiders finished second in the league in passing but seventh in rushing. The defense allowed the fewest yards in the AFL and was the best against the pass. The defensive line was anchored by Ben Davidson, Ike Lassiter, and newly acquired tackle Tom Keating from Buffalo. The secondary was also very good: Kent McCloughan had four interceptions, and so did Roger Bird. But the anchor of the defensive backfield was veteran Dave Grayson, who along with McCloughan was named first team

All-Pro after the season. After the 1964 season Al Davis traded Fred "The Hammer" Williamson for Grayson, who had helped lead the Texans to the 1962 championship. This African American player was a smart, skilled defender who grew up in San Diego's Logan Heights district; he attended Lincoln High School before playing for the University of Oregon. In 1961 he was signed as a free agent by the Dallas Cowboys, but Tom Landry did not have room for him on the roster. Gil Brandt, the Cowboys' general manager, called Texans coach Hank Stram and suggested they take a look at Grayson, who was signed. During the 1961 season Grayson returned an interception 99 yards, which set the AFL record, and he had a key interception in the 1962 championship game when he picked off George Blanda. He was selected to the AFL All-Star team in 1962, 1963, and 1964 as a member of the Texans and in 1965 after his first season with the Raiders. Grayson played with the Raiders through the 1970 season and was viewed as one of the greatest defensive backs to play in the AFL; his career arguably warranted consideration in the Pro Football Hall of Fame.[29]

Like Grayson, Ernie Ladd warrants Hall of Fame consideration. He was voted AFL All-Pro in 1961, 1964, and 1965, but the "Big Cat" was picked up by the Oilers after playing out his option with the Chargers in 1966. Ladd cut off his signature facial feature—his goatee—when he joined Houston, not because he was forced to, he said, but "out of respect for Wally Lemm," the Oilers' new coach. At a time when most professional athletes were not permitted to wear facial hair, Ladd was an outspoken black athlete who did not conform. As the face of the boycott in New Orleans, Ladd had become more opinionated, and in an interview before the start of training camp he indicated that his goatee had caused much discussion while he played with the Chargers but that he "could care less." Ladd went on to say that "the commissioner can't tell me how to do my face. Nobody can make me close my mouth. When I signed my contract I didn't sign a contract for voice or speech, I signed to play football." Ladd was also asked about the merger and again he did not mince words: "I think it's terrible in that it's going to cut the salaries of players coming out of school and it's given the advantage back to the owners." The final topic that Ladd commented on was the recent announcement by running back Jim Brown that he was retiring from the Cleveland Browns. New owner Art Modell had tried to persuade Brown to return while he was in London playing a part in the movie *The Dirty Dozen*. Modell decided to fine Brown, which caused him to announce his retirement. Ladd weighed in on the NFL losing arguably its greatest runner: "He's done everything for the NFL except make footballs. And then the Browns give him an ultimatum. I don't have much respect for his teammates who didn't go to bat for him and his employer either if that's all the regard he has for Jimmy. They treated him like dirt."[30]

When it came to outspoken black players, the Denver Broncos had one of the most well known in Cookie Gilchrist. Since being traded after the 1964 season, Gilchrist had not caused many problems on the team aside from arriving late for training camp and various team meetings. When he arrived late for camp in 1966, he made a request to head coach Mac Speedie: Gilchrist wanted his former Bills teammate Willie Ross to be given a tryout. Ross was a running back, and Speedie told Gilchrist first that he would be fined $1,000 for arriving ten days late and second that the Broncos were loaded at the running back position. According to Gilchrist, the meeting became confrontational only when Speedie brought up Ross's Muslim faith. As Gilchrist recalled, Speedie "didn't want that militant Muslim attitude around the team, because he already had enough trouble just dealing with him." Gilchrist took issue with what he perceived as Speedie's having jumped to the incorrect conclusion that because of his religion "Willie must be a follower of the black supremacy movement." Before leaving Speedie's office, Gilchrist requested a trade and refused to report to training camp. Once reporters got wind of the story, Speedie summed up Gilchrist's absence in an interview by saying, "Well, Christmas came early for me this year." Unfortunately for Speedie, it was not Christmas that came early but his release as coach. The Broncos opened the season by losing to the Oilers 45–7, and the following week they lost to Boston 24–10. Speedie then resigned as head coach, and assistant Ray Malavasi guided the team the rest of the way as they once again finished last in the West at 4–10. The Broncos purged themselves of both player and coach when they traded Gilchrist to the Dolphins in mid-October.[31]

As Gilchrist's career was ending, several African American running backs stepped in and filled the void. In Boston, Jim Nance lost weight and set the league on fire in his second year as a pro. Using pure power plus surprising speed, Nance pounded away at defenses in workhorse fashion, gaining an AFL record 1,458 yards while scoring eleven touchdowns. The Jets' Matt Snell finished fourth in the AFL in rushing with 644 yards, and rookie halfback Emerson Boozer rushed for 455 yards, but his 4.7 yards per carry placed him fourth in the league. Boozer gave New York its first legitimate outside threat. Although he was a very good high school player at Laney High in Augusta, Georgia, his only scholarship offer was to the University of Maryland Eastern Shore. At merely 5'11" and 190 pounds, he excelled in the open field, and his speed brought comparisons to Gale Sayers. Both Snell and Boozer were key contributors in the Jets' win over the Patriots in the last game of the season. The Jets' 38–28 victory made the Bills Eastern Division champions, despite the Patriots' two wins over Buffalo during the season. The win by the Jets was an upset because Joe Namath, based on several accounts, was in no condition to play. Facing knee surgery after the season, Namath stayed out drinking until early Saturday morning, just hours before kickoff. "We were out all night," said Frank Cicatiello, a friend who was visiting Namath. "Joe went from drinking B&B to Sambuca to Grand Marnier. I called back home and told a buddy to bet on Boston who was favored by seven or ten points. He said why? I said because we're not home yet and it's like six-thirty in the morning." Unfortunately for the Patriots, Namath needed only a couple hours of sleep: he threw for 287 yards and three touchdowns in the Jets' victory.[32]

The Houston Oilers dominated the AFL during their first two seasons, but now they were confined to the basement of the Eastern Division. They tied the expansion Miami Dolphins with the worst record in the league at 3–11. Despite the acquisition of Ernie Ladd the Oilers were last in the AFL in total defense, next to last in passing defense, and seventh against the run. The one bright spot on this bad team was receiver Charley Frazier, who was a former member of the U.S. international team that set a world record in the 4x100-meter relay. This African American player with blazing speed joined the Oilers in 1962 as an undrafted player from Texas Southern University. They patiently waited as he finally developed into a very good receiver in 1966, catching fifty-seven passes for 1,129 yards and twelve touchdowns. Unfortunately, Frazier could not prevent the Oilers from becoming the first team in history to lose twice in one season to an expansion team. The Dolphins beat Houston 20–13 on October 23 and then won 29–28 in the last game of the season on December 18. To make matters worse, the team plane had mechanical problems leaving Miami; players were told after it was repaired that the craft was fine but that they could find alternative transportation if they chose. One mostly white faction led by quarterback Don Trull voted to stay in Miami, while a mostly black faction led by Ladd voted to go home. Another group tried to get back through New Orleans. The Oiler plane made several stops along the way, and the Ladd group ended up stranded in Oklahoma. The plane came to a final rest in San Antonio, with players scattered from there to Miami, Tulsa, and New Orleans. This journey gave Coach Wally Lemm the opportunity to reflect, and he vowed that "we may lose next year but it won't be with the same people."[33]

Some 42,000 fans came out for the 1966 AFL Championship game, played in Buffalo's Memorial Stadium on January 1 between the two-time defending champion Bills and Kansas City. For the AFL, this was the most desirable game in its short history because the winner would have the opportunity to play the NFL Champion in the first Super Bowl. The game conditions were typical for Buffalo at that time of year—overcast gray skies, 32 degrees, and winds at 45 miles per hour, which made it feel more like 22 degrees. According to Len Dawson, "the weather was terrible, we might have been the last plane or the only plane to land in Buffalo. Today, they probably wouldn't have attempted it. Back then, we weren't that valuable." Hank Stram put together a very good game plan: it started with a high short kickoff that was fumbled by the Bills' Dudley Meredith at their 31-yard line and recovered by the Chiefs' Jerrell Wilson. Dawson quickly hit a wide-open Fred Arbanas for a 7–0 lead. Stram felt that Buffalo was a very good team "but they were like a lot of NFL teams, they used a 4–3 defense and they didn't do a lot of different things. We used a lot of variety, I can still see that Arbanas touchdown, he was so wide open it looked like he had run out of the bleachers." But four minutes later the Bills tied the game on a 69-yard pass from Jack Kemp to Elbert Dubenion. These were the last points of the day for Buffalo, and the Chiefs reeled off 24 unanswered points that included a 29-yard touchdown pass in the second quarter from Dawson to Otis Taylor. After a 22-yard field goal by Mike Mercer, in the fourth quarter Mike Garrett scored two touchdowns on runs of 1 yard and 18 yards, making the final score 31–7.[34]

The Chiefs celebrated by dousing each other in champagne despite the $2,000 fine from league president Milt Woodard, who mandated that there be no alcoholic beverages in the winning locker room. Later that afternoon the team gathered in a conference room at the Holiday Inn and watched the Green Bay Packers edge the Dallas Cowboys 34–27. Though there would have been an undeniable allure to facing their old Dallas rivals, most of the Chiefs' squad was glad for the opportunity to face the NFL's dominant team, Vince Lombardi's Packers, which had won the NFL title four times in six seasons. The anxious Chiefs arrived in California on January 4, eleven days before kickoff. Green Bay arrived four days later, and only then at Rozelle's insistence. Lombardi wanted to fly in on January 14, the morning before the game, just as the Packers did for any other road contest. But this was not simply another road game—it was Super Bowl I and would be played in the Los Angeles Coliseum. What Lombardi feared was exactly what he encountered: a large media contingent building up impossible expectations. The question before the game was whether the young, complex approach of these representatives from the "Mickey Mouse" league could compete with the experienced meat-and-potatoes attack of the Packers. Las Vegas believed the odds were long, and the Chiefs were installed as eight-point underdogs early but the spread quickly grew to thirteen. For one of the Chiefs this did not sit well, and he voiced his opinions repeatedly.[35]

Fred "The Hammer" Williamson decided that this was an opportunity to introduce himself to America and take some of the pressure off his nervous teammates. "We had about 20 writers and they were all following me because everybody was afraid to talk. My whole purpose was to put myself in some notary position so that I could sell myself after the game." Williamson told reporters that Packers receivers Carroll Dale and Boyd Dowler would be victims of his "Hammer Tackle," a swinging arm chop that he described as "a blow delivered with great velocity perpendicular to the earth's latitudes." Williamson bluntly proclaimed, "We're going to whip their asses, all of them, and if Dowler or Dale or any of those guys have the nerve to catch a pass in my territory they're going to pay the price." Realizing that the reporters were eating this up, he made sure to provide vivid details: "I'm going to lay a few hammers on 'em and they're going to go back into the huddle with their heads ringing like they're hearing chimes and their eyes full of stars and dots and their legs twanging like rubber bands." Williamson grew up in Gary, Indiana, the son of a welder who worked in an American Motors plant making Nash Ramblers. He was an A student who went to Northwestern University on a track scholarship to study architecture. But he learned quickly that in the Big Ten, football was more lucrative than track. "They sweetened the deal," he says slyly. Then he was on to the pros, drafted as a defensive back by the 49ers. Williamson played ten years, most of them All-Pro seasons for Oakland and Kansas City, and with typical modesty called himself "an innovator." This black athlete modeled himself after Muhammad Ali and felt that he "was one of the first guys with gall, to talk trash with such a purpose, that he could be a star in popular culture."[36]

Williamson was the first athlete to recognize the potential for publicity that the Super Bowl generated. Pete Rozelle also clearly understood that this was an opportunity for pro football to continue its ascension past major league baseball as America's first sport. Mickey Herskowitz, a writer for the *Houston Post* who covered the AFL, was given $250,000 from Rozelle, who said, "I don't care how you spend it. But when the news media leaves Los Angeles, I want them to be talking about all the things we did that they don't do at the World Series." Rozelle also realized that pro football's relationship with television could deteriorate if a compromise was not worked out regarding which network would cover the game. Both CBS's contract with the NFL and NBC's with the AFL called for exclusive broadcast rights of the league championship game. Rozelle made a deal that allowed both networks to broadcast the contest, each network spending $1 million for the rights and another $1 million on promotion. In the first half of January both networks devoted more than half of their nighttime promotional spots to the upcoming game. CBS, which provided the video feed of the game, charged $42,000 for a thirty-second spot or $85,000 for one minute of commercial time, about $10,000 more than NBC.[37]

The game was watched by more than 65 million people, the largest audience ever to watch a sporting event in America. But attendance was only 63,036, and there were more than 32,000 empty seats in the vast Coliseum—arguably pro football fans were simply not used to traveling to neutral sites. Kickoff was scheduled for 1:00 P.M. local time on Sunday, January 15, and the temperature was 54 degrees with bright sunny skies. After seven seasons of disparagement by the older league, it was inevitable that the game would feel like a crusade to the Chiefs players. As they stood in the tunnel, waiting to take the field before the pregame introductions, Buck Buchanan and Bobby Bell were so fired up that they had tears in their eyes. But this would be the ultimate test for the AFL Champions: the Packers entered the game with a 13–2 record and had come within four points of a perfect season. Green Bay was a team of great stars, its roster listing future Hall of Famers such as Bart Starr, Jim Taylor, Paul Hornung, Forrest Gregg, Ray Nitschke, Willie Davis, Henry Jordan, Willie Wood, and Herb Adderley.[38]

Super Bowl I began with both teams making first downs on their initial series before having to punt. But with 6:04 left in the first quarter the Packers scored first when Starr read a blitz and hit receiver Max McGee with a 37-yard pass that he caught with one hand and scored untouched. McGee was playing only because starter Dowler had been hurt in the first minutes of the game; McGee had spent most of the year on the bench as a backup, catching only four passes for 91 yards. He fully expected not to play in the game and decided to enjoy himself in Los Angeles. Days before the game, reporter Jerry Izenberg called McGee's room to try to get a quote from the colorful receiver. His roommate, Zeke Bratkowski, answered the phone and told Jerry that Max was not there because it was "only 10:59." Jerry then asked, "What time is curfew?" Bratkowski replied, "Eleven. Call back in the middle of the night." And despite the stern warning from Lombardi that any players caught out the night before the game would be fined $2,500, McGee told Hornung that he had just "waddled in about 7:30 in the morning and could barely stand up for the kickoff." Hornung kept teasing him, asking, what would you do if you had to play? McGee replied, "No way, there's no way I could make it."[39]

Unfortunately for the Chiefs, McGee had no choice but to play the entire game and arguably was the major factor in this historic contest. The Chiefs responded to McGee's touchdown when Len Dawson found Curtis McClinton on a 17-yard pass in the second quarter to even the score. But the Packers' veteran fullback Taylor scored on a 14-yard run, which was followed by a 31-yard field goal by Mike Mercer of the Chiefs as the teams broke for halftime with the Packers leading 14–10. Most fans across the country were surprised that Kansas City was this close to the mighty Packers, and Dawson felt that if they continued to play mistake-free football his Chiefs had a real chance. But in the third quarter at midfield on third-and-5 Dawson dropped back and the Packers sent a blitz that caused him to be intercepted by Willie Wood, who returned it to the Chiefs' 5-yard line. Dawson vividly described the play that changed the game: "They hadn't blitzed the whole game. We hadn't seen any film of them blitzing. They just happened to guess right, blitzing from my weak side when I didn't have any protection. My arm was hit, or the ball was hit." Green Bay scored on the next play as running back Elijah Pitts carried it over, and the game was never the same. From that point on, the Packers seemed to ooze confidence as the AFL Champions looked outmanned. McGee scored later in the third on a 13-yard pass from Starr, and Pitts added a 1-yard touchdown run in the fourth quarter that made the final score 35–10.[40]

Starr was named the game's MVP, but McGee could have been too, after catching seven passes for 138 yards and two touchdowns. The Packers received $15,000 each and the Chiefs $7,500; for Green Bay's offensive lineman Bill Curry, whose annual salary was $13,500, his winner's share capped off a great season. Reporters peppered Lombardi with questions comparing the Chiefs' talent to that of other NFL teams until they got the sound bite they wanted: "I don't think they are as good as the top teams in the National Football League. They're a good team with fine speed but I'd have to say NFL football is tougher." For many, the game proved that the AFL was inferior, but supporters of the "Mickey Mouse" league argued that the Chiefs were inferior not to the NFL but only to the Green Bay Packers.[41]

Like the Super Bowl, the first common draft, scheduled for March 14–15, was highly anticipated and clearly indicated that pro football was building for its future. There were twenty-six picks and seventeen rounds as the New Orleans Saints joined the NFL as an expansion team. In a trade with New Orleans the Baltimore Colts selected defensive lineman Bubba Smith with the first overall pick. Smith's teammate from Michigan State University, running back Clint Jones, was chosen next by the Minnesota Vikings, who acquired the pick from the New York Giants. The Miami Dolphins were the first AFL team to pick, as they followed the San Francisco 49ers; Dolphins owner Joe Robbie badly wanted quarterback Steve Spurrier from Florida, but the 49ers selected the 1966 Heisman Trophy winner. The Dolphins decided to pick quarterback Bob Griese from Purdue University, the Heisman runner-up. This draft had very talented players; in fact, eight would become members of the Pro Football Hall of Fame. Those eight included Griese, along with running back Floyd Little, who was picked sixth overall by the Denver Broncos out of Syracuse. Notre Dame defensive end Alan Page was picked fifteenth by the Minnesota Vikings, and offensive guard Gene Upshaw from Texas A&I University was chosen by the Raiders seventeenth in the first round. Jackson State University's Lem Barney was selected in the second round by the Detroit Lions to play defensive back, and linebacker Willie Lanier was chosen by the Chiefs out of Morgan State University with the fiftieth pick in round two. Future Hall of Famer Rayfield Wright out of Fort Valley State University was chosen with the 182nd pick in the seventh round as an offensive tackle by the Dallas Cowboys. And in the ninth round with the 214th selection the Houston Oilers found defensive back Ken Houston, who along with Barney, Lanier, and Wright came out of the historically black college ranks from Prairie View A&M University. All told, forty-seven players from historically black institutions were selected, and twenty-two made NFL or AFL rosters.

Buck Buchanan sacks the Green Bay Packers' Bart Starr in the first quarter of Super Bowl I. (*Courtesy of the Pro Football Hall of Fame.*)

Abner Haynes, an outstanding running back for the Dallas Texans, helped lead them to the 1962 double overtime AFL Championship over the Houston Oilers. (*Courtesy of the Pro Football Hall of Fame.*)

Ernie Ladd, also known as "The Big Cat," was a dominant defensive lineman for the Chargers, Oilers, and Chiefs. He was also elected the spokesman for the black players' boycott of the AFL All-Star game in New Orleans in 1965. (*Courtesy of the Pro Football Hall of Fame.*)

RIGHT: Cookie Gilchrist was the first AFL running back to rush for 1,000 yards in a season, when he played for the Buffalo Bills in 1962. (*Courtesy of the Pro Football Hall of Fame.*)

Buck Buchanan was the first African American in pro football from a historically black school to be selected as the AFL's number-one overall draft pick, when he was drafted by the Kansas City Chiefs in 1963. (*Courtesy of the Pro Football Hall of Fame.*)

In 1968 Marlin Briscoe of the Denver Broncos became the first African American quarterback in the modern era to start a game. (*Courtesy of the Pro Football Hall of Fame.*)

FACING PAGE: Willie Lanier of the Kansas City Chiefs was the first African American to play middle linebacker in pro football. Here he closes in to make the tackle on a New York Giants running back. (*Courtesy of the Pro Football Hall of Fame.*)

Lamar Hunt and Bud Adams were the principal founders of the "Foolish Club." (*Courtesy of the Pro Football Hall of Fame.*)

THE NEW NFL

The Super Bowl clearly indicated that a new era of pro football was about to begin. Although teams from both leagues would not play each other during the regular season until 1970, they began to play exhibition games in 1967. This change brought much anticipation from fans during the preseason and only added to the excitement of the Super Bowl at the end of the year. Change was the theme as pro football portrayed itself as entering in essence its phase of expansion. The AFL had added the Dolphins the previous year, and this was the first season for the NFL's New Orleans Saints. For African Americans, this change did not include the opportunity to play any position on the field or serve as head coaches of teams. The 1967 draft illustrated that positional segregation in pro football was real but could change if teams were willing to extend opportunities to black players. One such team was Kansas City. The Chiefs were willing to give a black player the opportunity to play a position that historically had been solely manned by white players: middle linebacker. Willie Lanier as a rookie became the first African American to play the position for the Chiefs during the 1967 season, and he quickly dispelled the notion that African Americans did not have the intellect to be the quarterback of the defense. Unfortunately for quarterback Hank Washington of West Texas State University, no AFL or NFL teams were ready to extend the same opportunity at the most important position on the field.

Washington was not selected despite being 6'3" and 205 pounds and setting the all-time record at West Texas State University for total offense during the 1965–1966 seasons. The fact that this strong-armed quarterback was not drafted was addressed in a scathing editorial by Bill Nunn Jr. of the *Pittsburgh Courier*. Nunn wrote that some scouts characterized Washington as the best quarterback in the country, and that the most skeptical analyst listed him among the top ten at the position. Nunn noted that several teams in pro football needed quarterbacks and that he understood how players like Steve Spurrier from the University of Florida, Bob Griese from Purdue University, Don Horn from San Diego State University, Tim Jones from Weber State University, John Foruria from the University of Idaho, and Bob Davis from the University of Virginia were picked before Washington. But he added that the only reason quarterbacks such as Vidal Carlin from the University of North Texas, Corey Colehour from the University of North Dakota, Rich Egloff from the University of Wyoming, Terry Southall from Baylor University, Steve Laub from Illinois Wesleyan University, Bruce Matte from Miami University (Ohio), and Bill Buckner from Delta State University were selected before Washington was that they had white skin. Nunn reiterated that there had never been a regular African American quarterback on any team and that numerous scouts had gone on the record stating that Washington would likely be the first. Nunn ended his editorial criticizing pro football and its color line at the quarterback position: "Hank Washington there is no doubt that you have become a victim of your color. True, there may be some teams in professional football who are stocked well enough in quarterbacks that they couldn't use your services. But those teams are few. So this week you, Hank Washington, have a right to be confused. You also have a perfect right to be bitter, disillusioned, frustrated and bewildered."[1]

The New York Giants brought Washington into camp as a free agent, but he was released before the regular season began. Professional football was a year away from extending an opportunity to an African American to play quarterback as a starter. The AFL was also one year away from adding its last team, ironically to one of its staunchest critics, Paul Brown. After being pushed out as head coach of the Cleveland Browns in 1963 by owner Art Modell, Brown wanted to return to pro football. He put together an ownership group that sought to bring a pro team to either Cincinnati or Columbus, Ohio. Cincinnati was chosen because its major league baseball team, the Reds, was threatening to leave town if Crosley Field was not replaced with a new stadium. The Reds' owner, Bill DeWitt, was holding up the new stadium deal because he did not like several of the provisions.

As a result he sold the Reds to the *Cincinnati Enquirer* in December 1966 for $8 million, and the new owners entered into a forty-year lease agreement to play in the new stadium. In essence the AFL's expansion into Cincinnati ensured that the Reds remained in the city. On May 24, 1967, Cincinnati became the second expansion franchise in AFL history. The city council promised to begin construction of a new stadium on a forty-eight-acre downtown plot that bordered Second Street and the Ohio River. Riverfront Stadium would be built for baseball and football and was scheduled to open in 1970, with a capacity of 56,200. Brown chose the name "Bengals" after the 1937 Cincinnati team that had played in the second of the three AFLs. ("Bengals" was chosen over the overwhelmingly popular "Buckeyes" because Brown did not want it to be confused with Ohio State University's nickname, and he wanted a name that people in Kentucky, West Virginia, Indiana, and Ohio could relate to.) The first Bengals franchise played in the city from 1937 to 1942, and possibly as an insult to Modell, Brown chose their exact shade of orange as the team's primary color with black as the secondary color. Brown chose a very simple logo that was displayed on the players' helmets: the word "BENGALS" in black lettering.[2]

Just as the AFL now seemed poised to enter the NFL with ten teams, the Denver Broncos realized that stadium expansion was no longer a choice. As the worst team in the league, the Broncos had toyed with the idea of moving to Birmingham, Alabama, where crowds of 40,000 routinely turned out for exhibition games. The club's future was not assured, because its playing facility, Bears Stadium, could not accommodate the minimum 50,000 paying customers the NFL required. But in March 1967 a $25 million bond issue was passed that allowed the stadium to be expanded from 34,000 to 54,000. The Broncos also faced another challenge, the fact that they had never signed a first-round draft choice. With the first AFL/NFL common draft, the only competition now came from the Canadian Football League. With the sixth pick in the first round, the Broncos selected Floyd Little, running back from Syracuse University. Born in New Haven, Connecticut, this African American player led the nation in all-purpose yards during his senior year. Little wanted the Jets to draft him so he could remain on the East Coast, and he thought about playing in the CFL after he was picked by the Broncos. "I thought Denver was a place where you could get attacked by Indians. The only people who went to Denver were in a Conestoga wagon. But when we flew out, it was the most gorgeous thing I'd ever seen."[3]

To help mentor Little, the Broncos reacquired Cookie Gilchrist in a trade, which reunited him with his old coach, Lou Saban, who had tired of Gilchrist's antics off the field and traded him to Denver after the Bills' 1964 championship. Gilchrist, Little, and the other Broncos were the first AFL team to play an NFL team during the exhibition season. On August 5 the Detroit Lions traveled to Bears Stadium to take on Denver. Defensive tackle Dave Costa was Denver's captain, and he met Lions captains Mike Lucci and Alex Karras at midfield for the coin toss. Costa remembers, "I put my hand out, and Karras just looked at it." Karras then looked around the stadium and said, "If we lose this game, I'll walk back to Detroit." Clearly Karras meant this remark figuratively because Denver won 13–7, making them the first AFL team to beat an NFL team. The Denver fans were ecstatic and felt that even though they were the worst team in the AFL, they could defeat an NFL team. For the next week, a local radio station started giving reports on Karras's walk back to Detroit: "Alex Karras has now reached Des Moines, Iowa," or "Karras was reportedly seen in a suburb of Cedar Rapids."[4]

The Broncos' victory illustrated that the AFL had teams that could be competitive with NFL teams, but the Kansas City Chiefs decided that they had much more to prove. NFL Films was founded by Ed Sabol, who started a company called Blair Motion Pictures in 1962. After submitting the winning bid to film the 1962 NFL Championship game, Sabol's company was renamed NFL Films in 1965. Sabol was given $20,000 from each of the fourteen NFL owners, and in return he filmed every NFL game and produced a highlight film for each team. The Chiefs took on the Chicago Bears on August 23, and Hank Stram had just received NFL Films' highlight film from the Super Bowl, which he showed his team the day of the game. Sabol's narration of the film centered on how the dominant Packers were eventually able to overpower the young, inexperienced Chiefs, and needless to say, after watching the film the Chiefs players were absolutely ready to play. The fact that George Halas was one of the principal opponents of Lamar Hunt's idea to start the AFL helped fuel the players' intensity. Now some seven years later he had to bring his team to Kansas City to face the best that the "Foolish Club" had to offer. The Bears featured two of the NFL's greatest stars in halfback Gale Sayers and middle linebacker Dick Butkus. Sayers had chosen the Bears over the Chiefs in 1965 largely because of money, but he also stated that he wanted to join the league that had better competition. All of these factors produced an explosion by the Chiefs' offense; quarterback Len Dawson threw four touchdown passes in the first half and helped lead Kansas City to 32 points in the second quarter. The Bears' defense could not stop the Chiefs' multiple formations, moving pocket, and double–tight end alignments. The final score sent a message heard throughout the NFL: Kansas City 66, Chicago 24. The Chiefs had a custom that each time they scored a touchdown, the team's mascot, a horse named War Paint, would run down the sideline in celebration. According to Sayers, "We knew it was going to be a tough game, but we didn't think they would beat us like that. The horse they had running around the track after each touchdown almost died. It was awful."[5]

Scoring was the theme of the 1967 AFL regular season as the Oakland Raiders dominated the league on their way to a record of 13–1. Al Davis had been stockpiling talent, and he decided that for the type of offense the Raiders wanted to run they needed a strong-armed quarterback. Raiders coach John Rauch felt that starter Tom Flores, who was the league's third-leading passer in 1966, was too injury prone. So Davis traded Flores and receiver Art Powell to the Bills for backup quarterback Daryle Lamonica and receiver Glenn Bass. The Raiders also added one of the best defensive backs in the league by acquiring Denver's Willie Brown for offensive tackle Rex Mirich and a draft choice. The final piece to the puzzle was Davis's signing of veteran kicker and backup quarterback George Blanda, who had been recently released by Houston. The Oilers felt that thirty-nine-year-old Blanda was washed up, but playing in his eighteenth year of professional football he led the AFL in scoring with fifty-six extra points and twenty field goals in thirty tries.[6]

In order to try to keep up with their division counterparts, Kansas City orchestrated its own blockbuster trade four games into the season. Coach Hank Stram characterized the acquisition of Ernie Ladd and quarterback Jacky Lee from Houston in exchange for quarterback Pete Beathard as "the most significant trade in the Chiefs eight year history." Ladd was expected to pair with Buck Buchanan and anchor the defensive line the way they did at Grambling State University. But the defending AFL Champion Chiefs struggled in big games to defend the pass and finished fifth in the league in passing defense. Kansas City finished second in the division at 9–5, largely because it was swept by Oakland and San Diego. Coach Stram decided to insert rookie linebackers Willie Lanier and Jim Lynch from the University of Notre Dame into the starting lineup in place of Chuck Hurston and Sherrill Headrick. Stram also changed the scheme in the secondary because cornerbacks Willie Mitchell and the "Hammer" had difficulty covering fast receivers. But aside from closing out the season with three straight wins, the high point of the year was the unveiling of two spectacular team rookies. Norwegian place-kicker Jan Stenerud was the AFL's second-leading scorer; he was perfect on forty-five extra-point tries and made twenty-one of thirty-six field goals. Kick returner Nolan

Smith returned more kickoffs (41) and gained more yards (1,148) than any other returner. The two players were clearly on one of the strongest teams in pro football, and fans showed their support, setting a new Western Division attendance record that included a franchise record of 33,119 season ticket sales. Only the New York Jets drew more fans. Although they took a step back after reaching the Super Bowl, the Chiefs, by playing several rookies, were strengthening their team, particularly on defense.[7]

Willie Lanier became the backbone of this developing Chiefs defense. Born in Richmond, Virginia, and growing up in the segregated South, he decided to attend Morgan State University in Baltimore. Lanier was a physically gifted athlete who took his academics very seriously. Scout Lloyd Wells was sent to sign Lanier and informed him that he needed to sign a contract that contained a $2,500 bonus along with three one-year contracts for $14,000, $15,000, and $16,000. Wells presented this as a take-it-or-leave-it deal, suggesting that if Lanier did not sign, he could go play football in Canada. This intimidating strategy had worked well for Wells when he was dealing with raw and sometimes guileless young men from black schools in the Deep South. But with Lanier, he confronted something else, a prideful man who was smart and connected enough to have found out, through calls made by his coach, Earl Banks, exactly how much money had been offered Lynch, who was selected just two picks before Lanier. Lanier's offer was for less money, and Lanier told Wells, "Firstly, no one talks to me like that. I am a college student, and I'm about to get my degree in business administration. Secondly, you will not tell me that I have to take your offer or go to Canada. I am done with you here." Lanier called Stram the next day and expressed how unhappy he was with the scout's approach. A few days later Wells returned with a much more conciliatory manner, and Lanier signed a contract that was in line with Lynch's.[8]

The Denver Broncos had the distinction of being the first AFL team to defeat an NFL team, but the fans' euphoria from this first victory was quickly replaced with the cold reality of another losing season. Although the team went 3–11, they were able to defeat two NFL teams in the preseason, Detroit and Minnesota. With their new rookie running back Floyd Little and Cookie Gilchrist blocking for him, the Broncos easily won 14–3 over the Vikings. Little recalled that Minnesota started rookie Alan Page from the University of Notre Dame at defensive end, where he had terrorized college offensive linemen. But the Broncos ran right at Page with Gilchrist blocking, and "he just destroyed Page. It was so one-sided that the next week the Vikings moved him to defensive tackle, where he went on to make the Pro Football Hall of Fame. This also allowed Carl Eller to take Page's position and he too went to the Hall of Fame."[9]

New head coach and general manager Lou Saban tried to rebuild the Broncos, first by trading two first-round draft choices to San Diego for quarterback Steve Tensi. By pairing him with Little, the Broncos were hoping for both players to mature together. Saban also tried to improve a very bad defense, which had its greatest difficulty in stopping the pass. He started fifteen rookies on offense and defense, but it was clear that Little had the most potential. He led the AFL in average yards on punt returns and led the team in rushing yards. This was quite an achievement for an African American who grew up in poverty in New Haven, Connecticut, and made it to college despite being told that his IQ was too low to qualify for higher education.

Little was recruited to Syracuse University by Coach Ben Schwartz-walder and the first African American Heisman Trophy winner, Ernie Davis. In an interview recalling their first meeting, Little said, "You can't imagine people like that coming to our neighborhood at that time of night." After introducing themselves, Little was invited to dinner: "In my house, a free dinner was like hitting the lottery. They took me to Jocko Sullivan's, a nice bar and grill restaurant on the campus of Yale University. At the restaurant my main concern wasn't talking football, it was eating. I had already finished reading the entire menu from front to back. I didn't know what steak or lobster looked like. So I decided to order one of each." Davis convinced Little that he should attend Syracuse over West Point, despite the fact that General Douglas MacArthur had told him he would ascend to the rank of general if he played football for Army.[10]

In the Eastern Division, second-year coach Wally Lemm led the Houston Oilers to the title with a revamped roster. Arguably no other team benefited from the common draft as much as the Oilers. General Manager Don Klosterman decided not to use the previous drafting strategy, which focused on selecting white players from the segregated Southwest and Southeast Conferences. Instead, he hired former Grambling State University assistant head coach Tom Williams specifically to scout black colleges. Klosterman also decided to bring in seniors for personal evaluations. Week after week, the Oilers reviewed a parade of players, until the Dallas Cowboys complained to Pete Rozelle, who made Houston stop even though there was nothing in the rules of either league to prevent it. But this rare Oiler innovation led directly to the scouting combines of today.[11]

The Oilers finished the season 9–4–1, one game ahead of the Jets. They led the AFL in rushing offense but were dead last in passing offense.

Fullback Hoyle Granger rushed for 1,194 yards, running back Woody Campbell chipped in 511 rushing yards, and running back Sid Banks added another 206 yards. After starting the year 2–2, Coach Lemm and GM Klosterman decided to trade starting quarterback Jacky Lee, Ernie Ladd, and their 1968 number-one draft choice to the Kansas City Chiefs for quarterback Pete Beathard, who quickly brought stability to the position. Houston led the AFL in team defense, largely because of first-round draft choice George Webster, a rookie linebacker from Michigan State University, and its vastly improved secondary. Segregation brought this great player to East Lansing; he had grown up in Anderson, South Carolina, and Clemson coach Frank Howard, a close friend of Michigan State's head coach Duffy Daugherty, encouraged Daugherty to take a look at Webster because the African American player could not play at Clemson.[12]

Webster was very fast and played "roverback" for the Spartans, which was a hybrid of linebacker and safety. He was voted consensus All-American in 1965 and 1966 before being chosen with the fifth pick in the first round by Houston. He would go on to have a ten-year career in pro football, but more importantly he sought to change health benefits for players after their careers were over. Webster suffered several major injuries during his playing days, and in 1989 he applied for benefits as totally and permanently disabled. Webster was found to have lost most of the use of a hand, foot, knee, and ankle due to football-related injuries but did not meet the NFL's definition of totally disabled. In 1998 the U.S. Supreme Court let stand a finding by the NFL's retirement board that Webster's disability was not related to his football career. In 2002 Webster had his right leg amputated above the knee because the limb had little circulation despite four previous surgeries. Webster died in 2007, but his courage paved the way for other health-related lawsuits by players, which eventually led to an NFL settlement in April 2015 of $765 million. The lawsuit was brought by 4,500 former players, and the terms of the settlement primarily provided medical benefits and injury compensation for retired NFL players. Critics of the settlement felt that these players deserved much more than $765 million from the NFL, which in 2015 was generating $10 billion per year.[13]

Webster's speed was an immediate asset to Houston's linebacker play, and the team improved its secondary during the off-season when they traded two players to Denver for talented cornerback Miller Farr. He quickly paid dividends for the Oilers when he tied for the league lead in interceptions with ten while returning three for touchdowns. Joining Farr in this new secondary was rookie Ken Houston, who was drafted out of Prairie View A&M University in the ninth round. Houston played safety and finished the year with four interceptions, returning two for touchdowns, and one fumble recovery.[14]

The Oilers' secondary exemplified a dramatic change in terms of the team's racial policies. GM Don Klosterman was most responsible for this change: he hired Williams as the team's first black scout and also gave him the job of improving community relations among African American fans. When Williams was interviewed by the *Houston Informer* in early November, he made some frank and pointed statements about the Oilers' past racial policies. Williams accused the Oilers of having a quota system that limited the number of black players to two in 1960 and six in 1965, the last year of its existence. Williams said that the Oilers "used to put check marks in the files by the names of Negro fans who held season tickets." Clearly a profound change had come to Houston by 1967, when there were some fifteen black players, including three starters in the secondary. Joining Farr and Houston was cornerback W. K. Hicks out of Texas Southern University, who led the AFL in interceptions in 1965 before being injured during most of the 1966 season.[15]

This trio, along with safety Jim Norton from the University of Idaho, set an AFL record for interception return yardage against the Jets in a game on October 15 in Shea Stadium. The Oilers intercepted six Joe Namath passes and returned them for 245 yards and three touchdowns, two by Houston and one from Farr. Walt Schlinkman, the Oilers' defensive backfield coach, was interviewed after the game and spoke glowingly about his players. He characterized Farr as the leader of the group and a "real cool guy who gives the other players a little chatter to pep 'em up." Schlinkman said that Norton called the coverages and was very good at spotting formations. Hicks was described as a player who had good but not exceptional speed but had the instincts to tell when a pass was being thrown to a receiver. Finally, his assessment of Houston was one that followed him throughout his illustrious fourteen-year Hall of Fame career. "He is tough, a tackler who will hit you, he has real quick feet and he's tall. He's got to learn some things but once he does he can be great."[16]

Ironically the backdrop to this great season was the complaining of owner Bud Adams regarding attendance. At the end of the season Adams threatened to move the Oilers to Seattle, largely because, he said, season ticket sales had dropped by more than 4,000. In an interview with the *Houston Chronicle* in December he stated, "If we go down to 7,000 in 1968 there's no question I'd move the team." Adams went on to say that his decision was "strictly business. Why should I lose $300,000 a year to go out and watch seven home games?" Adams indicated that this figure was about half of what he lost in 1966, but more importantly the Oilers drew only 185,129 fans, which was more than the Patriots, who finished last with 138,861. Because they were last in attendance, Adams feared that Boston would beat him to Seattle, noting, "Let's be honest, Seattle is going to get a pro football team. There probably won't be another expansion franchise granted until the AFL and NFL complete their merger in 1970. Somebody is going to grab off that rich market." An argument can be made that Adams's bluster worked: the Oilers moved into the Astrodome in 1968, but Adams still complained about the terms of the lease.[17]

In New York the Jets' quarterback clearly was still learning how to play the position in a consistent fashion. Namath led the Jets to a record of 8–5–1: he led the AFL in passing yardage, throwing for 4,007 yards, and was the first player to pass for 4,000 yards in pro football. He led in touchdown passes with twenty-six, attempted passes with 491, and completions with 258. But Namath also led the league in interceptions with twenty-eight. These drive killers helped create scoring opportunities for opponents, and several were returned for touchdowns. At twenty-four years old with the largest contract in professional football, Namath had great difficulty balancing on-the-field responsibilities with off-the-field socializing. Before he played the Oilers in his six-interception perfor-mance, Namath had been out drinking until early in the morning hours before the game. He spent the night on his friend Art Heyman's couch, and when he woke up, Heyman recalled, Namath had a very unusual pre-game request: "a shot of peppermint schnapps for his breath."[18]

The Jets were 5–1–1 at the halfway point of the season, but on Novem-ber 5 they lost 42–18 to the Chiefs, and more importantly they lost run-ning back Emerson Boozer for the remainder of the season with torn knee ligaments. Then, on December 3, they suffered their worst loss of the season, falling to Denver 33–24. The game was in Shea, and Namath's teammates by now were growing weary of his drinking. Defensive end Gerry Philbin was interviewed after the game by Paul Zimmerman, beat writer for the New York Post, and he was very direct: "All I know is he came in late, when everybody was already dressed. Prima donna." Matt Snell remembered Namath being out all night before the game: "He had to get in the sauna. You could just smell the booze." Arguably had Namath been more mature and responsible, the Jets could have won the Eastern Divi-sion over Houston. The following year Namath clearly realized that New York would go only as far as he could take them.[19]

As Namath struggled to mature, Boston fullback Jim Nance led the AFL with 1,216 rushing yards. Most of these yards came because he simply ran over defenders. But it was not enough, and the team finished 3–10–1. Fans showed their displeasure as the Patriots finished last in league attendance, drawing to Fenway Park an average crowd of only 23,142. It was not just the team's poor performance on the field that kept fans away; New Englanders spent most of the fall focused on the Red Sox, who were in a pennant race for the first time since 1949. To make matters worse, the Patriots were forced out of Fenway on October 8 because of the World Series and had to play a "home" game in San Diego against the Chargers. And of course the outcome of the Series put Bostonians in a foul mood when the St. Louis Cardinals prevailed over Boston 7–2 in game seven at Fenway. For owner Billy Sullivan, whose team sold only 13,000 season tickets, it was time to think about moving. Three cities had contacted him to gauge the interest of the Patriots in relocating: Memphis, Birmingham, and Tampa. In an interview after the season Sullivan was asked what might make the team move. "If we felt absolutely certain Boston would never build a stadium, then we'd have to give serious thought to moving the club."[20]

For the Houston Oilers, the mood going into the December 31 AFL Championship game against the one-loss Raiders was optimistic despite the fact that they were major underdogs. The idea that anything could happen in one game was the mindset for Oilers players. The two teams met only once during the regular season, in Oakland, where the Raiders won 19–7. But the score was 7–0 Oilers at halftime and 7–3 going into the fourth quarter before the Raiders scored sixteen unanswered points to win the game. The game was again played in Oakland, in front of 53,330. The former Oiler George Blanda opened the scoring with a 37-yard field goal. In the second quarter Raider running back Dave Dixon ran around left end for a 69-yard touchdown, and with eight seconds left until halftime, quarterback Daryle Lamonica prepared to hold for a short field goal. Instead of holding for the kick, Lamonica jumped up and threw a touchdown pass to receiver Dave Kocourek. The Oilers dug a deeper hole after Zeke Moore fumbled the kickoff to begin the third quarter; Lamonica scored from the 1-yard line. Nothing went right for Houston except for a touchdown pass from quarterback Pete Beathard to receiver Charley Frazier. Blanda outscored his former team by himself, kicking four field goals, and when the gun sounded, the 40–7 victory put the Raiders into the Super Bowl.[21]

On the other side of the country the Green Bay Packers and Dallas Cowboys played in Green Bay before 50,861. The game might as well have been played in Alaska because temperatures at kickoff were 13 degrees below zero, with a brisk 15-mile-per-hour wind. Tex Schramm had come up with the idea of adding another round to the playoffs, so both teams were required to take an extra step to get to the championship. Since New Orleans was the sixteenth NFL team, the league reorganized from two divisions into four divisions made up of four teams. Dallas easily beat the Cleveland Browns 52–14, and Green Bay took care of the Los Angeles Rams 28–7. The 1967 NFL Championship game has become a part of American sporting legend. Vince Lombardi had an $80,000 heating system installed under Lambeau Field that was designed to keep the field from freezing, but it failed. Players had difficulty maintaining their footing, and officials' whistles were useless. The cold was especially difficult for Cowboys players, none more so than receiver Bob Hayes, who ran pass routes with his hands in his pants. On the Cowboys' bench Walt Garrison turned to Don Perkins and said, "We must be crazy to be out here playing." Perkins replied, "We're not crazy. Look behind you. There's about fifty thousand crazy sonuvabitches up there. They *paid* to come out here and freeze to death." The Packers won this historic game on a block by guard Jerry Kramer that allowed quarterback Bart Starr to score the final touchdown in this 21–17 classic.[22]

Super Bowl II was played on January 14, 1968, in Miami's Orange Bowl. Despite losing only one regular-season game, the AFL's Raiders were underdogs to the NFL's Packers, who had lost four. Vince Lombardi was trying to win his third straight championship, something no other team had ever done; he also planned to retire as head coach after the game. The Raiders were known as a passing team, but their running game was underrated. Lamonica led the AFL in passing touchdowns, but running backs Hewritt Dixon and Clem Daniels were arguably the backbone of the offense. The outcome of the game might have been different had Daniels not broken his ankle against the Chargers on October 29. Dixon rushed for 601 yards and five touchdowns on the season, while Daniels had rushed for 575 yards and four touchdowns through only nine games. Quietly Daniels, who joined the AFL in 1960 as Abner Haynes's backup in Dallas and then was traded to Oakland in 1961, had become the AFL's all-time leading rusher by 1967. Daniels had rushed for 5,008 career yards, making him only the tenth player to rush for over 5,000 yards in the history of pro football: the other players were Jim Brown (12,312), Joe Perry (9,723), Jim Taylor (8,425), John Henry Johnson (6,800), Steve Van Buren (5,860), Rick Casares (5,534), Hugh McElhenny (5,233), Ollie Matson (5,173), and Lenny Moore (5,163). But when the Raiders took the field in the Orange Bowl, Daniels could only watch from the sideline.[23]

Daniels grew up in segregated McKinney, Texas, a town of about ten thousand some thirty-two miles northeast of Dallas. In 1955 he graduated from all-black Doty High, where he was chosen as the commencement speaker. Daniels decided to take this opportunity to discuss bigotry, oppression, and "how folks called black boys they didn't know by three names. We were all George or Willie or Lee Roy. Before I got halfway through the speech, the audience was standing." Thanks to Daniels's agitation, there would be no more commencement speakers at Doty, which closed in the late 1960s. If there was a single moment that galvanized young Clem, it came the afternoon he saw the raw agony experienced by his mother, Ida Louise. She worked as a housekeeper for Gibson Caldwell, a bank chairman and civic leader who was among McKinney's wealthiest white citizens. Daniels was summoned to the Caldwell estate shortly after graduating from Doty. He rode his bicycle over, rang the bell, and was invited in by a servant who escorted the boy to the study, where Caldwell sat behind a desk. "He got up and shook my hand, told me he wanted to commend me on the job I did, graduating from high school and getting the opportunity to go to college [historically black Prairie View A&M University] on a full scholarship," Daniels recalls. "He said, You've done very well for yourself and I wanted to wish you well." Clem expressed his appreciation and left, riding his bike back home. A couple of hours later he heard his mother in the kitchen preparing supper and humming a spiritual, which she had a tendency to do when something was gnawing at her soul. She called him into the kitchen and said, "When you left today, Mr. Caldwell came in to see me and he said next time you come to the house, you make sure you come through the back door." That's when Daniels noticed the tears streaming down her face. He consoled his mother and made a vow: "I would do whatever I could to see that things got better for all of us."[24]

Daniels maintained his promise after settling in Oakland in 1962, opening several businesses and becoming a civic and business leader. Oakland's Sequoyah Country Club, founded by developer Wayne Valley, one of the original Raiders owners, had zero black members in 1985, and Daniels quietly pressed the matter until he reached Valley at his business office. Valley conceded his bigotry but told Daniels he was welcome to join. He was one of the "good" ones. Clem declined, reminding Valley of the larger issue. Not until the next year, a few months after Valley's death, did the Sequoyah integrate. Unfortunately for the Raiders, this very good player and great leader was on the bench when Super Bowl II began.[25]

Before a festive crowd of 75,546 and a national television audience, at approximately 3:00 P.M. the Raiders took the field after the kickoff and decided to start the game with a weak side sweep, a play they had run with great success all year. Dixon headed around left end and was met by linebacker Ray Nitschke, who promptly flipped the 230-pound back heels-over-helmet for no gain. The Packers' defense had set the tone for the day. Green Bay's offense scored field goals on its first two possessions, resulting in a 6–0 lead, while the Raiders could not scratch out a first down. Then, in the second quarter, Green Bay added a touchdown on a 62-yard pass from Starr to Boyd Dowler on first down that caught the Raiders totally off guard. Oakland responded with a drive that culminated in a 23-yard touchdown pass from Lamonica to Bill Miller. The half ended with Green Bay adding another field goal, which made the score 16–7.[26]

Using their ball-control offense, the Packers nursed their lead through the second half and built it up to 33–14 on a Donny Anderson touchdown, a Don Chandler field goal, and Herb Adderley's return of an interception for a touchdown. Lamonica threw another touchdown pass to Miller in the fourth quarter, but that only made the final score a clear-cut 33–14. As a result of this game it was commonly believed that the AFL was so inferior that the ultimate game needed to be reworked. "We started talking in the league office that, if the game wasn't going to be competitive for several more years, we'd have to change the format once the merger was completed," said Don Weiss, then the NFL's director of publicity. "There was a feeling that it could be a long time before the AFL could field a competitive team." This line of thinking would be erased the following year in dramatic fashion by the New York Jets, led by Joe Namath.[27]

After the Super Bowl the NFL/AFL draft was held over two days, from January 30 to 31. It was a historic draft for African American players at black colleges. An all-time high of sixty-eight players were selected, and thirty-four made teams, but much more importantly, for the first time in NFL/AFL history a black quarterback was drafted in the first round. Eldridge Dickey, from Tennessee State University, was chosen with the twenty-fifth pick in the first round by the Oakland Raiders. Dickey grew up in Houston, Texas; he played at TSU from 1964 to 1967 and was a three-time HBCU All-American who amassed an amazing 6,523 yards passing with sixty-seven touchdowns while setting many historically black college records. He led his team to bowl berths in 1965 and 1966. The 1966 squad, which sent twenty-two players on to professional football, also featured future defensive lineman Claude Humphrey, who was selected third overall in this draft by the Atlanta Falcons. The group recorded TSU's first undefeated, untied season and their first National Black College Football Championship. With Dickey at the helm they averaged forty-one points per game and their stingy defense allowed only four points per game.[28]

In Dickey's senior year Al Davis was spotted scouting him at a game against Central State University in Wilberforce, Ohio. At the time, many wondered whether Davis was looking to be a maverick and turn the team over to a black quarterback or whether he saw another athletic black quarterback who needed to be converted. Most people believe that he saw a tremendously gifted athlete whose speed and athleticism were greater than his passing. Other rumors suggested that the Raiders wanted to keep Dickey away from their rival, the Kansas City Chiefs, who also had their eye on him. For whatever reason, the Raiders made the decision to grab Dickey in the first round, which was unthinkable for a black quarterback at the time. They then compounded their dilemma by selecting University of Alabama quarterback Ken Stabler in the second round. The Raiders' roster was crowded at the position with Lamonica and part-time quarterback/kicker George Blanda, who had already played with the first black quarterback in the NFL, Willie Thrower, for the Chicago Bears in 1953. They had to figure out what to do with Dickey when he arrived. The Raiders did not know it at the time, but they had selected a player who vehemently wanted only to be a quarterback. Joe Gilliam Sr., former coach at TSU during Dickey's time there, recalled, "If Eldridge couldn't play quarterback, he didn't want to play at all."[29]

In this draft another black quarterback was selected, but he was told that he was being chosen to play defensive back. Marlin Briscoe played quarterback at the University of Nebraska at Omaha and was selected in the fourteenth round by the Denver Broncos. Briscoe was only 5'10" and 170 pounds, but he set twenty-two records at his school and during his senior year averaged 263.9 yards of total offense per game, which ranked him fifth nationally. After he was drafted, Briscoe's head coach Al Caniglia gave him some very good advice: "The Broncos are one of the few teams in pro ball that have their training camp open to the public and media. Which means you can showcase your talent, and people other than the coaches and personnel directors will see you." This was important because Briscoe wanted the opportunity to play quarterback. Caniglia urged Briscoe to negotiate his own contract with the stipulation that he be given a look at quarterback. When Briscoe met over dinner with Stan Jones, a scout for the Broncos, and Fred Gerhke, their director of player personnel, to discuss his contract, he agreed to play cornerback but also demanded a three-day tryout at quarterback. Briscoe had this clause written into the contract and ultimately it helped to change history.[30]

Racial tensions in the country continued to escalate as President Johnson increased the number of troops in Vietnam. By the end of 1966 there were 385,000 U.S. troops there. African Americans made up 10 percent of the armed forces in the early 1960s, but that percentage increased substantially by 1967, in large part because of draft deferments for college and graduate students, who were predominantly white and middle class. Civil unrest in Newark, New Jersey, from July 12 to 17, was sparked by the beating of a black cab driver in police custody. More than 1,500 persons were injured and 1,300 arrested, and over the course of these five days the police and National Guard killed twenty-five black people—most of them innocent bystanders, including two children. And in Detroit from July 23 to 30, civil unrest broke out after police raided an after-hours drinking establishment. When order was restored, forty-three people had been killed and federal troops were called out in the city for the first time since 1943. Both incidents were sparked by white police and black citizens, but the causes were much deeper: high levels of unemployment, poor housing, inadequate health care, and poverty were the gasoline that fueled the fire.

It was in this environment that the American Basketball Association was founded in the fall of 1967, and the similarities between the ABA and the AFL were quite obvious. Like the AFL, the ABA sought to challenge the established NBA, which was viewed as more conservative, particularly in its style of play. However, the major difference between the two upstart leagues was that the ABA was never able to sign a major television contract, which caused it to struggle throughout its existence. Several teams folded because of the financial strain, which did not happen in the AFL. But like the AFL, the ABA had a very exciting style of play that featured prominent African American players, many of whom wore Afros, which were viewed as a cultural expression of black pride. The ABA had a thirty-second shot clock, compared with the NBA's twenty-four-second clock, and it introduced the three-point shot, which forever changed the game of basketball. And while the NBA used the classic brown basketball, the ABA used a red, white, and blue ball and encouraged players to shoot from three-point range and dunk. The league folded in 1976, but not before four teams were brought into the NBA.[31]

MARLIN BRISCOE AND THE DAWN
OF BLACK QUARTERBACKS

The 1968 season began after the assassinations of Dr. Martin Luther King Jr. and Senator Robert Kennedy, along with numerous protests against America's involvement in the Vietnam War. King's assassination on April 4 in Memphis sparked civil unrest in more than one hundred cities. Forty-six people were killed, and it took twenty thousand federal troops and thirty-four thousand National Guardsmen to quell disturbances. Eight days after King was slain, black students at Boston University occupied the administration building in demand for Afro-American history courses and additional black students. On April 26, black students seized the administration building at Ohio State University, and on May 3, black students seized the finance building at Northwestern University. Both groups of students demanded a black-oriented curriculum and campus reforms.[1]

In the American Football League historic change came in the form of a player who was only 5'10" and 170 pounds. Marlin "The Magician" Briscoe became the first African American to start as quarterback in the modern era of professional football, when he took the field for the Denver Broncos against the Cincinnati Bengals in the fourth game of the season on Sunday, October 6, in Denver. Briscoe's three-day tryout in camp was open to the media and fans, who witnessed his ability to throw accurate deep passes, display sound fundamental footwork, and make precise throws on the run. The Broncos had planned to start 6'5", 220-pound

Steve Tensi in the position. Tensi had played at Florida State University, where his primary target was Fred Biletnikoff, but he had broken his collarbone in camp. Denver turned to Jim Leclair and Joe Divito, but both failed miserably as the team began the season 0–3. Coach Lou Saban then turned to Briscoe, who started game four and led the Broncos to a 10–7 victory. In this game Tensi replaced Briscoe in the second half, but in game nine, against the Raiders, Tensi was hurt again and Briscoe started the rest of the season. The media covered this story extensively, while Saban tried to downplay the historic opportunity: "Everybody thought it was a touchy situation. It wasn't with me. First, what choice did I have? He was five foot eight or nine. You've not seen quarterbacks that size make it in big-time football, but he was exciting." Briscoe was more than exciting—he could play. The Broncos started him in seven games, and for the season he threw fourteen touchdowns and thirteen interceptions. Briscoe's greatest attribute was his ability to run and scramble: he was ahead of his time in terms of playing style. Quarterbacks were supposed to drop back, stay in the pocket, read defenses, and pass the ball. Briscoe finished second on the team in rushing, behind Floyd Little; he rushed for 308 yards on forty-one carries for a team-high average of 7.5 yards per carry, and he tied Little for second on the Broncos with three rushing touchdowns. Starting quarterback Steve Tensi ran the ball six times all season for two yards.[2]

The Broncos went 1–4 to end the season with Briscoe starting, but he finished second in Rookie of the Year voting to Cincinnati's running back Paul Robinson, who had the benefit of starting all year. Briscoe rightly felt that what he had done for the team warranted that he get another opportunity to compete at quarterback the following season. But a teammate told him during the off-season that the quarterbacks were having informal meetings with Saban, without him. Briscoe decided to fly to Denver unannounced and confront Saban, which he did. He was completely ignored by Saban, who just walked by Briscoe without acknowledging his existence. When Briscoe came to camp, he was the third-string quarterback so he received very few reps during practice. Briscoe was released, and his views regarding Coach Saban and race were made crystal clear in his autobiography: "I believe—and always will—that it was racial, that he simply wouldn't have a black quarterback. Saban could probably line up a hundred black players from other positions who had good careers for him, and they would say he was not racist. . . . But it will always be my belief that he did not want me to be his quarterback for the simple reason that I was black."[3]

Briscoe was the first black quarterback to start in the NFL or AFL. However, he was not the first black quarterback since reintegration of the league, which began in 1946. That distinction goes to Willie Thrower of the Chicago Bears. Thrower played sparingly for the 1953 Bears team, throwing only eight passes. Briscoe recalled, "You won't believe this. Right after my rookie season, one of my receivers was named Jimmy Jones. He used to play for the Bears. I went to Chicago to see my girlfriend. I contacted Jimmy and he took me to this bar called The Presidents. So, Jimmy is introducing me to the bartender, 'This is Marlin Briscoe. He is the first black quarterback in the NFL.' This guy was sitting next to me. He said, 'You weren't the first black quarterback.' I said, 'I was.' He said, 'No, you weren't.' I said, 'Well, who was?' He said, 'I was. My name is Willie Thrower.' It couldn't happen in a million years. I knew that he existed, and he was sitting right next to me. We sat there and we talked for a couple of hours. I met him by happenstance going to this lounge with my receiver. I knew who he was, and for him to be sitting right next to me. It was kind of crazy, but I am glad that I got a chance to meet him. That was one of the highlights of my life."[4]

Briscoe felt that Saban had problems with his skin color and ability to play the position. According to Briscoe, his fellow quarterback Joe Namath had neither of these problems. When the Broncos met the Jets on October 13, although Briscoe did not play in the game, Namath came up to him after the game ended and simply said, "There's the quarterback." Namath greeted Briscoe like this throughout his playing days and after their careers were over. For Namath, like Briscoe, this was a historic season, and he finally turned potential into rock-solid productivity. The Jets steamrolled through the league, finishing 11–3 and running away with the Eastern Division. Although Namath threw seventeen interceptions and only fifteen touchdowns during the season, he was a much more efficient quarterback on the field when it came to decision making. The Jets finished second in total offense to the Raiders, and while they were third in passing yards, their rushing attack was eighth out of ten teams. Although Namath was viewed as the team's franchise player, the defense was arguably the strength of this team. Ranked fourth on the basis of total yards allowed, the Jets finished atop the AFL in rushing defense and were second in passing defense. The team began the year by winning the first game of the season 20–19 over the Chiefs, and after losing to the Broncos 21–13, they won the next four heading into Oakland and stood 7–2. The Raiders were also 7–2, and many fans believed that this game was only an appetizer before the main course, when they surely would meet again for the AFL title.[5]

On November 17, 1968, the Jets met the Raiders in Oakland–Alameda County Stadium, where kickoff was scheduled for 1:00 P.M. Pacific time and 4:00 P.M. on the East Coast. The game was part of NBC's "national doubleheader" and was broadcast everywhere in the country except the Bay Area, where it was blacked out. Although millions of fans missed the ending of the game, it forever changed the way football games are broadcast by television networks. The back-and-forth affair had millions of viewers captivated after Namath engineered a desperate drive that put the Jets ahead 32–29 with just over a minute to play. With fifty seconds to go, it was 7:00 P.M. on the East Coast, and at that instant NBC's national feed of the game disappeared and tens of millions of viewers were treated to the opening credits of *Heidi*, a made-for-TV movie that had been scheduled at 7:00. Immediately NBC's switchboard was flooded with an estimated ten thousand calls, but this did not change the fact that most of the nation missed how the Raiders scored two touchdowns in nineteen seconds. Daryle Lamonica hit halfback Charlie Smith on a 43-yard touchdown that made the score 36–32, and Jet kick returner Earl Christy fumbled the ensuing kickoff, which was returned for a touchdown by Preston Ridlehuber to make the final score 43–32.[6]

Julian Goldman, the president of NBC, issued a public apology the next day, and he called the decision by Dick Cline, the broadcast control supervisor, "a forgivable error committed by humans concerned about the children. . . . I missed the end of the game as much as anyone else." People phoned not only NBC but also other TV stations, newspapers, and even the New York City Police Department's emergency number to try to find out why the game had been switched to *Heidi*. The lasting effect was to forever change NBC's policy toward pro football. In 1975 the network put out a small fortune to promote another children's movie, *Willie Wonka and the Chocolate Factory*. But when the game between the Raiders and Washington Redskins ran into overtime, NBC stayed with the game to the end.[7]

Sonny Werblin had arguably saved the Jets and the AFL when he helped negotiate the league's 1964 television contract with NBC. Werblin was a part owner of the team, along with Leon Hess, Don Lillis, Phil Iselin, and Townsend Martin; in essence Werblin owned 23 percent of the team. After the partners purchased the team five years earlier, Werblin had increasingly been seen as the sole owner. This caused resentment and friction, which boiled over after it was discovered that Werblin had renegotiated Namath to a new contract the previous summer without informing his partners. An offer of $7 million was made to Werblin to buy the team, and he countered with a proposal to put $1.5 million down with the promise to pay off the balance in seven years. This was quickly declined and a counteroffer was made to buy out Werblin, which he accepted. He received $1,638,000 on an investment of slightly more than $200,000. The offer of $7 million for Werblin to buy the team was extremely low—in 1965 the Dolphins paid $7.5 million to join the AFL, and in 1966 the Chargers were sold for $10 million. Clearly Werblin's partners recognized his limited access to this amount of money; the Jets franchise had an estimated value of $15 million.[8]

When Hess, Lillis, Iselin, and Martin found out about Namath's new contract, it was the last straw that ended a very acrimonious relationship. Werblin had renegotiated the star quarterback's second contract with no publicity and no knowledge by his partners, who were responsible for four-fifths of the deal. The Jets were to pick up their one-year option on Namath for the 1968 season. There was a new no-cut, no-trade clause that ran from 1969 to 1971. His salary was raised to $35,000, but as in the previous contract, the real money was in the bonuses. Namath received a $10,000 bonus for 1967 and $25,000 for 1968, and a deferred payment of $150,000 that was not due until 1972. The total came to $340,000. For Werblin, who realized the power of publicity, Namath was worth every penny. With the retirement of Vince Lombardi, Namath was now the dominant figure in pro football. With his Fu Manchu mustache, white shoes, and mink coats, the "Broadway Joe" persona was similar to that of Muhammad Ali. Without question, Namath was the first white athlete to attack the stereotypes of his sport. Just as Ali refused to be the modest, unassuming heavyweight champion that Joe Louis, Rocky Marciano, and Floyd Patterson had been, Namath shunned the uncontroversial public lifestyles that Johnny Unitas and Bart Starr led. Namath owned a gold Cadillac and kelly-green Lincoln, and his Manhattan apartment was famous for its leather bar, llama rug, and lovely ladies. He appeared in ads featuring everything from boots to pantyhose, but this great player was not all style. His throwing ability and arm strength were uncanny; he seemed oblivious in the pocket even though numerous knee surgeries made him virtually a statue. But his quick release and tight spirals were enough to excite even purists. Lombardi succinctly and directly summed up his ability when he stated, "Joe Namath is an almost perfect passer."[9]

Namath and the Jets were clearly the team that the Oakland Raiders had to defeat if they hoped to return to the Super Bowl. The reigning champions of the Western Division finished tied with the Chiefs with a league-best record of 12–2. Al Davis had incredibly transformed the culture and attitude of this organization, which had gone 1–13 in 1962. The philosophy of the Raiders was summed up in their team press release. On the first page inside the release was a letter written by Lee Grosscup, director of public relations, and its last sentence was prophetic: "We are dedicated to the development of the Oakland Raiders as a professional football power." By 1968 arguably the Raiders were just that; they led the AFL in team offense and scoring. They were second in passing offense and rushing offense, but they led the league in punt return yardage with 666: no other team had even 500 yards. They finished second to the Chiefs in team defense, but statistics cannot necessarily portray intimidation. Defensive lineman Ben Davidson took great pride in hitting quarterbacks around the head and late, particularly Namath. In a game against the Jets in 1967 Davidson made *Life* magazine for a hit on Namath that knocked his helmet off. Raiders defensive linemen Tom Keating and Ike Lassiter were very physical and nasty as well, but the addition of a 6'0", 185-pound defensive back from Morris Brown College was also important to the team's defense. George Atkinson was a great punt returner in college, and he led the AFL during his rookie season in 1968. The Raiders really did not know what they were getting from this historically black school beyond an excellent athlete with sprinter speed. Throughout his career he would be one of the smaller safeties in the game, but also one of the most feared by receivers. Atkinson liked to wrap his right arm from wrist to elbow in tape for use as a hook to deliver blows to the heads of receivers left defenseless while reaching to make a catch: "My attitude was that receivers were burglars breaking into my house and needed to be treated as such."[10]

The success of the Raiders kept their first-round draft pick from playing. Eldridge Dickey was the first African American quarterback to be drafted in the first round of the NFL draft, but he never threw a pass during the season. He did return six punts and one kickoff. Daryle Lamonica was clearly entrenched as the starter; he threw for 3,245 yards, twenty-five touchdowns, and fifteen interceptions. His backup, George Blanda, threw for 522 yards, six touchdowns, and two interceptions. Dickey was listed as a receiver, where he made one catch for 34 yards the entire year. By selecting Dickey in the first round, Al Davis clearly planned to make him the Raiders' starting quarterback at some point. But it is difficult to follow the Raiders' plan, largely because Lamonica was only twenty-seven years old and in the prime of his career, and they drafted quarterback Ken Stabler in the second round. Davis may not have totally believed in Dickey's ability to be a successful AFL/NFL quarterback, but he probably intended to play him at some point so that the Raiders could be given credit for making history by starting Dickey. But circumstances in Denver caused Marlin Briscoe to become the first black quarterback to start an AFL/NFL game.

Dickey's opportunity or lack thereof was followed by many on the West Coast, including Bill Nunn Jr., reporter for the *Pittsburgh Courier*. Nunn wrote several articles that discussed Dickey's treatment by the Raiders, and two in particular were quite interesting. In a story published on August 10, Nunn wrote that he witnessed a meeting of Raiders officials with Sam Skinner, sports editor of the black newspaper *San Francisco Sun-Reporter*, and "black militants." Nunn stated that a boycott was threatened by the militants if Dickey was not played, and Skinner warned Coach John Rauch that trouble "will develop unless the Raiders remember that Dickey can think and throw." Al Davis spoke for the team, stating, "We think he has super potential both as a quarterback and at other possible positions. We reserve the right to play him where we think he can do the club most good." Nunn closed the article by speculating that if a boycott was organized, Davis would trade Dickey quickly. Nunn was never specific regarding what organization the "black militants" belonged to, but by 1968 the Black Panthers were extremely visible in the city. Nunn ended his article with a quote from one of the "militants," someone he labeled as a part of the Black Nationalist fringe. In response to Davis's possibly trading Dickey instead of giving in to a boycott, Nunn wrote that this member flatly said, "He wants the Raiders headquarters fire-bombed until nothing but cinders remain." Nunn followed this story up with an article on September 7, in which he said he believed that Davis was going to use Dickey at another position, and that threats of a boycott would not change his thinking.[11]

In Kansas City, change came in the form of a much improved regular-season record. The Chiefs had won nine games the previous season and won three more this season to finish in a tie with the Raiders for the Western Division. Quarterback Len Dawson was named to the Pro Bowl after throwing seventeen touchdowns and nine interceptions. The Chiefs selected Robert Holmes in the fourteenth round of the draft from Southern University. Holmes was a short fullback but led the team in rushing as a rookie. He rushed for 866 yards and seven touchdowns, and his nickname was "Tank" because he was only 5'9" and 221 pounds but had thighs that were thirty inches in diameter. He ran low to the ground, and Coach Stram decided to start three backs after the team suffered injuries to their receivers. Mike Garrett rushed for 534 yards, and Wendell Hayes chipped in another 340. Although they had a potent rushing attack, the team's strength was its defense. It ranked number one overall in the league and number two against the run. Statistically the Chiefs struggled against the pass, finishing next to last in the AFL. The defense yielded only 170 points over fourteen games, an average of 12 points per game and an AFL record. The Raiders' defense was ranked second after giving up 233 points during the season. The Chiefs had to play Oakland for the right to meet the Jets in the AFL Championship, which unfortunately produced an uncharacteristic performance by Kansas City's defense.[12]

The Chiefs were a very cohesive team when it came to race. Willie Lanier and Jim Lynch were the first black and white teammates on the Chiefs to room together on the road. The linebackers became close as rookies and realized that formal and informal conversations about responsibilities could only help each other. By the late 1960s the Chiefs as a team had decided that it was better to overcome long-held prejudices for the sake of a deeper sense of unity. Most of the team spent the off-seasons in Kansas City, many playing on the Chiefs' barnstorming basketball team. After Dr. King was assassinated in April, Curtis McClinton and Buck Buchanan drove to O.G.'s Lounge, one of the city's black clubs, and urged their fellow citizens not to riot.[13]

The black and orange color combination that was a part of the long success enjoyed by Paul Brown's Cleveland Browns did not help his expansion Cincinnati Bengals. The team finished 3–11, but the old master was back in pro football after being fired in Cleveland by owner Art Modell. Brown had to sell his five shares of Cleveland Browns stock, which were reportedly worth $500,000. According to the AFL bylaws, one person in an ownership group must control 51 percent of the voting power. That individual did not have to own 51 percent of the team, however, and Brown had put together a group that allowed him to own 10 percent of the new team. Brown was made coach, general manager, and part owner, and he put together a team made up primarily of young, inexperienced players. This occurred because Cincinnati, unlike the Dolphins in 1966, was given additional picks in its first college draft, including nine picks in the sixth round. In all, Cincinnati made forty-one selections in seventeen rounds. It also had to play its first two seasons at the University of Cincinnati's Nippert Stadium, which seated only 25,000, until Riverfront Stadium was ready to open in 1970. The team's organization was small, with Brown's family at the core. Brown took these inexperienced players and fielded a reasonably competitive team led by the defense. It was surprisingly good, finishing sixth overall in the AFL, largely because of its success against the pass. But the offense struggled, being ranked next to last in the league, and was very weak throwing the football.[14]

Cincinnati lost its first game of the season to San Diego 29–13, but in its second game, which was the home opener at Nippert, it beat Denver 24–10. The Bengals had a revolving door at quarterback: John Stofa started but was injured early in the season, and next they turned to Dewey Warren, but he too was injured. This forced the team to elevate Sam Wyche from the taxi squad. The biggest surprise of this team was rookie Paul Robinson, who was drafted in the third round and had played only one year of football, at the University of Arizona. This African American player grew up near Tucson, where his father was a cotton-picker contractor. He ran track in junior college and for the University of Arizona. Robinson's one year of football was enough for Paul Brown to draft him. He led the Bengals in rushing with 1,023 yards, rushing touchdowns with eight; he had the longest run from scrimmage at 87 yards, and he was the AFL rookie of the year. Robinson is still the only player in the history of pro football ever to rush for over 1,000 yards with an expansion team. In an interview Robinson recalled his playing days with the Bengals, particularly teammates Wyche and Bruce Coslet, who would go on to be head coaches in the NFL. His memory centered on a favorite prank of theirs: "Wyche and Coslet, I can't see how these crazy guys became head coaches. They'd put turtles in your thigh pads. You're running and all of a sudden you see this thing moving in your pants. You had to jump out there in front of everybody and take your clothes off."[15]

Ironically the creation of the Cincinnati Bengals caused Cookie Gilchrist and Paul Brown to once again be connected. The Denver Broncos left Gilchrist unprotected following knee surgery, and he was designated to the Bengals. After forfeiting his college eligibility by signing with the Browns out of high school, Gilchrist still had much animosity toward Brown. The combination of his knee injury and disdain of Brown caused Gilchrist to retire instead of reporting to camp. When Brown was interviewed about any resentment Gilchrist might still harbor, his response was succinct and without emotion—typical from this long-standing head coach: "If any men have possibilities in business or feel it's to their advantage to start life's work elsewhere, then we'll make no effort to change their minds. We're only interested in players who want to play football, who recognize this as an employment opportunity and enjoy football."[16]

The Bengals ended their inaugural season with a loss to the Jets, who had wrapped up the Eastern Division several weeks earlier. Now the Raiders and Chiefs had to play a tie-breaking game to decide the champion of the Western Division. The game was played in Oakland on Sunday, December 22, when some 53,605 crammed into the Oakland Coliseum on a relatively cool 42-degree day. This matchup was obvious: could the Chiefs' defense, which allowed only eighteen touchdowns and held seven of their fourteen opponents to single digits in scoring, stop the Oakland passing game? The answer was no. Lamonica threw three first-quarter touchdown passes, one to Warren Wells and two to Fred Bilentnikoff. The Chiefs responded with two field goals in the second quarter. But Bilentnikoff caught another touchdown from the Bomber—this one was 54 yards—and Lamonica did not forget about Wells throwing another 35-yarder to him in the fourth quarter. When the game was over, the final score was 41–6. Lamonica had thrown five touchdown passes while the Chiefs' Lenny Dawson threw four drive-stopping interceptions. After this game many fans and individuals in the media came to two conclusions. First, the Chiefs still had not figured out how to play in a big game, dating back to their dismal performance in Super Bowl I. Second, clearly the Raiders had learned from their loss the previous year and the Jets had no real chance in the upcoming AFL Championship.[17]

The game was scheduled for Shea Stadium the following Sunday, and it was clear what the Raiders' strategy would be. Ben Davidson told reporters that Namath could expect more rough treatment. "He gets paid enough to get hit, doesn't he? On Sunday, we'll hit him again hard enough to let him know he's earning his money." Davidson and his defensive teammates wanted to go after the Jets' unquestioned leader. By 1968 Namath was clearly that on the field, but many did not realize he was also the leader in breaking down informal team racial divides. Writer Paul Zimmerman covered the Jets for the *New York Post* and marveled at Namath's social skills: "I've seen Namath come into a dining room at training camp, check out the tables and sit down at a table composed entirely of black players." Zimmerman wrote that "most teams, no matter how close they are, break down into some loose kind of black-white arrangement at mealtimes. A couple of black players come in together and find a table. Then a couple more join them. Before long, it becomes an all-black table, and the one next to it becomes predominantly white. But I have seen Namath plunk his tray down at one of those all-black tables, and then a few white players join him and soon it becomes a mixed table. I've seen this happen too many times to assume it's accidental. The same thing on buses. I've seen Namath integrate a little knot of black players by his presence."[18]

It was also no accident that Namath was seen coming out of the side entrance of the Summit Hotel a little after 8:00 A.M. on December 29 by a police officer who noticed that he was with a young woman and had what appeared to be a whiskey bottle in his hand. This caught the officer off guard because kickoff for the AFL Championship was at 1:00 P.M. The officer described the Jets quarterback as looking "disheveled. Disheveled, but happy." Maybe Namath anticipated what was in store for him and decided not to be depressed because this was one of the most physical football games he ever played in.[19]

The temperature was just above freezing, but the wind was gusting at fifty miles an hour, and to make matters worse the field was soggy in some places and hard as concrete in others. Namath drove the Jets down the field in the first quarter and threw a 14-yard touchdown pass to Don Maynard, making the score 7–0. Maynard got free of Raiders rookie George Atkinson, who lost his footing on the Shea infield. The Jets' Jim Turner added a field goal, and they were now up by ten. In the second quarter Lamonica found Bilentnikoff for a 29-yard touchdown, and the teams both kicked field goals to make the halftime score 13–10 Jets. Halftime presented Namath with the opportunity to get additional medical treatment—his left middle finger had been broken and his right thumb was badly bruised after he was sacked in the second quarter by Davidson and Ike Lassiter. It was the only sack of the day, but the quarterback went airborne and Davidson hit Namath with a knee to the head. The Jets quarterback was slow to rise and probably had a concussion, but concussions were not then part of football vernacular. Teammate Babe Parilli described Namath's condition as "a little punchy." Nevertheless, Namath would not let Parilli relieve him from the game.[20]

In the Jets' locker room the team's medical staff administered three shots to Namath's finger and another for each knee. The Raiders began the third quarter by marching to the Jets' 6-yard line, where they had first-and-goal. But defensive back Jim Hudson made three straight tackles, and the Raiders had to settle for a field goal. Namath then drove the Jets down the field, mixing in runs by Emerson Boozer and Matt Snell and passes to Maynard. He ended the drive with a 20-yard pass to Pete Lammons, making the score 20–13. The Raiders put another drive together, but it also ended in a George Blanda field goal, which cut the deficit to four. Namath then made a mistake, overthrowing Maynard, which turned into an easy interception for Atkinson. Namath tackled Atkinson, using as much force as possible and riding him all the way out of bounds. Atkinson told Namath he would kill him. But the 5-yard touchdown run by the Raiders' Pete Banaszak almost killed the Jets, as they were now down 23–20. It took Namath only thirty-one seconds to put together a drive that ended with a 6-yard touchdown pass to Maynard. But there were more than eight minutes still left in the game. The Raiders drove into Jets territory twice, only to come away with no points, and the game ended with Jets linebacker Ralph Baker recovering a pass that was ruled a lateral. After the game, left tackle Winston Hill had a broad grin on his face; he had battled Oakland's defensive end Davidson throughout the long, cold afternoon and kept him off his quarterback. It has been forgotten by many now, but reporter Sam DeLuca interviewed Hill in the locker room and posed the question, "Are the Jets going to win that Super Bowl?" Hill responded with a definitive "Yes, we are."[21]

Hill had flatly stated that the Jets would win the Super Bowl, but in the euphoria of the locker room his "prediction" became lost to history. Hill was an outstanding offensive lineman who grew up in segregated Joaquin, Texas, and attended Texas Southern University. He was drafted by the Baltimore Colts in 1963 but signed as a free agent in the same year with the Jets, where he spent his career protecting Namath's blind side at left tackle and opening holes for Boozer and Snell. He made 174 consecutive starts and was named AFL All-Pro in 1964, 1967, and 1968. Hill had done a phenomenal job against Davidson, who many felt did not have the best technique but was mostly a dirty player. The Jets' opponent in the Super Bowl would be the Baltimore Colts, who destroyed the Cleveland Browns 34–0. The Colts' defense was anchored by another very physical defensive end, Bubba Smith, seen by many as the best in pro football. The analysis quickly began: Hill and the Jets dominated Davidson, but Smith would be a greater challenge.

Super Bowl III did not have Vince Lombardi's Packers; instead, the NFL was represented by the Colts, who used an eight-man maximum blitz that was put together by head coach Don Shula and assistants Bill Arnsparger and Chuck Noll. The Colts' offense was led by journeyman quarterback Earl Morrall, who took over for Johnny Unitas after he was hurt early in the season. Las Vegas oddsmaker Jimmy "The Greek" Snyder listed the Colts as 18-point favorites, the largest spread in Super Bowl history. When the Jets arrived in Miami ten days before kickoff, Coach Weeb Ewbank encouraged his staff and players to begrudgingly accept the role of huge underdog. But as the Jets did interview after interview responding to how they could compete with Baltimore, Namath became more and more tired of playing underdog. More importantly Namath and his teammates had been watching film of the Colts and saw what they felt were glaring weaknesses in their defense. So when he attended the Miami Touchdown Club dinner on Thursday night to receive the award as the outstanding professional football player of 1968, Namath's patience was running out. He had a few drinks and during the course of the speech thanked his teammates for making the award possible, along with "all the single girls in New York." Before he could finish, someone shouted from the back of the room, "Namath, we're gonna kick your ass." Namath looked out into the dark expanse and said, "Hey, I got news for you. We're gonna win the game; I guarantee it."[22]

Unlike Hill, who was responding to a question about the Jets' chances against the Colts, Namath made a prediction that was not prompted by a question and emphatically guaranteed it. This was the distinctive difference between the two responses, as well as the context in which they were made—in Namath's case, in front of a room full of journalists three days before the Super Bowl. Namath relished the spotlight, and it was bright when the teams took the field on Sunday, January 12, in the Orange Bowl. In 1967 more than 30,000 seats had remained empty in the cavernous Los Angeles Coliseum. But this year the tickets were almost impossible to get. The $12 seats were now being scalped for $150, and the sellout attendance was 75,377. Curt Gowdy, NBC's play-by-play man, said in his opening, "They could have sold 150,000." He was probably right; the telecast, sponsored by Chrysler, Pall Mall Gold, Salem, Winston, TWA, RCA, Schlitz, Phillips 66, and Gillette Techmatic razors, paid for commercial time at $135,000 a minute. The Colts and the Jets were stereotyped as the crewcuts versus the longhairs. Maybe the players deserved better than that, but as seen on television, they had come to represent opposite ends of the decade.[23]

The Jets had the ball first, but their drive stalled and they were forced to punt. The Colts then drove to the Jets' 19-yard line and called on kicker Lou Michaels, who attempted a 27-yard field goal that slid right of the goal posts. The Colts then put another drive together, following a Jets turnover, and were inside their 10-yard line. On third-and-4 Morrall's pass to Tom Mitchell in the end zone deflected off the reserve tight end's shoulder pads and into the waiting arms of New York cornerback Randy Beverly for a touchback. After this play the game began to turn, as Namath drove the Jets, using runs by Snell with quick passes as he anticipated the Colts' blitz. In the second quarter Snell scored on a 4-yard run that capped a five-minute drive. The Colts drove again into Jets territory, but kicker Michaels missed a 46-yard field goal. For the Colts, this half was full of missed opportunities. Morrall drove his team again deep into Jets territory but was intercepted at the 2 by Johnny Sample on a pass intended for Willie Richardson. And on the last play of the half the Colts ran a flea-flicker, an option to halfback Tom Matte. Matte lateraled back to Morrall, whose primary receiver was split end Jimmy Orr. Instead, Morrall threw to fullback Jerry Hill, covered by Jim Hudson, who intercepted the pass. Orr was running wide open at the 10-yard line, and there was no one within 15 yards of him as he frantically waved his hands. After the game Orr said, "I did everything but shoot up a flare."[24]

Things only got worse for the Colts in the second half. In the third quarter Jim Turner added a 30-yard field goal, and in the fourth quarter he made a 9-yard field goal, bringing the score to 16–0. Desperate, the Colts turned to their injured veteran, Unitas, who quickly engineered a drive to the Jets' 25, but as he tried to find Orr in the end zone, he too was intercepted easily by Beverly. Finally, on his next possession, Unitas led the Colts on an 80-yard touchdown drive. With 3:19 left, the Colts scored on a Jerry Hill 1-yard touchdown run, making the score 16–7. This was the final score; the old gladiator Unitas fought hard but could not bring his team back. As the game was winding down, Commissioner Pete Rozelle made his way down to the field. He spotted Pat Summerall, who was working the Colts' sideline for NBC. "Tell me," Rozelle said, taking a long, nervous drag on a cigarette and preparing for the trophy presentation, "everything you know about the New York Jets."[25]

In the winners' locker room there was much jubilation, and Namath gave writers, especially those not from New York, who had picked the Colts a hard time. He also gave much credit to his defense, but even in victory it seemed like the focus was on what Baltimore did wrong. "What about the two passes that the Colts almost intercepted? What if the Colts had scored first?" Namath responded the only way he knew how: "If a frog had wings, it wouldn't bump its ass." For the Colts' Bubba Smith, the outcome of this game was not that simple: "I don't think the game was kosher. The line opened at 18 and went down to 15 or something like that because a big bet had been placed on the game. And I know where the bet came from. It came from Baltimore, from someone on the team from what I understand." Reporters flocked to Morrall, who threw three interceptions, none bigger than the pass intended for Matte when Orr was wide open. Morrall said he simply did not see Orr: "I should have seen him. Countless people have told me he was wide open."[26]

Few games have a profound and lasting effect on their sport, but Super Bowl III is one on the benchmarks of pro football history. Because it helped legitimize the American Football League in the eyes of many fans, the game has been recognized as one of the most important ever played. At the time of their victory, however, few of the Jets realized what they had accomplished. Winston Hill had opened holes that allowed Matt Snell to gain a then-record 121 yards rushing. Hill recalled, "We didn't realize the long-range effect of that game, the historical aspect of the impact it had on the game of football, we didn't realize any of that at the time. What I remember most about that Jets team was the great group of guys we had." Hill was right: the Jets' cohesiveness controlled the game, and Namath had matured after entering pro football under the cloud of his contract. He was named MVP after calling a masterful game that relied on his precise passing. The Jets quarterback completed seventeen of twenty-eight passes for 206 yards, but more importantly he kept the Colts' offense off the field with time-consuming drives. NBC announcer Kyle Rote approached Namath after the game; toweling off, Namath smiled at Rote. "Welcome," the Jets quarterback said, "to the AFL."[27]

After the Super Bowl there were two major events that were vital to the future of pro football. The first was the draft, which took place January 28–29, 1969, and it was a foregone conclusion that the Buffalo Bills would select O. J. Simpson with the first overall pick. The only question was whether Simpson would sign with the Bills or opt to play in Canada. After drafting Simpson, owner Ralph Wilson was made aware of Simpson's contract demands. "His agent wanted a $500,000 loan," Wilson recalled. "He said, we want a signing bonus and a salary that's acceptable, but we also want a $500,000 loan. I said, for what? The agent said they wanted to buy stocks with it so he can have something for his retirement. I said if you want a $500,000 loan, go to the bank. I'm not a bank, and I wouldn't give it to him." Simpson was viewed as the most talented player in the draft, but there were several others, including Joe Greene, a defensive tackle out of the University of North Texas who was selected by the Pittsburgh Steelers in the first round. Defensive back Roger Wehrli, out of the University of Missouri, was selected in the first round by the St. Louis Cardinals, and linebacker Ted Hendricks, out of the University of Miami (Florida), was picked in the second round by the Raiders; both players had outstanding careers. Once again teams scoured historically black colleges for potential players. Of the sixty-two players drafted from black schools, twenty-eight made teams. Defensive back Jim Marsalis, selected by the Kansas City Chiefs in the first round from Tennessee State University, was the highest-drafted player from a black school. The Houston Oilers found a great player in receiver Charlie Joiner from Grambling State University. The success of Marlin Briscoe and selection of Eldridge Dickey as black quarterbacks may have influenced the Boston Patriots to pick quarterback Onree Jackson out of Alabama A&M University in the fifth round, but he did not make the team. But African American quarterback James Harris made Buffalo's team after being selected in the eighth round out of

Grambling. Several black players from black schools went on to have stellar careers and played prominent roles for teams; among them were Ken Riley from Florida A&M University, L. C. Greenwood from the University of Arkansas at Pine Bluff, and John "Frenchy" Fuqua from Morgan State University.[28]

The second major issue the new NFL/AFL had to address was realignment. This was a difficult problem because it required balance in the new proposed American Football Conference and National Football Conference. At the February owners' meetings the NFL owners initially wanted to keep the new league status quo, with sixteen teams in the NFC and ten in the AFC. This made Paul Brown livid because the NFL had ten teams in the top television markets while the AFL had only one. Brown clearly indicated that when he decided to create the Bengals, the implication was that there would be a full merger and he was prepared to pursue legal measures if necessary. He was not alone; Al Davis also vehemently supported a full merger. A full merger required that three NFL teams move to the AFC, and to stimulate this process, Commissioner Rozelle stipulated that those teams would receive a one-time payment of $3 million from the league. Carroll Rosenbloom decided it was in the Colts' interest to start a rivalry in the same division with Namath and the Jets, and he jumped at the chance. But two more teams were needed. Interestingly Art Modell put the league ahead of his own interest and indicated that the Browns would move if the Steelers would join them. Steelers owner Art Rooney was willing to consider this, but his son Dan was adamant that his father should not move to the AFC. Dan said that there was "no way that the Pittsburgh Steelers are going to join the American Football Conference." But Art cut him off: "Now Danny, not so fast." Art decided to support Modell: the Steelers would join the Browns in retooling a rivalry with the Bengals, and they would have the opportunity to play in the state-of-the-art Astrodome. So the new AFC would be organized into three divisions: the Central Division, with Pittsburgh, Cleveland, Cincinnati, and Houston; the Western Division, with Oakland, San Diego, Kansas City, and Denver; and the Eastern Division, with Boston, Buffalo, Miami, New York, and Baltimore.[29]

Rosenbloom almost did not get his wish of a matchup with Namath and the Jets. Bachelors III, a restaurant and bar that Namath had invested in, was being investigated by the FBI for gambling and other criminal activity. Rozelle met with Namath and asked that he sell his interest and distance himself from the establishment. On June 6 a tearful Namath announced his retirement from football, saying, "I'm not selling." After several meetings over the summer, a compromise was worked out that required Namath to sell his interest and not enter the club in the "foreseeable future," but he could invest in Bachelor III franchises elsewhere in the country. Namath quickly acquiesced and realized that he was not above rules, policies, or the law. He told reporters of how as a rookie he was fined for not wearing a tie: "I was wearing a $190 sport coat, a $25 shirt, $125 shoes, $50 slacks—and I get fined $100 for not wearing a $2 tie."[30]

As Namath's Jets were clinching the Eastern Division in November, Americans were deciding who the next president of the United States would be. The process of selecting the Democratic nominee became exciting when Senator Eugene McCarthy of Minnesota entered the race as an antiwar alternative to Lyndon Johnson. Robert Kennedy, U.S. senator from New York, entered the race in mid-March, when many of the delegates had already pledged to Johnson. After Johnson withdrew, those delegates transferred to Vice President Hubert Humphrey. Kennedy was assassinated in June, and the beating of antiwar protesters at the convention in Chicago left a cloud over the party. In November, Republican Richard Nixon narrowly defeated Humphrey 43.1 percent to 42.7 percent in the popular vote and 301 to 191 in the electoral vote. George Wallace, the segregationist former governor of Alabama, in his first serious bid for the presidency, won 13.5 percent of the popular vote and forty-six electoral votes. Running as the candidate of the American Independent Party, Wallace denounced civil rights legislation and court-ordered desegregation. Although Wallace had not changed his racial views, the American political scene was now different. Shirley Chisholm was elected to the House of Representatives from New York's Twelfth Congressional District, making her the first black woman elected to Congress.[31]

Almost a month before the November elections the Olympics took place in Mexico City. Black athletes had discussed the idea of an organized protest of the Olympics but could not decide what to do as a group. So it was agreed that individual athletes would choose for themselves ways to protest racial discrimination that was still taking place in America. African American sprinters Tommie Smith and John Carlos finished first and third in the 200-meter race, and during the playing of the national anthem after receiving their medals, Smith and Carlos raised their glove-covered fists in the air, a clear reference to "black power." Avery Brundage, head of the International Olympic Committee, immediately had them suspended and evicted from the Olympic Village. His justification was that the Olympics was not a place for protest. However, gymnast Vera Caslavska from Czechoslovakia protested the invasion of her country by the Soviet Union. She won six medals at the games, and each time the Soviet national anthem was played she turned her head down and away. Brundage did not reprimand this white athlete, and many black athletes pointed out that what Smith and Carlos were protesting was very real. Not all the black athletes supported the symbolic gesture of Smith and Carlos, however. Boxer George Foreman won the heavyweight division, and after being awarded the gold medal, he walked around the ring waving the American flag as an overt gesture of patriotism. Foreman was not the typical black athlete by the late 1960s, and most clearly identified with the idea that America needed to continue to improve in the area of race relations.

The Olympic protest was seen as an example of the growing militancy within African American communities all across America. One year earlier heavyweight champion Muhammad Ali had refused induction into the U.S. armed services because of his religious beliefs, but he also noted that racism still existed in America and that he would not serve as an advocate for "Brown people to go kill other Brown people." Ali's refusal caused him to lose his boxing license for three years, but he felt that his principles were more important than lost income, media scrutiny, and unearned patriotism. Ali's refusal of induction and the Olympic protest of Smith and Carlos both followed the successful 1965 AFL All-Star Game boycott by black players. Cookie Gilchrist, Abner Haynes, Ernie Ladd, and the other participants clearly illustrated that black athletes could take on issues of racial injustice despite the view that they should relish the opportunity professionalism affords. Before 1965 black athletes had not organized a group protest against segregation that had forced a professional league to change venues. For that matter, very few were willing to speak out publicly against racial discrimination because they feared it could cost them their jobs. Although Gilchrist and Haynes felt that their participation in the boycott caused them to be traded afterward, they set an example that the fear of reprisals should not keep athletes from standing up to racial discrimination.

THE BIRTH OF
MODERN PRO FOOTBALL

The American Football League's last season took place in 1969, and appropriately the league's founder, Lamar Hunt, and his Kansas City Chiefs would leave as World Champions. The New York Jets had let the NFL know that the AFL could compete with its best, and the Chiefs validated that what the Jets accomplished was no accident. More importantly the merger and creation of the Super Bowl had helped the popularity of pro football grow in America. Specifically, pro football was not merely growing but muscling its way to primacy, at baseball's expense. From 1960 to 1968 baseball's attendance had gradually grown from 19,931,780 to 23,102,745, but after having peaked at 25,182,209 in 1966, its attendance had gradually declined. Many felt that the game had become dull because of low-scoring games and the dominance of great pitchers. In bars and living rooms, football had surpassed baseball in popularity among mainstream sports fans.[1]

In 1968 there were twenty major league baseball teams, five of which averaged less than 10,000 fans per game. Still, baseball decided to expand in 1969, adding San Diego, Seattle, Montreal, and Kansas City. While Montreal brought in almost 15,000 fans per game, the San Diego Padres played in front of 6,333. This was a stark contrast to the 46,311 that filled Jack Murphy Stadium to watch the Chargers. In a story that exemplifies the difference between the Chargers and Padres, Buzzie Bavasi, the general manager of the Padres, was sitting in his office when he received a phone call that a player was on his way up to borrow some money. Bavasi groaned and asked trainer Doc Mattei where he could hide. Mattei replied, "You might try down by the ticket windows, nobody's ever there. Or maybe the upper deck. Nobody's ever there either. Just be careful not to fall. They'd never find you until football season."[2]

The Kansas City Chiefs of 1969 were not hard to find: they began the year 9–1 on their way to a record of 11–3. The AFL created a new play-off system for this season that matched the division winner of the East against the team that finished second in the West, and the division winner in the West against the second-place team in the East. Although the Chiefs finished second to the Raiders in the West, the new playoff system afforded them the opportunity to extend their season. This team was driven by a defense that led the league in total yards allowed, forced turnovers, points allowed, and yards allowed per offensive play. The offense led the AFL in total rushing yards, rushing touchdowns, and rushing yards per game. The Chiefs had to rely on the run because quarterback Len Dawson was lost for six weeks with a knee injury. Running backs Mike Garrett and Warren McVea, along with fullbacks Robert Holmes and Wendell Hayes, stepped up to fill the void. These four African American players epitomized the Chiefs' philosophy of playing the best players regardless of race. On defense this policy was crystal clear: of the eleven starters, eight were African American. The defensive line of Buck Buchanan, Aaron Brown, Jerry Mays, and former NCAA wrestling champion Curley Culp recorded a league-high forty-eight quarterback sacks. The secondary was manned by rookie Jim Marsalis along with veterans Emmitt Thomas, Jim Kearney, and Johnny Robinson.[3]

But it was the linebackers who were the heart and soul of this defense. Bobby Bell and Jim Lynch played on the outside, and Willie Lanier manned the middle. Lanier was routinely compared to the Bears' famous linebacker Dick Butkus, and many scouts felt he covered more ground and hit harder when he got there. So hard, in fact, that Lanier often blacked out after making tackles. His frequent concussions and ensuing headaches landed him at the Mayo Clinic in 1968 and prompted him to begin wearing a distinctive helmet with water pockets lining the inside of the shell and a wide strip of foam padding bisecting the outside. These three linebackers led by Lanier were the best in the AFL and arguably in all of pro football. Lanier led the defense, Dawson led the offense, and Coach Hank Stram led the team. Players often referred to him as "Little Caesar" or "The Little Man," but black and white players were united in their impatience with his vanity and excesses. They also, to a man, believed their coach to be utterly without prejudice. Said one player, "There were some people who thought he put form over substance, but it was clear when it came to race, he didn't care about color, he only cared if you could play."[4]

The same could be said of the Raiders' new coach, who was hired after John Rauch resigned to take the head coaching job with the Buffalo Bills. John Madden became the youngest coach in pro football when he was named Raiders head coach in February 1969 at the age of thirty-two. Madden had coached linebackers for the team since 1967, and he quickly led the 1969 Raiders to a record of 12–1–1. They won their first three games before the Dolphins were lucky enough to tie them, and somehow the Cincinnati Bengals provided their only defeat at 31–17. They possessed the league's most potent offense as they led in points scored, total yards, and touchdowns. More importantly they swept the Chiefs, but the games were extremely close: the Raiders won 27–24 in Kansas City and 10–6 in Oakland. Once again the strong arm of Daryle Lamonica lit up defenses as he threw thirty-four touchdowns and twenty-five interceptions. His receiving corps of Warren Wells and Fred Bilentnikoff showed a contrast of speed and moves. Wells provided speed on the outside, which enabled him to lead the AFL in yards per catch at an incredible 26.8, receiving yards with 1,260, and touchdown receptions with fourteen. Bilentnikoff used moves and great hands to finish second in the league in catches with fifty-four and second to Wells in touchdowns with twelve.[5]

The Raiders of the late 1960s have been remembered largely for the play of their quarterback and receivers, but the offensive line was arguably one of most overlooked aspects of these great teams. Center Jim Otto was a perennial All-Pro, and tackles Harry Schuh and Bob Svihus were solid performers, but in 1967 they drafted Gene Upshaw out of tiny Texas A&I University to play guard. This African American player grew up in Robstown, Texas, a small segregated town in south Texas. He went to a four-room school with eight other students from first grade through middle school. He spent the rest of his time either picking cotton or playing baseball. As Upshaw remembers, "blacks could only go to the movies on Saturday afternoon, and they had to sit in the balcony." Baseball was his favorite sport, and he attended college after his father gave him an ultimatum not to sign a major league contract but take $75 and go register at Texas A&I University. He was watching football practice one day when he was spotted by the coach, who made Upshaw come out for the team. By the time he was a senior, he was invited to the College All-Star Game and Senior Bowl. Drafted in the first round by the Raiders, he had the speed and athleticism to be a starter in his first year. His teammates called him "The Governor," not just because of his political ambitions but also because he talked all the time. During this season the Raiders began to work in another offensive lineman who was a massive tackle drafted in 1968 from Maryland State College. Art Shell played sparingly next to Upshaw, but this tandem would become one of the greatest blocking duos in the history of pro football.[6]

In San Diego, Coach Sid Gillman retired due to health problems from a stomach ulcer and chest hernia. Gillman and Kansas City's Hank Stram were the only head coaches left in the AFL who had been in place since the league's inception in 1960. Gillman had built an impressive 78–42–6 record during his term. But arguably his greatest contribution was not his tenure as coach of the Chargers but his overall offensive philosophy, which spawned a coaching tree that is still producing coaches today. Al Davis, Chuck Noll, Chuck Knox, Dick Vermeil, George Allen, and Don Coryell were the first to coach under Gillman. Many have credited Gillman with creating the modern passing game in professional football. Gillman was the first to use game film and later practice film as coaching tools. In 1968 Gillman required players during training camp and on the road to room together by position, which forced black and white players to share a room. One year earlier Gale Sayers and Brian Piccolo of the Chicago Bears became the first black and white teammates to room together in pro football when Sayers chose Piccolo as his road roommate. Gillman insisted that his entire team follow this policy, and when questioned on the subject, he told the *Los Angeles Times*: "We've really been thinking about it a long time. We just decided to Americanize our football team. That's all there is to it. We don't segregate Jews and don't segregate Catholics why should we segregate them because of their race? If we are designing our future with the idea that we're going to get this racial situation straightened out, then let's get with it."[7]

The Houston Oilers were also clearly focused on the future and not the past as they brought on young, talented African American players. The Oilers epitomized the changing racial landscape of pro football, at a time when teams were adding more black players to their rosters. The overwhelmingly white Oilers who won the first two AFL Championships were now long gone, replaced by a team with numerous African American players who were establishing league-wide reputations at their respective positions. George Webster was the AFL's rookie of the year in 1967 after averaging ten tackles per game as a linebacker. Blessed with incredible speed, he was modest in describing his ability: "I have to feel that I've been very lucky." The New York Jets realized that luck had nothing to do with

Webster's ability to cover backs. In a game in the Astrodome on October 20, Joe Namath tried to throw several passes with Webster matched up man for man with Jets running backs—Webster knocked down three and almost intercepted a fourth. He was joined on defense with Miller Farr, who played cornerback and was named All-AFL in 1967. Like Webster, Farr possessed tremendous speed; he ran a 9.6 in the 100-yard dash but more importantly improved his cover skills. He was the defensive back responsible for covering opponent's top receiver, so week after week he faced Lance Alworth, Don Maynard, Warren Wells, and others.[8]

Middle linebacker Garland Boyette was another member of this improving defense. Ernie Ladd was his nephew, and like Ladd, Boyette attended Grambling State University. He finished sixth in the 1960 Olympic Trials as a shot putter and was forced to run a leg in the 440 relay; at 230 pounds he helped Grambling finish third in the race. The Oilers were also developing talent on offense, again using key African American players. Running back Woodie Campbell was voted All-AFL after rushing for 511 yards during his rookie season in 1967, and he remained a relatively productive back the next two seasons. But without question the sensation of 1969 was rookie Jerry LeVias. He was the first African American scholarship player at Southern Methodist University, breaking the color barrier in the Southwest Conference. The 5'9", 177-pound wide receiver and kick returner set career records for the Mustangs despite constant racial slurs. SMU coach Hayden Fry tried to keep LeVias's spirits up as he endured these indignities, but in a game against Texas Christian University during his senior year LeVias nearly broke. After being spit in the face, he retreated to the SMU sideline in tears, threw his helmet on the ground in disgust, and flatly stated, "I quit." But by the time TCU had to punt, he had regrouped, telling Fry, "I'm running this back for a touchdown." Described by Fry as one of "the most spectacular punt returns I've ever seen," LeVias went untouched for an 89-yard touchdown that made the difference in a 21–14 Mustang victory. "That was the first time I openly hated. When you let hate get into your system, your mindset is terrible. That's why that one touchdown, I'm more ashamed of than anything else. Once you let the taste of hatred into your body, it's like a poison."[9]

LeVias was voted All-AFL as a rookie, and he led the league in punt returns, punt return yardage, and all-purpose yardage. He also had the longest touchdown reception in the AFL, an 86-yard catch and run against the Denver Broncos. Joining LeVias in the receiving corps was rookie Charlie Joiner, who played at Grambling State. Joiner was one of the many talented players who helped Coach Eddie Robinson go 23–6–1 from 1967 to 1969. But Joiner played only seven games for the Oilers before he broke his arm.[10]

Without question the greatest anticipation surrounding the arrival of a rookie in the AFL centered on O. J. Simpson. No player had facilitated such coverage by the media since Namath arrived in New York. The Bills expected that Simpson would be a major part of the team's offense, and they hoped his running ability would translate into wins on the field. But that was not the case, as Buffalo finished 4–10, although Simpson had a relatively solid season. He rushed for 697 yards but scored only two rushing touchdowns. He was voted All-Pro, but players such as Marlin Briscoe did not care for his prima donna attitude. Briscoe was invited to the Bills' camp in late August and was given the opportunity to make the team as a wide receiver. The Bills had drafted quarterback James "Shack" Harris out of Grambling in the eighth round, and Briscoe helped mentor Harris. The Bills decided to start Harris over veteran Jack Kemp and rookie Dan Darragh. When Harris met Briscoe, the younger man was very direct and appreciative: "I never thought I'd get to meet you, you were the reason I was drafted this year. What you did last year set the stage for other blacks. Now we're on the same team!" Although Harris recognized the great historical accomplishment of Briscoe, Simpson did not. Harris pulled a groin in camp, and Briscoe was called on to play quarterback temporarily. During one drill he threw to Simpson, who according to Briscoe made no real attempt to catch the pass. As Simpson headed back to the line of scrimmage, he said to Briscoe, "You aren't a quarterback, brother, you're a wide receiver." Briscoe snapped; after not receiving a real opportunity to play quarterback in Denver and being cut, he was not going to let Simpson criticize him. Because Simpson had such a large head, the team had to order a helmet for him that had not yet arrived, and Briscoe picked up a football and tried to hit Simpson in the head. Realizing that he had just thrown a ten-dollar football at the head of the Bills' prize rookie, Briscoe thought that he was going to get cut for sure. But it caused him to be respected by his teammates, particularly Harris and even Simpson, who apologized to Briscoe: "Sorry, for what I said. That wasn't cool."[11]

The testament of Briscoe's athletic ability was that he made the Bills team as a receiver and finished the season with thirty-two receptions for 532 yards and five touchdowns. Haven Moses led the Bills with thirty-nine receptions for 752 yards and five touchdowns. Although Harris started the first game of the season, Kemp started eleven, but his play was less than stellar—he threw twenty-two interceptions and only thirteen touchdowns. Briscoe and Harris talked a lot during the season, and this was vital to Harris's development as a quarterback. Briscoe realized that Harris's intelligence was astounding, once he was willing to talk with you. But Harris, who had grown up in a small segregated town in Louisiana, was wary of his new surroundings. The responsibility of leading a predominantly white group of athletes was foreign to him. Harris received death threats, and the media criticized his throwing ability. The criticism was not based on accuracy or lack of velocity on his passes; instead, he was accused of throwing too hard. According to Briscoe, this was ludicrous because he, Moses, and the other receivers had no problems catching his passes. "Sure, he had a strong arm, but to even imply that he threw the ball too hard was absurd."[12]

Harris was a pioneer for the black quarterback once the merger took place. He was signed by the Los Angeles Rams in 1972 and took over as their starting quarterback in 1974. He led the Rams to the NFC division title that year and their first playoff victory since 1951. He was the first African American player to start a season as quarterback and the first black quarterback to start and win an NFL playoff game. More importantly he served as a constant reminder during the early 1970s that the NFL needed to fundamentally change at the quarterback position. Racism kept Harris from getting a full opportunity to play the most important position in football, but his brief career made other black quarterbacks think about the possibilities for success if they had a legitimate chance.

The end of the 1969 regular season brought to a near close the story of the AFL. The league that had fought to survive against the NFL and the fans' and media's prejudices for ten seasons was about to be incorporated into the senior league. Through the second half of the 1960s the AFL's growth had been tremendous. New stadiums were built in New York, Oakland, San Diego, and Houston, and the Oilers became the first pro team to play its home games inside a dome. Attendance at AFL games had increased steadily. After averaging under 20,000 fans per game the first two seasons, the AFL in 1969 was drawing twice that many, averaging 40,619 per game and a total of more than 2.8 million during its final season. And the AFL's distinct style of play, its star performers, and its championship teams provided memorable moments and captured the imagination of millions of fans.[13]

On Saturday, December 20, the Kansas City Chiefs played the New York Jets in Shea Stadium in the AFL's new playoff system. The winner would play either the Oakland Raiders or Houston Oilers, who were scheduled to play the following day in Oakland. The conditions for the game were chilly and windy, and game-time temperatures were 33 degrees.

Several key players for the Jets had injuries, including receiver Don May-nard, who had a broken foot, and quarterback Joe Namath, who had taken several hard hits during the season—none harder than the one delivered by Denver defensive lineman Dave Costa, who burst through the Jets' line and planted his helmet between Namath's rib cage and solar plexus. Namath's ribs were bruised, and this only decreased his limited mobil-ity. But Costa may not have been the toughest opponent Namath faced that season: days before the game, singer Janis Joplin cornered him, using large quantities of tequila. The earthy singer was not the prototype Namath bunny, but she was determined to sleep with the superstar quar-terback. On Friday, December 19, before she took the stage at Madison Square Garden, the sold-out crowd was informed that "Miss Joplin would like to dedicate the entire set to the New York Jets for their victory over the Kansas City Chiefs tomorrow."[14]

The "Queen of Psychedelic Soul" may have been a great live performer, but she knew little about the Chiefs' defense, which controlled this game. The Jets scored first on a Jim Turner 27-yard field goal, and the Chiefs responded with fields goals by Jan Stenerud of 23 and 25 yards. In the third quarter, with the score still 6–3, a pass interference call gave the Jets the ball first-and-goal on the Chiefs' 1-yard line. Quarterback Len Dawson on the Chiefs' sideline turned his head from the field and covered his eyes. What he did not see was linebacker Willie Lanier in the Chiefs' huddle, with tears running down his face, imploring his teammates not to let the Jets score. "He was crying and screaming," cornerback Emmitt Thomas said. "He started running up and down the defensive line begging us to stop the Jets." On first and second down the Chiefs stopped the Jets' run-ning backs cold. On third down Namath faked a handoff to running back Bill Mathis and rolled to his right, looking for Matt Snell in the flat. But Bobby Bell had not bought the fake and covered Snell, so under pressure Namath had to throw the ball away, and the Jets were forced to settle for a tying field goal. Namath said to reporters after the game, "He was out there with Snell, and he had no right being there. If he's not there, it's a touchdown."[15]

But it was not, and after receiving the kickoff, the Chiefs took over at their own 20. As the offense took the field, receiver Otis Taylor convinced Dawson that by lining up a few yards behind the line of scrimmage the Jets would be forced to cover him with a safety. Dawson agreed, and on first down he hit Taylor on a 61-yard pass that devastated the Jets' defense. On the next play, from the New York 19, Dawson found Gloster Richardson for the go-ahead touchdown. The Kansas City defense repelled two more drives, concluding with a Jim Marsalis interception in the end zone. The champions were vanquished, and walking to the sidelines after the final interception, Namath threw his helmet to the ground in frustration. The great quarterback who was the face of the AFL completed fourteen of forty passes, with three interceptions. The Jets' reign as champions came to an end, and Coach Weeb Ewbank broke down weeping in the locker room.[16]

The following day, the other half of the AFL Championship match-up was settled when the Raiders dominated the Oilers 56–7. In the first quarter Daryle Lamonica threw three touchdown passes, and defensive back George Atkinson returned an interception 57 yards for a touchdown. Lamonica threw three more touchdown passes, and the Oilers did not score until late in the fourth quarter, when Pete Beathard hit Alvin Reed on an 8-yard touchdown pass. Without a real pass rush to pressure Lamonica, the Oilers were simply at his mercy. The Raiders had 412 total yards to the Oilers' 197; Lamonica played pitch and catch passing for 276 yards while completing thirteen of seventeen passes with six touchdowns and one interception. The Chiefs were now headed back to Oakland, where they had not won since their Super Bowl season in 1966.[17]

The AFL Championship game was held the following Sunday, January 4. By 1969 the Oakland–Kansas City series had become one of the most intense in pro football. The two teams had dominated the Western Division since 1966, in the process creating a rivalry that Hank Stram called "bitter." The Raiders were favored going into the game, having beaten the Chiefs in seven of their eight previous meetings. Although the offenses were led by Dawson and Lamonica, most predicted another defensive struggle. The Chiefs had the best overall defense in the league, and they were also first against the run and pass. The Raiders were second in team defense and had led the AFL in sacks the last three seasons. In 1967 they set the single-season record with 67, which would not be broken until the 1985 Bears. This was a very hard-hitting physical football game, described by many of the participants as "a war."[18]

The Raiders' comments leading up to the game reflected their confidence. "I played my first exhibition game against K.C.," Lamonica said. "I scored my first TD pass against K.C. in my rookie year. I feel—I *know* I can beat them. I know I can score on them, on the ground and in the air. Just watch us Sunday. We are ready." Lamonica appeared to be prophet as he drove the Raiders late in the first quarter to a 7–0 lead, when Charlie Smith scored on a 3-yard run. Dawson was having a difficult time against the Raiders' defense as he threw seven straight incompletions. But late in the second quarter, he hit Frank Pitts with a 41-yard bomb that brought the ball to the Oakland 1-yard line. From there Wendell Hayes smashed over, and the Chiefs went into halftime tied 7–7.[19]

Early in the second half Lamonica tore tendons in his hand following through on a pass, when his fingers caught in the face mask of the Chiefs' onrushing Aaron Brown. George Blanda relieved Lamonica and not only struggled passing but also missed three field-goal attempts. Late in the third quarter he was able to move the Raiders deep into Chiefs territory, but Emmitt Thomas intercepted Blanda in the end zone and ran it out to the 6. After an incompletion and a 4-yard loss, the Chiefs faced third-and-14 from their own 2-yard line. Dawson then made the play of the game as he eluded the rush and found Otis Taylor at the 35-yard line to continue a drive that ended with fullback Robert "The Tank" Holmes scoring on a 5-yard run. With only a few minutes left in the third the play gave the Chiefs an improbable 14–7 lead. According to Raiders coach John Madden, "the Chiefs would be open and flamboyant when they got ahead, but they tended to be a little conservative when the game was tighter and they were behind." In essence the Raiders were not expecting such a risky call, and Madden had to give the Chiefs credit for their willingness to call the play. "That was a hell of a call, and a hell of a throw by Len Dawson. Because that could have turned the game around the other way. That's a dangerous place to throw. Then Otis makes a heck of a catch on the sideline. If we knock the thing down, if we pick it off, we win the game."[20]

Lamonica returned to the game, but he could not grip the ball and in the final period he threw three interceptions. The Chiefs added a Stenerud field goal from 22 yards out to make the final score 17–7. Despite finishing second behind the Raiders in the regular season, they were headed to the Super Bowl to face the Minnesota Vikings, who defeated the Cleveland Browns 27–7 in the NFL Championship game. Once again the AFL Champion was considered a substantial underdog. Jimmy "The Greek" installed the Vikings as 13-point favorites, and many felt that a team that could not win its own division had no chance against the gritty Vikings. But for the third time in franchise history, Lamar Hunt's team became champions of the American Football League. "We have a lot to be proud of," Hunt said. "Looking back over the years we've spent in the AFL, we've won three league championships. That is more than any other team. Buffalo and Houston each won two. Oakland won one, San Diego won one, and New York won one. That makes us the all-time AFL champions."[21]

There was obvious irony in the matchup between the Chiefs and Vikings. Hunt had founded the AFL, and Max Winter, owner of the Vikings, had initially committed to joining the upstart league before jumping to the NFL. At the time, the NFL hoped that the Vikings' departure would cause the AFL to unravel and fold before it ever began. But Hunt's vision and tenacity simply made him extend an opportunity to the Raiders to join his "Foolish Club." Hunt relished the role of underdog, and the Vikings were seen as the superior team, largely because of their defense and tough quarterback. More accurately they had bullied their way through the NFL with a frightening defense led by the front four of Jim Marshall, Carl Eller, Alan Page, and Gary Larsen. The offense was led by quarterback Joe Kapp, whose passes wobbled but often found the mark. He set the tone for the Vikings, using scrambling runs that included hurdling over defenders and running through tacklers. The Viking attack was unrelenting but unspectacular, and the team led the league in points scored primarily because the defense kept giving it the ball. Bud Grant's team rolled through the NFL to a 12–2 record by relying on physicality from both sides of the football.[22]

The Chiefs were ready to redeem themselves after getting destroyed by Green Bay in Super Bowl I. Quarterback Len Dawson did not put up great stats during the season, throwing nine touchdowns and thirteen interceptions. But days before the game he had bigger problems besides how to attack the Vikings defense: his name surfaced as part of a gambling investigation. He was later cleared of any wrongdoing, but the stress he endured in the week of Super Bowl IV drained him emotionally. Dawson's roommate, defensive back Johnny Robinson, witnessed the pressure he was under as Dawson tried to get to sleep each night. But Robinson also assured Dawson that the Vikings' offense was simplistic and easy to stop. According to Robinson, it was almost identical to that of the Packers, whose foundation was built on "We aren't going to try and trick anybody. Here's what we're going to do. We're not gonna run a halfback reverse pass when we can just kick your teeth in."[23]

Super Bowl IV forever changed pro football and the medium of television. The night before the game, Hank Stram was trying to relax in his room when Ed Sabol of NFL Films was adamant that he needed to talk with him. Although Stram had numerous family and friends in his suite, Sabol came over and said, "I want to wire you for sound tomorrow." Stram's immediate reply was, "Are you crazy? For the Super Bowl?" Sabol said it would be the greatest thing in the world—nobody had ever heard a coach live in a big game. Sabol was convinced that Stram could do it and not Grant, who he felt "never says anything." Stram promised Sabol that he could wire him two hours before the game, and for the first time in television history, viewers would be able to hear the voice of a coach during a pro football game. The verbiage of Stram enthusiastically calling plays has become one of the most recognized pieces ever produced by NFL Films.[24]

Since the AFL was playing its final Super Bowl, Stram and Hunt ordered special patches to be sewn on the shoulders of the Chiefs' jerseys. The patch was the AFL logo, and its effect on Kansas City's players was uplifting. "It lit us up," Lanier said. "We all knew what it meant." The players were loose and ready to take the field even though the weather in New Orleans was rainy and cold. A record crowd of 80,897 crammed into Tulane Stadium on Sunday, January 11, 1970. This game would be won in the trenches, and it quickly became clear that 235-pound Viking center Mick Tingelhoff was having problems blocking 6'7", 285-pound Buck Buchanan and 6'1", 265-pound Curley Culp. They alternated lining up right over Tingelhoff, virtually destroying the Vikings' interior running game. On the game's opening drive the Vikings drove to the Chiefs' 39 but elected to punt into the wind. The Chiefs took over and drove to the Vikings' 48, where they attempted a field goal with the wind at their backs. If Jan Stenerud made the kick, it would be the longest in Super Bowl history. According to Stram, when he sent his kicker in, players on the Minnesota bench were punching each other. "Look at that. The guy's crazy!" Stenerud split the uprights for the game's first score and only points of the first quarter.[25]

In the second quarter Stenerud added two more field goals and Stram unleashed a play that the Chiefs had not run all year. To offset the speed of defensive tackle Alan Page, the Chiefs ran 65 toss power trap, which allowed their running backs to gain yards inside. With almost six minutes left in the quarter, Chiefs halfback Mike Garrett scored from 5 yards out on this now famous play. Once again the AFL was poised to pull the upset, and across the country the statement the Jets had made one year earlier was now being verified as no fluke. Viking fans finally had something to cheer about when a drive early in the third quarter ended with a 4-yard touchdown run by Dave Osborn. This made the score 16–7, but any real hopes of the Vikings winning the game were dimmed when Dawson hit Otis Taylor on a short 6-yard pass at the Minnesota 46. Taylor broke a tackle and sprinted the last 40 yards, which gave the Chiefs a 23–7 lead. The defenses controlled the rest of the game, and neither team was able to score again.[26]

The wiring of Stram during the game produced a celebrated monologue but more importantly allowed fans more access to the game. This play that gave the Chiefs a lead at halftime is still considered one of the NFL's most memorable moments. NFL Films continues to air this clip of coach Stram stating that 65 toss power trap might just work and allow the running back to score. The vision of Sabol and charisma of Stram arguably validated how well the sport of football works with the medium of television. Sabol used this footage to continue to mike coaches and players and used slow motion and the voice of John Facenda to produce what some have called the greatest public relations machine in pro sports history.

A Hollywood script writer could not have penned a better finish to the American Football League. Lamar Hunt had placed his team in the last Super Bowl just as he had the first, but this time he was victorious. Once again he took on the established NFL, which ten years earlier had turned down his request to join its league and which mocked the AFL. The "Foolish Club" had defied the odds and won. The league's television deal paved the way for revenue sharing that would enrich pro football and its owners for decades to come. As Hunt celebrated with his players, a reporter asked him if there was any special significance to the moment. Hunt smiled and said, "It's been a lot of fun. I don't even care who started it. But it's nice to know that the Chiefs finished it."[27]

The merger became official on February 1, 1970. The National and American Football Leagues entered into marriage and a new age of discovery. Astronaut Neil Armstrong took the United States into the space age when he became the first human being to step on the moon's surface on July 20, 1969, but the flight of Apollo 11 went relatively smoothly compared with the talks that formalized the merger. The competition committee, made up of Tex Schramm, Vince Lombardi, Paul Brown, and Al Davis, was still trying to decide in March whether to use the AFL's two-point option after touchdowns or stick with the NFL's single-point rule. After agreeing to put players' names on their jerseys and selecting the type of football to be used, the committee decided to use the NFL's one-point rule. The NFL ball was chosen over the AFL ball, but the AFL's use of the scoreboard as the official clock became a part of the new NFL. The two leagues officially became the American and National Football Conferences of the National Football League, with Kansas City Chiefs owner Lamar Hunt and Chicago Bears owner George Halas chosen as figurehead presidents. The league was divided evenly with thirteen teams in each conference, which were broken into three divisions. The best record among the nondivision winners would be awarded a "wild card" berth in the playoffs.[28]

The Pittsburgh Steelers won the first overall draft pick in a coin flip over the Chicago Bears and selected strong-armed quarterback Terry Bradshaw from Louisiana Tech University. Bradshaw went on to live up to his high rating and was one of the many wise draft selections that

enabled the Steelers to become an American Football Conference power-
house after years of mediocrity in the old NFL. Three African American
players from historically black schools were also picked in the first round:
wide receiver Ken Burrough from Texas Southern University was chosen
by the New Orleans Saints, followed by guard Doug Wilkerson from North
Carolina Central University by the Houston Oilers, and Raymond Chester,
tight end out of Morgan State University, by the Oakland Raiders. A total
of sixty players were drafted from historically black schools, and twenty-
seven made teams, including future Hall of Famer Mel Blount, who was
picked by the Steelers in the third round out of Southern University as a
defensive back. With the merger the Colts and the Steelers moved to the
AFC, and both teams experienced success in the new NFL. The Colts won
the Super Bowl after the merger by defeating the Dallas Cowboys 16–13
in January 1971. The Steelers became the dominant team of the decade,
winning four Super Bowls and propelling pro football to new heights. The
NFL's success was directly tied to the expansion of television when the
league signed a new deal with ABC to televise games on Monday nights.[29]

For slightly more than $8 million each season, ABC agreed to telecast
thirteen prime-time games on Monday nights. This meant that each of
the twenty-six NFL teams would receive approximately $1.7 million in
1970, $500,000 more than what each NFL team got in 1969 and $800,000
more than what AFL teams received. Howard Cosell, Don Meredith, and
Keith Jackson broadcast the games, and for the first time the game itself
became secondary to the show put on by the announcers. Cosell made his
commentary in highly dramatic tones, while Meredith mixed his analysis with homespun country witticisms. Jackson tried to concentrate on
reporting the game but lasted for only one year before he was replaced by
Frank Gifford. The network used multiple cameras in its broadcast, which
made the games appear more vivid at night. The show earned a share of
over 35 percent on its opening night and a consistent Nielsen rating of 18,
which was approximately 60 million homes. In its first season Monday
Night Football had a share of 31 and by early October had knocked ABC's
Dick Cavett Show off the air on Mondays, with Cavett moving to a four-
night-a-week schedule through the end of the football season.[30]

Without question the AFL was successful in facilitating the evolution
of modern football. The merger, the brilliant use of television, and the
commitment to revenue sharing propelled pro football past baseball as
America's favorite sport. African American players were also a fundamental factor in the growth of this American sport. Charles Follis, Fritz
Pollard, Paul Robeson, Joe Lillard, and several other early black players

generated curiosity among fans during the initial days of the sport's development up to 1933. African Americans were not given opportunities to play during pro football's "Dark Ages," from 1934 until 1946, when an informal color ban was in place. The reintegration process that began with Kenny Washington, Woody Strode, Bill Willis, and Marion Motley was the third phase for black players, who simply wanted opportunities to play. The AFL must be given credit for eradicating many of the historic barriers African American players faced in their efforts to play pro football. When the league was formed in 1960, every team had at least two black players, and the 1963 Chargers made conscious efforts to socialize together off the field as teammates regardless of race. The AFL was willing to move its All-Star Game in 1965 from New Orleans to Houston after black players staged a successful boycott against segregation. When Marlin Briscoe started for the 1968 Denver Broncos at quarterback, he became the first African American to do so in the history of pro football. And the Super Bowl champion Kansas City Chiefs were the first team in pro football to field a lineup in which more than half the twenty-two starters were African Americans.

When the AFL merged with the NFL, it brought more than the names of players on the backs of jerseys, the game clock as the official clock, or even the eventual use of the two-point conversion. The AFL served as an example to the NFL that football was changing: the 1969 Chiefs were very similar to the 2015 Chiefs. The AFL clearly represented where pro football was going, and the merger caused the NFL to follow.

EPILOGUE

THE STATE OF THE GAME II

The creation of the AFL and subsequent merger with the NFL propelled pro football into its modern era. The AFL recognized the power of television and how it could be used to make the new league stronger or destroy it in its infancy. This new league also realized that African American players could contribute to the success of a team without having to be outstanding players at white collegiate institutions. The NFL historically struggled with extending opportunities to African American players from the time it was founded in 1920. Its thirteen-year color barrier from 1933 to 1946 cost many qualified black players the opportunity to earn a living but more importantly to contribute to the history of this great game. The reintegration process was slow and still going on when the AFL was founded in 1960. The Washington Redskins remained all-white under the leadership of owner George Preston Marshall until 1962; in contrast, the AFL, formed under the vision of Lamar Hunt, from its inception had black players on every team.

Interestingly it appears that the AFL was more responsible for facilitating opportunities for black players at historically black schools. During the 1958 NFL draft a total of 360 players were selected; of those, only six were chosen from historically black institutions. Only two made respective teams—defensive end John Baker from North Carolina Central University was kept by the Los Angeles Rams, and defensive back Johnny Sample from the University of Maryland Eastern Shore made the Balti-

more Colts team. Again in 1959 the NFL selected some 360 college players, only twelve of whom played at HBCUs, and perhaps coincidentally
only two made NFL rosters. Halfback Jamie Caleb from Grambling State
University stuck with the Cleveland Browns, and defensive tackle Rufus
Granderson from Prairie View A&M University played one year with the
Detroit Lions. Somehow, after the AFL's first draft in November 1959, the
NFL discovered that more than two players from historically black schools
can help teams, and some seven made respective teams after being drafted. The AFL immediately recognized the talent that these black players
possessed, and arguably the new league's existence forced the NFL to take
a more active approach to scouting and extending opportunities to this
population of African American players. Clearly the AFL valued the talent
of players from historically black schools in the early 1960s more than
the NFL did, although it can be debated that the success of Julius "Buck"
Buchanan as a player was based on his ability to stay relatively injury-free
during his stellar career or maybe it was the system he played in with the
Chiefs. What cannot be debated is the fact that Kansas City drafted him
with the first overall pick of the 1963 draft out of Grambling based on the
talent they saw. This made him the first African American player from a
historically black school to be selected with the first overall pick in pro
football. The NFL, however, felt that this future Hall of Fame player was
worthy of being drafted only in the nineteenth round by the New York
Giants with the 265th pick.[1]

The success of modern football is inextricably tied to the use of television by both the NFL and AFL. The 1958 NFL Championship was watched
by millions of Americans, and this overtime victory by the Colts has been
given credit for launching pro football on its way to becoming America's
game. But a strong argument can also be made that the 1962 AFL double-
overtime championship game won by the Dallas Texans was instrumental
in this process. Millions watched as both teams fought in the longest pro
football game ever. Undoubtedly this sport infatuated Americans, and it
meshed very well with television. The three major networks submitted
lucrative bids for the rights to broadcast NFL games in 1964; CBS won, but
in the process helped to open a Pandora's box. NBC negotiated a deal with
the AFL that virtually guaranteed the existence of the league but also
helped to facilitate a costly bidding war over players. These two television
deals led to the merger in 1966 and the evolution of modern football.

The merger created the Super Bowl, the most-watched television event
in American history. Victories by the Jets and Chiefs in Super Bowls III
and IV unmistakably illustrated that the AFL was not an inferior league

but a highly competitive one. With realignment the notions of "us" and "them" turned to "we" when the Colts, Browns, and Steelers all moved to the newly formed AFC. With an integrated regular-season schedule, fans quickly forgot the territorial lines that once separated the AFL and NFL. Fans in the AFL also witnessed change on the field as African American players were given the opportunity to play positions that historically had been exclusively reserved for white players.

In 1967 Willie Lanier became the first African American to start at middle linebacker in pro football, with the Chiefs. Lamar Hunt and Hank Stram were pioneers who shared a vision for success largely based on opportunity. The 1969 Chiefs were the first team to have a majority of their starters on defense who were African Americans. This offered fans a glimpse into the future: African Americans now make up 68 percent of the players in the NFL. Fans today take for granted the idea that the vast majority of players on offense or defense will be African American. The AFL also provided a brief opportunity for African Americans to play the most important position on the field—quarterback.

Interestingly the Denver Broncos were the only AFL team never to have a winning season during the league's existence. Arguably much of this ineptitude can be blamed on their failure to find a successful starting quarterback. Injuries and desperation caused the Broncos to make Marlin Briscoe the first African American to start as a quarterback in pro football. One can only speculate on the fortunes of the Broncos had they decided to extend this opportunity beyond the 1968 season. The specter of Briscoe possibly haunted this team until 1983, when they drafted John Elway, who eventually led them to Super Bowl victories in 1997 and 1998. But since Briscoe started for Denver in 1968, only one other African American has started at quarterback for the Broncos, and that was Jarious Jackson, who started one game in 2003.

In many ways the racial progress of pro football has been measured by the opportunities extended to black notable quarterbacks. Briscoe tutored James Harris, who joined the Bills in 1969 and was the first to serve as a full-time starter in the NFL. Joe Gilliam had a brief stint with Pittsburgh beginning in 1972, followed in 1977 by Vince Evans, who had a long career mostly as a backup with the Bears and Raiders. In 1978 Doug Williams from Grambling State University became the first African American to be drafted as a quarterback in the first round of the NFL draft. The Tampa Bay Buccaneers drafted him with the seventeenth pick overall, and he played three seasons there before leaving in a salary dispute. Williams played two seasons in the United States Football League and then joined the Washington Redskins, where he started for them in Super Bowl XXII. He was the first African American to start at quarterback and lead his team to victory as it easily defeated the Denver Broncos. Warren Moon entered the league in 1984 after having to prove himself initially in the CFL. He dispelled the idea that black quarterbacks cannot read defenses and be "pocket" passers. He was a nine-time Pro-Bowler and the first and only African American to be inducted into the Pro Football Hall of Fame as a quarterback. In 1985 Randall Cunningham entered the league and became the first accepted duo-threat African American quarterback, with the Philadelphia Eagles. His ability to extend plays with his legs made him a virtual nightmare for defenses. His charisma and athletic ability made him a superstar who endorsed national products and drew comparisons with NBA basketball star Michael Jordan. In 2001 Michael Vick became the first African American quarterback to be selected first overall in the NFL draft. The Atlanta Falcons chose Vick, and immediately comparisons were made to Cunningham, as Vick was a polished passer and runner. In 2013 Russell Wilson led the Seattle Seahawks to the Super Bowl and a decisive victory over the Denver Broncos as the second African American to do so. Wilson's success prompted articles and media reports about progress at this important position within the context of the NFL's history.[2]

In 2015 the NFL consisted of thirty-two teams, of which six have what would be considered full-time starters at the quarterback position who are African American: Tyrod Taylor, Buffalo Bills; Cam Newton, Carolina Panthers; Teddy Bridgewater, Minnesota Vikings; Colin Kaepernick, San Francisco 49ers; Russell Wilson, Seattle Seahawks; and Jameis Winston, Tampa Bay Buccaneers. Interestingly these six African American starters are viewed as possessing both passing and running abilities. Before Wilson and Newton signed new deals at the end of the 2014 season, only Kaepernick was listed among the ten highest-paid quarterbacks in the NFL. In essence, before Wilson and Newton signed their new deals, the top five highest-paid quarterbacks in the NFL were all white, starting with Aaron Rodgers of the Packers, whose contract is for $110 million with $54 million guaranteed. Matt Ryan of the Falcons has a contract for $103 million with $42 million guaranteed. Joe Flacco of the Baltimore Ravens is next with a $120 million contract and $29 million guaranteed. Drew Brees of the New Orleans Saints plays for $100 million with $40 million guaranteed. And Peyton Manning is paid $96 million with $18 million guaranteed. Wilson's new contract pays him $87 million with $60 million guaranteed, and Newton is now paid $103 million with $60 million guaranteed, placing them both in the top five highest-paid quarterbacks in the league.[3]

The question remains, has the playing field been truly leveled for African Americans playing the quarterback position? Russell Wilson led the Seahawks to back-to-back Super Bowls, defeating the Denver Broncos in Super Bowl XLVIII and losing to the New England Patriots in Super Bowl XLIX. His innate ability to combine accurate passing on the run with making plays with his legs is arguably second to none in the NFL. But Wilson's greatest strengths might be his intellect for the game and leadership over the team's offense. The Carolina Panthers awarded Cam Newton a new contract largely based on the perception that he is the most physically gifted quarterback in professional football. His size, incredibly strong arm, and intimidating running ability propelled a very average team into the playoffs in 2013 and 2014. Colin Kaepernick signed a new contract in 2013 after leading the San Francisco 49ers to Super Bowl XLVII; it called for him to be paid $114 million but with only $12 million guaranteed. So the three highest-paid black quarterbacks in the NFL consist of two who took their teams to the Super Bowl and one who is viewed as superhuman.

Obviously comparisons can be made to white quarterbacks who have not accomplished nearly as much on the field—particularly in terms of being successful in the playoffs—but who have large contracts, such as Matt Ryan; Jay Cutler (Bears), $126 million with $38 million guaranteed; Tony Romo (Cowboys), $108 million with $40 million guaranteed; Matt Stafford (Lions), $53 million with $41 million guaranteed; and Sam Bradford (Eagles), $78 million with $50 million guaranteed. Clearly there is work to be done in terms of equity at the most important position on NFL teams. The fact that African Americans make up 68 percent of the players in the NFL yet are an overwhelming minority at the quarterback position is troubling. Arguably the challenges that Marlin Briscoe, James Harris, and others faced in the late 1960s have not been fully addressed in the first quarter of the twenty-first century.[4]

The physical nature of football as a sport has always had repercussions for its players. Ferocious hits and hard tackles have helped to attract fans and create identities for players. The intensity with which both teams hit each other in the 1963 AFL Championship is still recalled by those participants as extremely brutal. The hit by Mike Stratton of the Bills on Keith Lincoln of the Chargers in the 1964 AFL Championship not only broke Lincoln's ribs but also changed the momentum of the game. The NFL of the twenty-first century has attempted to make the game safer, with improvements in equipment and revolutionary rule changes. Players such as the Raiders' Ben Davidson, who routinely hit late, speared, and tried to hit quarterbacks in the head, would be fined heavily today and suspended from games. But the NFL's attempt to make the game safer has also been challenged in terms of the league's sincerity. Is the NFL truly concerned about the health and welfare of its players, or does it want to protect itself from costly litigation? The key issue is head injuries and their effects on active players, but more importantly on those who have left the game. In August 2013 a settlement was announced from a lawsuit against the NFL filed by more than 4,500 former players seeking compensation from the league for injuries suffered during their careers. The case was nicknamed the "concussion lawsuit," and the NFL offered $765 million to the plaintiffs. However, in January 2014 U.S. District Judge Anita Brody rejected the settlement, "fearing the sum may not be enough to cover injured players." Judge Brody specifically was concerned whether the amount would be enough to cover some 20,000 retired players. Critics had argued that the NFL, with its more than $9 billion in annual revenue, was getting away fairly lightly. But in April 2015 Judge Brody approved the settlement, which allowed players with specific neurological disorders to receive payments up to $5 million. It also provided funds for medical monitoring of all players to determine if they qualify for a payment and $10 million for education about concussions.[5]

The popularity of the NFL has caused the league to look to the future regarding several key issues. The settlement of the concussion litigation is paramount to the image of the league and how it is viewed by fans and supporters. The NFL continues to emphasize its concern for players by modifying rules and improving equipment. However, league owners and Commissioner Roger Goodell have advocated for expansion of the league's regular season by adding two games. This would increase revenue but also increase the players' chance for injury. One of the primary lessons the AFL taught the NFL was the importance of exploring new markets. The NFL has played regular-season games in England and Canada; these two countries could one day be awarded expansion teams and thus open up vast new streams of revenue. Meanwhile the Los Angeles market represents a void and challenge to the league. The NFL has explored the possibility of building a stadium that could house two franchises, and there are several teams that might be willing to relocate to Los Angeles. The Raiders are not happy with their home venue, the Jacksonville Jaguars are in a market that has revenue-generating limitations, and the St. Louis Rams might be willing to move back to the West Coast.

Without question the eight original AFL franchises have enjoyed prosperity that few could have imagined. Those teams that joined the league in 1960 for a nominal $25,000 were worth between $800 million and $1.8 billion on average in 2014. Players who made an average salary of $6,000 in the early 1960s now roughly make $2 million. In 1960 the combined AFL and NFL fan attendance was 4.1 million; in 2013 some 17.3 million fans attended NFL games. Lastly the 1966 merger was reluctantly initiated by the NFL, but it produced the Super Bowl, which has become a television and cultural phenomenon that can be compared to no other American sporting event. In 1967 CBS and NBC simultaneously broadcast Super Bowl I. Each network attracted some 25 million viewers and charged advertisers about $42,000 for a thirty-second commercial. Super Bowl XLIX, played in January 2015, was broadcast by NBC, and the network charged advertisers $4.5 million for a thirty-second spot. The game was watched by 114.4 million viewers, making it the most-watched television program in American history. Lamar Hunt, the visionary who carved out the idea for the AFL on a napkin while flying on American Airlines, coined the term "Super Bowl" but probably never imagined that this championship game would grow to be an iconic American event.

CHAPTER 1

1. *New York Times,* September 19, 2001; Charles K. Ross, *Outside the Lines: African Americans and the Integration of the National Football League* (New York: New York University Press, 1999), 114, 166–169.

2. *Standard Times,* September 9, 1960; Ed Gruver, *The American Football League: A Year-by-Year History, 1960–1969* (Jefferson, N.C.: McFarland, 1997), 10–15 (Adams quotation); Michael MacCambridge, *America's Game: The Epic Story of How Pro Football Captured a Nation* (New York: Random House, 2004), 119–120; Pro Football Hall of Fame Series, "First A.F.L. Game," Pro Football Hall of Fame, Canton, Ohio, Boston/New England Patriots file; "The First AFL Game," *Coffin Corner* (Official Newsletter of the Professional Football Researchers Association) 2, no. 11 (November 1980).

3. MacCambridge, *America's Game,* 119; David A. F. Sweet, *Lamar Hunt: The Gentle Giant Who Revolutionized Professional Sports* (Chicago: Triumph Books, 2010), 28.

4. Sweet, *Lamar Hunt,* 29–30 (Hunt quotation); Larry Felser, *The Birth of the New NFL* (Guilford, Conn.: Lyons Press, 2008), xiv–xv; MacCambridge, *America's Game,* 120.

5. Gruver, *American Football League,* 16; Rick Wolff, ed., *The Baseball Encyclopedia* (New York: Macmillan, 1993), 8.

6. Gruver, *American Football League,* 17.

7. Sweet, *Lamar Hunt,* 32–33; *New York Times,* July 29, 1959; Gruver, *American Football League,* 18 (Hilton quotation).

8. Ross, *Outside the Lines,* 120.

9. Ibid.; Sweet, *Lamar Hunt,* 36; Gruver, *American Football League,* 7–8.

10. Gruver, *American Football League,* 24–26; David S. Neft, Richard Cohen, and Rick Korch, *The Football Encyclopedia* (New York: St. Martin's Press, 1994), 318.

11. MacCambridge, *America's Game,* 124–126; Neft, Cohen, and Korch, *Football Encyclopedia,* 318.

12. MacCambridge, *America's Game,* 128 (Wismer quotation).

13. Gruver, *American Football League*, 31–32.

14. Ibid., 35–36; AFL Official Minutes, Memo No. 97, Pro Football Hall of Fame, Canton, Ohio, dated September 14, 1960, author AFL Commissioner Joe Foss.

15. Sweet, *Lamar Hunt*, 41.

16. Gruver, *American Football League*, 38–41; Neft, Cohen, and Korch, *Football Encyclopedia*, 318; "Dimples Tell Coach Ramsey Pleased with Bills Q-Backs," *Buffalo Bills Bulletin* 1, no. 1, Pro Football Hall of Fame, Canton, Ohio, Buffalo Bills file, July 1960.

17. Dave Steidel, *Remember the AFL: The Ultimate Fan's Guide to the American Football League* (Cincinnati, Ohio: Clerisy Press, 2008), 32–57; "Civic Stadium Ready for Bills' July 30 Pre-season Opener with Boston," *Buffalo Bills Bulletin* 1, no. 1, Pro Football Hall of Fame, Canton, Ohio, Buffalo Bills file, July 1960.

18. Jon Morgan, *Glory for Sale* (Baltimore, Md.: Bancroft Press, 1997), 83–84; MacCambridge, *America's Game*, 132, 173 (Rozelle quotation); Gruver, *American Football League*, 30; AFL Official Minutes, Memo No. 17, Pro Football Hall of Fame, Canton, Ohio, March 16, 1960, author AFL Assistant Commissioner Milt Woodard.

19. *Dallas Morning News*, January 8, 1960; Neft, Cohen, and Korch, *Football Encyclopedia*, 328.

20. MacCambridge, *America's Game*, 146; Jeff Miller, *Going Long: The Wild Ten-Year Saga of the American Football League in the Words of Those Who Lived It* (New York: McGraw-Hill, 2003), 15–16 (Adams quotations).

21. MacCambridge, *America's Game*, 147; Felser, *Birth of the New NFL*, 23.

22. Felser, *Birth of the New NFL*, 24 (Bell quotation); Miller, *Going Long*, 16.

23. *Dallas Morning News*, January 15, 1960.

24. AFL Official Minutes, Memo No. 33, April 18, 1960, author AFL Assistant Commissioner Milt Woodard.

25. AFL Official Minutes, Memo No. 28, April 8, 1960, author AFL Assistant Commissioner Milt Woodard; Steidel, *Remember the AFL*, 24; Ross, *Outside the Lines*, 149, 173–175.

26. Steidel, *Remember the AFL*, 41.

27. Miller, *Going Long*, 25–26; Luther H. Hodges, Secretary, U.S. Department of Commerce, and Richard M. Scammon, Director, Bureau of the Census, "Current Population Reports: Consumer Income," *Income of Families and Persons in the United States: 1960*, January 17, 1962, Series P-60, No. 17, Washington, D.C.

28. Pro Football Hall of Fame, *AFL Legacy Games: Bills vs. Patriots in First Ever AFL Game*, Canton, Ohio, official website of the Pro Football Hall of Fame, www.profootballhof.com, September 9, 2009; *San Diego Union Tribune*, February 13, 2011 (Lowe quotation); Steidel, *Remember the AFL*, 53.

29. Kevin Carroll, *Houston Oilers: The Early Years* (Austin, Tex.: Eakin Press, 2001), 76–77.

CHAPTER 2

1. Michael MacCambridge, *America's Game: The Epic Story of How Pro Football Captured a Nation* (New York: Random House, 2004), 164 (Brown quotation); Charles K. Ross, *Outside the Lines: African Americans and the Integration of the National Football League* (New York: New York University Press, 1999), 130.

2. MacCambridge, *America's Game*, 164; Ross, *Outside the Lines*, 145–146.

3. *Dallas Morning News*, September 26, 1960; *Houston Informer*, August 20, 1960; Ross, *Outside the Lines*, 144–145.

4. *Houston Informer*, September 24, 1960.

5. *Strange Demise of Jim Crow*, Thomas R. Cole, Creator and Executive Producer, California Newsreel, 56 minutes, San Francisco, 1998; Andy Rhodes, "Monumental Change: Marker Commemorates Houston's First Sit-In, Dismantling of Segregation," *The Medallion*, Texas Historical Commission, January/February 2010, 2–3.

6. Jeff Miller, *Going Long: The Wild Ten-Year Saga of the American Football League in the Words of Those Who Lived It* (New York: McGraw-Hill, 2003), 36.

7. MacCambridge, *America's Game*, 162–163; Bob Carroll, "The American Football League Attendance, 1960–69," *Coffin Corner* 13, no. 4 (1991): 1; *Dallas Morning News*, September 23 and 26, 1960.

8. Jeffrey J. Miller, *Rocking the Rockpile: The Buffalo Bills of the American Football League* (Toronto: ECW Press, 2007), 112–113 (Fowler quotation); *Buffalo Evening News*, August 17, 1973.

9. Miller, *Rocking the Rockpile*, 113–114.

10. *Boston Globe*, January 19, 1986; David S. Neft, Richard Cohen, and Rick Korch, *The Football Encyclopedia* (New York: St. Martin's Press, 1994), 328.

11. Dave Steidel, *Remember the AFL: The Ultimate Fan's Guide to the American Football League* (Cincinnati, Ohio: Clerisy Press, 2008), 53–54.

12. *Chicago Defender*, January 20, 1961.

13. Neft, Cohen, and Korch, *Football Encyclopedia*, 328; Steidel, *Remember the AFL*, 41; Michael MacCambridge, *Lamar Hunt: A Life in Sports* (Kansas City, Mo.: Andrews McMeel Publishing, 2012), 117–119 (H. L. Hunt quotation). *Dallas Morning News*, November 9, 1960.

14. John Lombardo, *Raiders Forever* (New York: McGraw-Hill, 2001), 2.

15. Ross, *Outside the Lines*, 172–175; Steidel, *Remember the AFL*, 32–59.

16. MacCambridge, *Lamar Hunt*, 119; Ed Gruver, *The American Football League: A Year-by-Year History, 1960–1969* (Jefferson, N.C.: McFarland, 1997), 62 (Howsman quotation).

17. Neft, Cohen, and Korch, *Football Encyclopedia*, 329; Steidel, *Remember the AFL*, 61; Gruver, *American Football League*, 58–59.

18. Neft, Cohen, and Korch, *Football Encyclopedia*, 329; Gruver, *American Football League*, 59.

19. Gruver, *American Football League*, 59 (Blanda quotation); AFL Official Minutes, Memo to AFL Executive Committee, Pro Football Hall of Fame, Canton, Ohio, January 30, 1960, author AFL Assistant Commissioner Milt Woodard.

20. William J. Ryczek, *Crash of the Titans: The Early Years of the New York Jets and the AFL* (Jefferson, N.C.: McFarland, 2009), 100.

21. AFL Official Minutes, Memo to Members of Executive Committee, Pro Football Hall of Fame, Canton, Ohio, October 14, 1960, author unknown.

22. *Dallas Morning News*, November 22, 23, and 24, 1960.

23. Ross, *Outside the Lines*, 149–150; MacCambridge, *America's Game*, 165–166 (Kennedy quotation); *Chicago Defender*, April 7, 1961.

24. MacCambridge, *America's Game*, 171–172.

25. *San Francisco Examiner*, April 27, 1961 (Rozelle quotation); MacCambridge, *America's Game*, 173.

26. Neft, Cohen, and Korch, *Football Encyclopedia*, 342.

27. Steidel, *Remember the AFL*, 82; Gruver, *American Football League*, 66.

28. *New York Herald Tribune*, December 25, 1961; Gruver, *American Football League*, 71; Kevin Carroll, *Houston Oilers: The Early Years* (Austin, Tex.: Eakin Press, 2001), 248; Ross, *Outside the Lines*, 170–177.

29. *New York Herald Tribune*, December 25, 1961; Carroll, *Houston Oilers*, 248–249 (Banfield and Whitehurst quotations).

30. *Dallas Morning News*, November 21, 1961 (Rozelle quotation); AFL Official Minutes, Memo to AFL Executive Committee, Pro Football Hall of Fame, Canton, Ohio, November 8, 1961, author AFL Assistant Commissioner Milt Woodard; AFL Official Minutes, Memo to AFL Presidents, General Managers and Coaches, Pro Football Hall of Fame, Canton, Ohio, December 13, 1961, author AFL Commissioner Joe Foss; *Houston Chronicle*, December 20, 1961 (Foss quotation); William J. Ryczek, *Crash of the Titans: The Early Years of the New York Jets and the AFL* (Jefferson, N.C.: McFarland, 2009), 201–202 (Wismer quotation).

31. Ryczek, *Crash of the Titans*, 202; AFL Official Minutes, Memo No. 168, Pro Football Hall of Fame, Canton, Ohio, November 22, 1961, author AFL Commissioner Joe Foss.

32. Ryczek, *Crash of the Titans*, 202–203 (Wismer quotation, 203); Ross, *Outside the Lines*, 155; AFL Official Minutes, Memo to Officials of AFL Clubs, Pro Football Hall of Fame, Canton, Ohio, March 20, 1962, author AFL Assistant Commissioner Milt Woodard.

33. Ryczek, *Crash of the Titans*, 204; Ross, *Outside the Lines*, 155; *Buffalo Evening News*, December 22, 1961 (Modell quotation).

CHAPTER 3

1. ABC Press Release, "ABC Sports Page," Pro Football Hall of Fame, Canton, Ohio, August 1, 1962; AFL-TV, "Pigskin for Profit," Television Age, Pro Football Hall of Fame, Canton, Ohio, August 6, 1962.

2. Jeffrey J. Miller, *Rocking the Rockpile: The Buffalo Bills of the American Football League* (Toronto: ECW Press, 2007), 160; Ed Gruver, *The American Football League: A Year-by-Year History, 1960–1969* (Jefferson, N.C.: McFarland, 1997), 84 (Gilchrist quotation); Cookie Gilchrist with Chris Garbarino, *The Cookie That Did Not Crumble* (Staten Island, N.Y.: U Are Superstar, 2011), 18–19.

3. Gilchrist and Garbarino, *Cookie That Did Not Crumble*, 24.

4. Ibid., 55 (Gilchrist quotation); Gruver, *American Football League*, 85; Miller, *Rocking the Rockpile*, 162–163 (Flint quotation, 163); *Los Angeles Sentinel*, November 8, 1962.

5. *Pittsburgh Courier*, November 10, 1962; Miller, *Rocking the Rockpile*, 169–171 (Kemp quotation, 169); *Chicago Defender*, January 5, 1963.

6. William J. Ryczek, *Crash of the Titans: The Early Years of the New York Jets and the AFL* (Jefferson, N.C.: McFarland, 2009), 269–270; Mark Kriegel, *Namath: A Biography* (New York: Penguin Books, 2005), 117; Harold Rosenthal, "Glib Wismer Wrapped in Riddle: Bumpkin or Victim of Bum Luck?" *Sporting News*, January 5, 1963; *Newark Star Ledger*, February 7, 1963.

7. Gruver, *American Football League*, 89; Michael MacCambridge, *Lamar Hunt: A Life In Sports* (Kansas City, Mo.: Andrews McMeel Publishing, 2012), 125.

8. MacCambridge, *Lamar Hunt*, 130 (Hunt quotation); *Pittsburgh Courier*, September 1, 1962.

9. Gruver, *American Football League*, 62; Dave Steidel, *Remember the AFL: The Ultimate Fan's Guide to the American Football League* (Cincinnati, Ohio: Clerisy Press, 2008), 68; Miller, *Rocking the Rockpile*, 118.

10. AFL Official Minutes, Memo No. 221, Pro Football Hall of Fame, Canton, Ohio, December 11, 1962, author AFL Commissioner Joe Foss; AFL Official Minutes, Memo

No. 222 to Executives of AFL Clubs, Pro Football Hall of Fame, Canton, Ohio, December 18, 1962, author AFL Assistant Commissioner Milt Woodard.

11. Tex Maule, "The Sad Case of the Missing Quarterback," *Sports Illustrated*, November 26, 1962; David S. Neft, Richard Cohen, and Rick Korch, *The Football Encyclopedia* (New York: St. Martin's Press, 1994), 342; Steidel, *Remember the AFL*, 65–66; MacCambridge, *Lamar Hunt*, 123.

12. National Pro Football Hall of Fame, *The Longest Football Game Ever Played*, Pro Football Hall of Fame, Canton, Ohio, Kansas City Chiefs File, 3–4; Jeff Miller, *Going Long: The Wild Ten-Year Saga of the American Football League in the Words of Those Who Lived It* (New York: McGraw-Hill, 2003), 62.

13. John Pirkle, *Oiler Blues: The Story of Pro Football's Most Frustrating Team* (Houston, Tex.: Sportline Publishing, 2000), 38 (Dewveall quotation); National Pro Football Hall of Fame, *Longest Football Game*, 5.

14. Miller, *Going Long*, 63 (Haynes quotation); National Pro Football Hall of Fame, *Longest Football Game*, 5.

15. Miller, *Going Long*, 64 (Stram and Haynes quotations); Pirkle, *Oiler Blues*, 38.

16. Miller, *Going Long*, 65–66 (Brooker quotation and Haynes quotation); Gruver, *American Football League*, 77; MacCambridge, *Lamar Hunt*, 130 (Stram and Povich quotations).

17. MacCambridge, *Lamar Hunt*, 133; Sporting News, "Too Many Chiefs Made Too Many Touchdowns," September 16, 1963.

18. *Kansas City Star*, February 9, 1963; MacCambridge, *Lamar Hunt*, 139; *Dallas Morning News*, January 14, 1963; *Kansas City Star*, January 14, 1963; Steidel, *Remember the AFL*, 128.

19. *Dallas Morning News*, December 10, 1962; *Chicago Defender*, January 5, 1963; *Los Angeles Sentinel*, January 10, 1963; *Chicago Defender*, January 12, 1963; *Pittsburgh Courier*, January 12, 1963.

20. Charles H. Martin, *Benching Jim Crow: The Rise and Fall of the Color Line in Southern College Sports, 1890–1980* (Urbana: University of Illinois Press, 2010), 281–282. See also Charles Eagles, *The Price of Defiance: James Meredith and the Integration of Ole Miss* (Chapel Hill: University of North Carolina Press, 2009), 19–20.

21. Martin, *Benching Jim Crow*, 282–283.

22. Gruver, *American Football League*, 96 (Gowdy quotation); AFL Official Minutes, Memo No. 230, Pro Football Hall of Fame, Canton, Ohio, April 18, 1963, author AFL Assistant Commissioner Milt Woodard; AFL Official Minutes, Memo No. 236, author Milt Woodard; Bob Carroll, "The American Football League Attendance, 1960–69," *Coffin Corner* 13, no. 4 (1991): 1–3.

23. ABC Press Release, "ABC-TV to Provide Exclusive Coverage of American Football League for 4th Straight Year," Pro Football Hall of Fame, Canton, Ohio, June 18, 1963; ABC Press Release, "AFL Highlights, a Saturday Afternoon Roundup of Activities in the American Football League, Will Premiere September 7," Pro Football Hall of Fame, Canton, Ohio, June 21, 1963; ABC Press Release, "Forty American Football League Games Plus Championship Contest to Be Covered by ABC-TV Starting September 8," Pro Football Hall of Fame, Canton, Ohio, July 31, 1963.

24. Miller, *Going Long*, 73–75 (Haynes quotation, 73; Burford quotation, 75); MacCambridge, *Lamar Hunt*, 140; *Chicago Defender*, September 10, 1963; Steidel, *Remember the AFL*, 140; AFL Official Minutes, Memo No. 245, Pro Football Hall of Fame, Canton, Ohio, August 14, 1963, author AFL Assistant Commissioner Milt Woodard.

25. "Chargers Busy during Off-Season," *Charge with the San Diego Chargers* 2, no. 1, Pro Football Hall of Fame, Canton, Ohio, LA/San Diego Chargers file, June 1963; Steidel, *Remember the AFL*, 153; Todd Tobias, *Charging through the AFL: Los Angeles and San Diego Chargers Football in the 1960s* (Paducah, Ky.: Turner Publishing, 2004), 17; San Diego Chargers, *1963 Pre-season Press, Radio-TV Guide*, Pro Football Hall of Fame, Canton, Ohio, LA/San Diego Chargers file, June 1963; AFL Official Minutes, Memo No. 251, Pro Football Hall of Fame, Canton, Ohio, September 6, 1963, author AFL Assistant Commissioner Milt Woodard.

26. Miller, *Going Long*, 78–79 (Kocourek quotation); Gruver, *American Football League*, 110 (Mix quotation).

27. Miller, *Going Long*, 78–79.

28. Gruver, *American Football League*, 100–103; *Oakland Tribune*, December 28, 1963; *Los Angeles Sentinel*, January 31, 1963; Neft, Cohen, and Korch, *Football Encyclopedia*, 370; *Pittsburgh Courier*, November 9, 1963; *Los Angeles Sentinel*, November 14, 1963 (Davis quotation).

29. John Lombardo, *Raiders Forever* (New York: McGraw-Hill, 2001), 3 (Davidson quotation); Jennifer B. Smith, "An International History of the Black Panther Party," Ph.D. diss., State University of New York at Buffalo, 1997.

30. *Los Angeles Times*, January 26, 1986 (Eisenhauer quotation); Gruver, *American Football League*, 114 (Richardson quotation).

31. Gilchrist and Garbarino, *Cookie That Did Not Crumble*, 81–82; Miller, *Rocking the Rockpile*, 219–220.

32. Michael MacCambridge, *America's Game: The Epic Story of How Pro Football Captured a Nation* (New York: Random House, 2004), 186.

33. MacCambridge, *America's Game*, 188; AFL Official Minutes, Memo No. 260 to Executives of AFL Clubs, Pro Football Hall of Fame, Canton, Ohio, November 25, 1963, author AFL Assistant Commissioner Milt Woodard.

34. Tobias, *Charging through the AFL*, 17–18; Gilbert Rogin, "Run to a Title," *Sports Illustrated*, January 13, 1964; *San Diego Tribune*, January 6, 1963; MacCambridge, *America's Game*, 190 (Gillman and Rozelle quotations).

35. Gruver, *American Football League*, 121–122; Miller, *Going Long*, 85 (Ditka and Lincoln quotations).

CHAPTER 4

1. Zein Nakoda, "New Orleans Citizens Boycott for U.S. Civil Rights, 1960–61," *Global Nonviolent Action Database*, Project of Swarthmore College, Peace and Conflict Studies, Peace Collection, and Lang Center for Civic and Social Responsibility, 2010, available at http://nvdatabase.swarthmore.edu/content/new-orleans-citizens-boycott-us-civil-rights-1960-61; *New Orleans Times-Picayune*, November 12, 2014.

2. Michael MacCambridge, *America's Game: The Epic Story of How Pro Football Captured a Nation* (New York: Random House, 2004), 190–191.

3. AFL letter to Joe Foss, National Broadcasting Company, Pro Football Hall of Fame, Canton, Ohio, November 20, 1964, "AFL and Television" file; *New York Herald Tribune*, January 30, 1964; Ed Gruver, *The American Football League: A Year-by-Year History, 1960–1969* (Jefferson, N.C.: McFarland, 1997), 125 (Sullivan and Foss quotations); MacCambridge, *America's Game*, 201 (Rooney quotation).

4. MacCambridge, *America's Game*, 193.

5. Jeff Miller, *Going Long: The Wild Ten-Year Saga of the American Football League in the Words of Those Who Lived It* (New York: McGraw-Hill, 2003), 146–147.

6. Pete Hamill, "Cookie," *Sport*, August 1963; Bob Peterson, "Football Frenzy in Buffalo," *Sport*, January 1964; Stan Grosshandler, "When the Buffalo Bills Rode High," Pro Football Hall of Fame, Canton, Ohio, Buffalo Bills file, January 1973; Cookie Gilchrist with Chris Garbarino, *The Cookie That Did Not Crumble* (Staten Island, N.Y.: U Are Superstar, 2011), 94 (Gilchrist quotation).

7. William J. Ryczek, *Crash of the Titans: The Early Years of the New York Jets and the AFL* (Jefferson, N.C.: McFarland, 2009), 273; Gruver, *American Football League*, 126.

8. AFL Official Minutes, Memo No. 294, Pro Football Hall of Fame, Canton, Ohio, September 29, 1964, author AFL Assistant Commissioner Milt Woodard.

9. John Pirkle, *Oiler Blues: The Story of Pro Football's Most Frustrating Team* (Houston, Tex.: Sportline Publishing, 2000), 45–46.

10. Bob Halford and Pat Cross, Kansas City Chiefs News Release, Pro Football Hall of Fame, Canton, Ohio, Dallas Texans/Kansas City Chiefs file, July 1964; Dave Steidel, *Remember the AFL: The Ultimate Fan's Guide to the American Football League* (Cincinnati, Ohio: Clerisy Press, 2008), 170.

11. Gilchrist and Garbarino, *Cookie That Did Not Crumble*, 95–96; Jeffrey J. Miller, *Rocking the Rockpile: The Buffalo Bills of the American Football League* (Toronto: ECW Press, 2007), 268–269 (Byrd quotation); Gruver, *American Football League*, 134–135 (Lowe quotation).

12. Miller, *Going Long*, 135 (Lincoln quotation); Miller, *Rocking the Rockpile*, 270–271.

13. *New Orleans Times-Picayune*, August 8, 2010; Gilchrist and Garbarino, *Cookie That Did Not Crumble*, 100 (Gilchrist quotation); Miller, *Going Long*, 156–157 (Bell, Ladd, Westmoreland, and Faison quotations).

14. Gilchrist and Garbarino, *Cookie That Did Not Crumble*, 102–105 (Gilchrist and Foss quotations); *Houston Chronicle*, January 16, 2005; *New Orleans Times-Picayune*, January 16, 2005; *Chicago Defender*, January 16, 1965; *Afro-American*, January 16 and 23, 1965.

15. *Afro-American*, January 23, 1965.

16. *Chicago Defender*, April 16, 1965; Gilchrist and Garbarino, *Cookie That Did Not Crumble*, 112–113 (Gilchrist quotation); Edwin Shrake, "Tough Cookie Marches to His Own Drummer," *Sports Illustrated*, December 14, 1964, 71–80; Edwin Shrake, "Denver Broncos," *Sports Illustrated*, September 13, 1965; *Rome News Tribune*, January 21, 1965.

17. MacCambridge, *America's Game*, 209.

18. David A. F. Sweet, *Lamar Hunt: The Gentle Giant Who Revolutionized Professional Sports* (Chicago: Triumph Books, 2010), 61–62.

19. Gruver, *American Football League*, 126; Sweet, *Lamar Hunt*, 61.

20. Mark Kriegel, *Namath: A Biography* (New York: Penguin Books, 2004), 138–141; MacCambridge, *America's Game*, 206–207 (Davis quotation).

21. Kriegel, *Namath*, 141 (Modell, Ryan, Hayes, and Werblin quotations); Robert H. Boyle, "Show-Biz Sonny and His Quest for Stars," *Sports Illustrated*, July 19, 1965, 66–72; *New York Times*, July 13, 1966 (Daley quotation).

22. Pro-Football-Reference.com, *1964 AFL Opposition and Defensive Statistics*, available at http://www.pro-football-reference.com/years/1964_AFL/#team_stats.

23. John Dittmer, *Local People: The Struggle for Civil Rights in Mississippi* (Urbana: University of Illinois Press, 1995), 288.

24. MacCambridge, *America's Game*, 202.

CHAPTER 5

1. John Pirkle, *Oiler Blues: The Story of Pro Football's Most Frustrating Team* (Houston, Tex.: Sportline Publishing, 2000), 55; Mark Kriegel, *Namath: A Biography* (New York: Penguin Books, 2004), 167.

2. AFL Official Minutes, Memo to AFL Executive Committee, Pro Football Hall of Fame, Canton, Ohio, July 26, 1965, author AFL Commissioner Joe Foss; *Atlanta Journal Constitution,* July 2, 1965.

3. *Atlanta Journal Constitution,* July 2 and 3, 1965; Ed Gruver, *The American Football League: A Year-by-Year History, 1960–1969* (Jefferson, N.C.: McFarland, 1997), 145–146.

4. Kriegel, *Namath,* 160–161.

5. Jeff Miller, *Going Long: The Wild Ten-Year Saga of the American Football League in the Words of Those Who Lived It* (New York: McGraw-Hill, 2003), 188 (McDole quotation); Kriegel, *Namath,* 164.

6. *New York Times,* June 8, 1994 (Ewbank quotation); Kriegel, *Namath,* 238 (Grantham quotation).

7. *New York Times,* June 17, 1992; *Boston Globe,* May 25, 2011 (Garron quotation); John Underwood, "Another Good Joe for the AFL," *Sports Illustrated,* August 9, 1965, 46–49.

8. Pro-Football-Reference.com, *1965 AFL Opposition and Defensive Statistics,* available at http://www.pro-football-reference.com/years/1965_AFL/; Todd Tobias, *Charging through the AFL: Los Angeles and San Diego Chargers Football in the 1960s* (Paducah, Ky.: Turner Publishing, 2004), 19.

9. Cookie Gilchrist with Chris Garbarino, *The Cookie That Did Not Crumble* (Staten Island, N.Y.: U Are Superstar, 2011), 116 (quotation); Pro-Football-Reference.com, *1965 AFL Opposition and Defensive Statistics.*

10. Jeffrey J. Miller, *Rocking the Rockpile: The Buffalo Bills of the American Football League* (Toronto: ECW Press, 2007), 310.

11. AFL Official Minutes, Memo to AFL Executive Committee, Pro Football Hall of Fame, Canton, Ohio, October 21, 1965, author AFL Commissioner Joe Foss; Gruver, *American Football League,* 155.

12. Michael MacCambridge, *America's Game: The Epic Story of How Pro Football Captured a Nation* (New York: Random House, 2004), 214–215 (Borman and Brandt quotations); Gruver, *American Football League,* 155.

13. MacCambridge, *America's Game,* 216.

14. Lerone Bennett Jr., *Before the Mayflower* (New York: Penguin Books, 1988), 574–576; Darlene Clark Hine, William C. Hine, and Stanley Harrold, *The African American Odyssey* (Upper Saddle River, N.J.: Pearson–Prentice Hall, 2006), 573, 589.

15. Charles H. Martin, *Benching Jim Crow: The Rise and Fall of the Color Line in Southern College Sports, 1890–1980* (Urbana: University of Illinois Press, 2010), 284.

16. *New York Times,* June 20, 2011.

17. MacCambridge, *America's Game,* 214–218 (Schramm quotation, 218); Gruver, *American Football League,* 217–218.

18. Michael MacCambridge, *Lamar Hunt: A Life in Sports* (Kansas City, Mo.: Andrews McMeel Publishing, 2012), 156–157.

19. Edwin Shrake, "Thunder Out of Oakland: Unloved Al Davis and His Outcasts Jolted Houston and Climbed to Second in the AFL's Turbulent West," *Sports Illustrated,* November 15, 1965; Gruver, *American Football League,* 157.

20. MacCambridge, *Lamar Hunt,* 157; Gruver, *American Football League,* 159.

21. Miller, *Rocking the Rockpile,* 320 (Gogolak quotation); MacCambridge, *America's Game,* 221 (Rosenbloom quotation).

22. Gruver, *American Football League,* 160; MacCambridge, *Lamar Hunt,* 160.

23. MacCambridge, *Lamar Hunt,* 160–161.

24. MacCambridge, *America's Game,* 229.

25. Ibid., 212; Gruver, *American Football League,* 163–164.

26. *New York Times,* January 16, 1964.

27. American Football League Players Association Minutes, January 16, 1966, Pro Football Hall of Fame, Canton, Ohio, AFL Players Association File.

28. John Lombardo, *Raiders Forever* (New York: McGraw-Hill, 2001), 4.

29. Pro-Football-Reference.com, *1966 AFL Opposition and Defensive Statistics,* available at http://www.pro-football-reference.com/years/1966_AFL/; Todd Tobias, *Tales from the American Football League: Preserving the Legacy of the AFL,* blog titled "Why Is Dave Grayson Not in the Hall of Fame?" May 2, 2012, available at http://tales fromtheamericanfootballleague.com/why-is-dave-grayson-not-in-the-hall-of-fame/.

30. *Pittsburgh Courier,* August 20, 1966.

31. Gilchrist and Garbarino, *Cookie That Did Not Crumble,* 127–128; David S. Neft, Richard Cohen, and Rick Korch, *The Football Encyclopedia* (New York: St. Martin's Press, 1994), 412; Pro-Football-Reference.com, *1966 AFL Opposition and Defensive Statistics.*

32. Miller, *Rocking the Rockpile,* 316 and 320; Miller, *Going Long,* 226; Kriegel, *Namath,* 185 (Cicatiello quotation); Pro-Football-Reference.com, *1966 AFL Opposition, Offensive and Defensive Statistics;* Neft, Cohen, and Korch, *Football Encyclopedia,* 412; *Boston Globe,* December 18 and 19, 1966; *Springfield Sunday Republican,* December 18, 1966; Rick Cimini, "Boozer Remembers Clarence Clemons," ESPN, June 20, 2011, available at http://sports.espn.go.com/nfl/columns/story?columnist=cimini_rich&id=6682974.

33. Pirkle, *Oiler Blues,* 66–67.

34. *Kansas City Star,* January 2, 1967; Neft, Cohen, and Korch, *Football Encyclopedia,* 413; Pro-Football-Reference.com, *1966 Boxscore, January 1, 1967, Chiefs vs. Bills,* available at http://www.pro-football-reference.com/boxscores/196701010buf.htm; Miller, *Going Long,* 228 (Dawson quotation); Gruver, *American Football League,* 169 (Stram quotation).

35. MacCambridge, *Lamar Hunt,* 166; MacCambridge, *America's Game,* 238.

36. *Northwest Indiana Times,* February 2, 2013 (Williamson quotations); *New York Daily News,* January 14, 1996.

37. MacCambridge, *America's Game,* 238.

38. Gruver, *American Football League,* 174.

39. *Kansas City Star,* January 15, 1987.

40. Dave Steidel, *Remember the AFL: The Ultimate Fan's Guide to the American Football League* (Cincinnati, Ohio: Clerisy Press, 2008), 257–258; Neft, Cohen, and Korch, *Football Encyclopedia,* 418; Miller, *Going Long,* 238 (Dawson quotation).

41. Neft, Cohen, and Korch, *Football Encyclopedia,* 418.

CHAPTER 6

1. West Texas A&M University, *2011 Media Guide* (Canyon, Tex., 2011), 42–43; *Pittsburgh Courier,* April 1, 1967.

2. *Cleveland Plain Dealer,* June 9, 1966; *Cincinnati Enquirer,* October 26, 1966; *Cincinnati Enquirer,* November 24, 1966; *Cleveland Press,* December 6, 1966; *Cincinnati En-*

quirer, December 6, 1966; *St. Petersburg Times,* August 3, 1968; Bob Gill, "The Best of the Rest: Part One," *Coffin Corner* 5, no. 11 (1983): 3; Ed Gruver, *The American Football League: A Year-by-Year History, 1960–1969* (Jefferson, N.C.: McFarland, 1997), 180; *Cincinnati Enquirer,* October 28, 1967.

3. Jeff Miller, *Going Long: The Wild Ten-Year Saga of the American Football League in the Words of Those Who Lived It* (New York: McGraw-Hill, 2003), 245.

4. Ibid., 248; Cookie Gilchrist with Chris Garbarino, *The Cookie That Did Not Crumble* (Staten Island, N.Y.:U Are Superstar, 2011), 138–139; Larry Felser, *The Birth of the New NFL* (Guilford, Conn.: Lyons Press, 2008), 148–149 (Costa quotation).

5. *Kansas City Star,* August 24, 1967; Gruver, *American Football League,* 181–182; Michael MacCambridge, *Lamar Hunt: A Life in Sports* (Kansas City, Mo.: Andrews Mc-Meel Publishing, 2012), 177; Miller, *Going Long,* 249 (Sayers quotation).

6. Dave Steidel, *Remember the AFL* (Cincinnati, Ohio: Clerisy Press, 2008), 292; Miller, *Going Long,* 255.

7. Pro-Football-Reference.com, *1967 AFL Opposition and Defensive Statistics,* available at http://www.pro-football-reference.com/years/1967_AFL/; David S. Neft, Richard Cohen, and Rick Korch, *The Football Encyclopedia* (New York: St. Martin's Press, 1994), 430.

8. MacCambridge, *Lamar Hunt,* 194 (Lanier quotation); *Pittsburgh Courier,* October 21, 1967.

9. Felser, *Birth of the New NFL,* 149.

10. Floyd Little with Tom Mackie, "How Floyd Little Decided to Play Football at Syracuse: The Non-Hollywood Version," *Yahoo Sports,* January 11, 2013 (Little quotation); Rich Cimini, "Floyd Little Chooses Cuse All Over Again," ESPN, May 26, 2011, available at http://sports.espn.go.com/ncf/columns/story?columnist=cimini_rich&id=6596721.

11. John Pirkle, *Oiler Blues: The Story of Pro Football's Most Frustrating Team* (Houston, Tex.: Sportline Publishing, 2000), 68.

12. *Lansing State Journal,* April 19, 2007; *Houston Chronicle,* December 6, 1967; Pro-Football-Reference.com, *1967 AFL Opposition and Defensive Statistics.*

13. *Lansing State Journal,* April 21, 2007; *USA Today,* April 22, 2007; *New York Times,* August 29, 2013.

14. *Pittsburgh Courier,* October 21, 1967; Pirkle, *Oiler Blues,* 68–69.

15. *Houston Informer,* November 2, 1967; *Houston Chronicle,* November 30, 1967.

16. *Pittsburgh Courier,* October 28, 1967.

17. *Houston Chronicle,* December 22, 1967; *New York Daily News,* December 22, 1967; *Houston Post,* December 24, 1967; Edwin Shrake, "Almost All Alone at the Top," *Sports Illustrated,* December 25, 1967; *Houston Post,* January 28, 1967; *Houston Chronicle,* February 12, 1968.

18. Mark Kriegel, *Namath: A Biography* (New York: Penguin Books, 2004), 219.

19. *New York Post,* December 4, 1967 (Philbin quotation); Kriegel, *Namath,* 220 (Snell quotation).

20. Jeffrey J. Miller, *Rocking the Rockpile: The Buffalo Bills of the American Football League* (Toronto: ECW Press, 2007), 356–357; Neft, Cohen, Korch, *Football Encyclopedia,* 430; Edwin Shrake, "A Break, a Wrench and a March of New Quarterbacks," *Sports Illustrated,* September 25, 1976; Steidel, *Remember the AFL,* 271–272; Bob Carroll, "The American Football League Attendance, 1960–69," *Coffin Corner* 13, no. 4 (1991): 6, 5; *Cincinnati Post and Times-Star,* December 13, 1966; *Pittsburgh Courier,* October 28, 1967; *Sunday Herald Traveler,* December 24, 1967 (Sullivan quotation).

21. Neft, Cohen, and Korch, *Football Encyclopedia*, 436; *Oakland Tribune*, January 1, 1968.

22. Michael MacCambridge, *America's Game: The Epic Story of How Pro Football Captured a Nation* (New York: Random House, 2004), 242–244 (Garrison and Perkins quotations); Neft, Cohen, and Korch, *Football Encyclopedia*, 436.

23. *New York Times*, January 13, 2001; *Pittsburgh Courier*, November 16 and 18, 1967.

24. *San Jose Mercury News*, March 1, 2012.

25. Ibid.; *Oakland Tribune*, January 1, 1968.

26. Gruver, *American Football League*, 192; Miller, *Going Long*, 263.

27. Neft, Cohen, and Korch, *Football Encyclopedia*, 437; MacCambridge, *America's Game*, 248–249 (Weiss quotation).

28. Lloyd Vance, "Remembering Eldridge Dickey: A Pioneer before His Time," *Pro Football Researchers Association*, April 2007; Damali Binta Sara, "Oakland Raiders QB: What Happened to Eldridge Dickey?" *Bleacher Report*, April 16, 2010, Turner Broadcasting System.

29. Vance, "Remembering Eldridge Dickey."

30. Marlin Briscoe with Bob Schaller, *The First Black Quarterback: Marlin Briscoe's Journey to Break the Color Barrier and Start in the NFL* (Grand Island, Neb.: Cross Training Publishing, 2002), 80.

31. Terry Pluto, *Loose Balls: The Short, Wild Life of the American Basketball Association* (New York: Simon and Schuster, 2007), 41–71.

CHAPTER 7

1. Lerone Bennett Jr., *Before the Mayflower* (New York: Penguin Books, 1988), 583–585.

2. Jeff Miller, *Going Long: The Wild Ten-Year Saga of the American Football League in the Words of Those Who Lived It* (New York: McGraw-Hill, 2003), 253.

3. Marlin Briscoe with Bob Schaller, *The First Black Quarterback: Marlin Briscoe's Journey to Break the Color Barrier and Start in the NFL* (Grand Island, Neb.: Cross Training Publishing, 2002), 107.

4. Ken Crippen interview with Marlin Briscoe, *National Football Post*, December 13, 2013.

5. Briscoe with Schaller, *First Black Quarterback*, 84–96 (Namath quotation, 96); Pro-Football-Reference.com, *1968 AFL Offensive, and Opposition and Defensive Statistics*, available at http://www.pro-football-reference.com/years/1968_AFL/.

6. Michael MacCambridge, *America's Game: The Epic Story of How Pro Football Captured a Nation* (New York: Random House, 2004), 252; Dave Steidel, *Remember the AFL: The Ultimate Fan's Guide to the American Football League* (Cincinnati, Ohio: Clerisy Press, 2008), 329.

7. Ed Gruver, *The American Football League: A Year-by-Year History, 1960–1969* (Jefferson, N.C.: McFarland, 1997), 205 (quotation); David S. Neft, Richard Cohen, and Rick Korch, *The Football Encyclopedia* (New York: St. Martin's Press, 1994), 448.

8. *New York Post*, May 22 and 23, 1968.

9. *New York Post*, May 22, 1968; Gruver, *American Football League*, 197–198 (Lombardi quotation).

10. Pro-Football-Reference.com, *1968 AFL Offensive, and Opposition and Defensive Statistics*; John Lombardo, *Raiders Forever* (New York: McGraw-Hill, 2001), 157–158 and 102 (quotation).

11. *Pittsburgh Courier,* August 10 and September 7, 1968.

12. *Huntsville Item,* February 1, 2014; Pro-Football-Reference.com, *1968 AFL Offensive, and Opposition and Defensive Statistics.*

13. Michael MacCambridge, *Lamar Hunt: A Life in Sports* (Kansas City, Mo.: Andrews McMeel Publishing, 2012), 195.

14. *Dayton Daily News,* May 25, 1967; Larry Felser, "AFL Won't Unload Culls on Cincy," *Sporting News,* Pro Football Hall of Fame, Canton, Ohio, Cincinnati Bengals File, June 10, 1967; *Cincinnati Post and Times-Star,* May 24, 1967; Miller, *Going Long,* 268–269, 272; *Cincinnati Post and Times-Star,* September 27, 1967; Pro-Football-Reference.com, *1968 AFL Offensive, and Opposition and Defensive Statistics;* Pro-Football-Reference.com, *1968 NFL/AFL Draft,* available at http://www.pro-football-reference.com/years/1968/draft.htm; *Cincinnati Post and Times-Star,* January 17, 1968.

15. Steidel, *Remember the AFL,* 300; Miller, *Going Long,* 275, 279 (Robinson quotation).

16. Cookie Gilchrist with Chris Garbarino, *The Cookie That Did Not Crumble* (Staten Island, N.Y.: U Are Superstar, 2011), 140–141; Barry Cobb, "Paul Brown Picks Younger Players for Baby Bengals," *Sporting News,* Pro Football Hall of Fame, Canton, Ohio, Cincinnati Bengals File, February 3, 1968 (quotation).

17. Gruver, *American Football League,* 208–209.

18. MacCambridge, *America's Game,* 252–253.

19. Mark Kriegel, *Namath: A Biography* (New York: Penguin Books, 2004), 250.

20. Kriegel, *Namath,* 250–251 (Parilli quotation); Pro-Football-Reference.com, *Oakland Raiders 23 at NY Jets 27, Sunday, December 29, 1968,* available at http://www.pro-football-reference.com/boxscores/196812290nyj.htm.

21. Kriegel, *Namath,* 253–254; Gruver, *American Football League,* 214–215 (Hill quotation); Pro-Football-Reference.com, *Oakland Raiders 23 at NY Jets 27.*

22. Gruver, *American Football League,* 216; MacCambridge, *America's Game,* 253–254 (Joe Namath quotation).

23. Kriegel, *Namath,* 272–273; Miller, *Going Long,* 302.

24. Kriegel, *Namath,* 276 (Orr quotation); Pro-Football-Reference.com, *NY Jets 16 vs. Baltimore Colts 7, Sunday, January 12, 1969,* available at http://www.pro-football-reference.com/boxscores/196901120clt.htm.

25. MacCambridge, *America's Game,* 255.

26. Pro-Football-Reference.com, *NY Jets 16 vs. Baltimore Colts 7;* Kriegel, *Namath,* 280 (Namath quotation); Miller, *Going Long,* 311 (Smith and Morrall quotations).

27. Gruver, *American Football League,* 223–224 (Hill and Namath quotations); *New York Daily News,* January 22, 1969; *Pittsburgh Press,* January 23, 1969.

28. Jeffrey J. Miller, *Rocking the Rockpile: The Buffalo Bills of the American Football League* (Toronto: ECW Press, 2007), 428 (Wilson quotation); Pro-Football-Reference.com, *1969 NFL/AFL Draft,* available at http://www.pro-football-reference.com/years/1969/draft.htm.

29. MacCambridge, *America's Game,* 257–258.

30. Ibid., 259–260 (first Namath quotation, 259); *Houston Oilers Magazine,* Pro Football Hall of Fame, Canton, Ohio, Houston Oilers file, July 1969; *Boston Herald Traveler,* January 24, 1969; *New York Post,* July 19, 1969 (second Namath quotation).

31. Bennett, *Before the Mayflower,* 586–587; Darlene Clark Hine, William C. Hine, and Stanley Harrold, *The African American Odyssey* (Upper Saddle River, N.J.: Pearson–Prentice Hall, 2006), 603.

CHAPTER 8

1. Michael MacCambridge, *America's Game: The Epic Story of How Pro Football Captured a Nation* (New York: Random House, 2004), 261.

2. John Helyar, *Lords of the Realm: The Real History of Baseball* (New York: Ballantine Books, 1995), 111.

3. Dave Steidel, *Remember the AFL: The Ultimate Fan's Guide to the American Football League* (Cincinnati, Ohio: Clerisy Press, 2008), 372; Pro-Football-Reference.com, *1969 AFL Offensive, and Opposition and Defensive Statistics*, available at http://www.pro-football-reference.com/years/1969_AFL/.

4. Steidel, *Remember the AFL*, 372; Michael MacCambridge, *Lamar Hunt: A Life in Sports* (Kansas City, Mo.: Andrews McMeel Publishing, 2012), 196–197 (quotation).

5. Pro-Football-Reference.com, *1969 AFL Offensive, and Opposition and Defensive Statistics*.

6. John Lombardo, *Raiders Forever* (New York: McGraw-Hill, 2001), 165–168.

7. Todd Tobias, *Charging through the AFL: Los Angeles and San Diego Chargers Football in the 1960s* (Paducah, Ky.: Turner Publishing, 2004), 22–23, 23–24; *San Diego Union*, December 15, 1969; *Los Angeles Times*, November 15 and 16, 1969.

8. Sam Blair, "Webster of the Oilers . . . All the Instincts of Greatness," *1968 Houston Oilers Magazine*, Pro Football Hall of Fame, Canton, Ohio, Houston Oilers file, July 1968 (Webster quotation); Sam Blair, "A Stroke of Luck for a Super Thief," *1968 Houston Oilers Magazine*, Pro Football Hall of Fame, Canton, Ohio, Houston Oilers file, July 1968.

9. Sam Blair, "Boyette: Linebacker with All the Tools," *1968 Houston Oilers Magazine*, Pro Football Hall of Fame, Canton, Ohio, Houston Oilers file, July 1968; *Houston Chronicle*, August 22, 2013 (LeVias quotation); Sam Blair, "Stepping to the Roar of the Young Lions," *1968 Houston Oilers Magazine*, Pro Football Hall of Fame, Canton, Ohio, Houston Oilers file, July 1968.

10. Dick Peebles, "Oilers Set to Open Training in Kerrville," *Gusher* 4, no. 7, Pro Football Hall of Fame, Canton, Ohio, Houston Oilers file, July 1969; John Pirkle, *Oiler Blues: The Story of Pro Football's Most Frustrating Team* (Houston, Tex.: Sportline Publishing, 2000), 82.

11. Brock Yates, "Warts, Love and Dreams in Buffalo," *Sports Illustrated*, January 30, 1969; Marlin Briscoe with Bob Schaller, *The First Black Quarterback: Marlin Briscoe's Journey to Break the Color Barrier and Start in the NFL* (Grand Island, Neb.: Cross Training Publishing, 2002), 115–117 (Harris and Simpson quotations).

12. *Buffalo Evening News*, December 8, 1969, and October 21, 1969; Schaller, *First Black Quarterback*, 123–124 (Briscoe quotation).

13. Ed Gruver, *The American Football League: A Year-by-Year History, 1960–1969* (Jefferson, N.C.: McFarland, 1997), 235–236.

14. MacCambridge, *Lamar Hunt*, 199; Mark Kriegel, *Namath: A Biography* (New York: Penguin Books, 2004), 305–306, 311 (quotation).

15. Gruver, *American Football League*, 238–239 (Thomas and Namath quotations); MacCambridge, *Lamar Hunt*, 199.

16. MacCambridge, *America's Game*, 266–267; MacCambridge, *Lamar Hunt*, 200; Kriegel, *Namath*, 312.

17. Pro-Football-Reference.com, *Houston Oilers 7 at Oakland Raiders 56, Sunday, December 21, 1969*, available at http://www.pro-football-reference.com/boxscores/196912210

rai.htm; Pirkle, *Oiler Blues*, 83; Jeff Miller, *Going Long: The Wild Ten-Year Saga of the American Football League in the Words of Those Who Lived It* (New York: McGraw-Hill, 2003), 339.

18. Gruver, *American Football League*, 240 (Stram quotation); MacCambridge, *Lamar Hunt*, 201 (player quotation).

19. Gruver, *American Football League*, 241 (Lamonica quotation); David S. Neft, Richard Cohen, and Rick Korch, *The Football Encyclopedia* (New York: St. Martin's Press, 1994), 472.

20. MacCambridge, *Lamar Hunt*, 201 (Madden quotations); Miller, *Going Long*, 341–342; MacCambridge, *America's Game*, 267.

21. *Kansas City Star*, January 5, 1970; Gruver, *American Football League*, 245 (Hunt quotation).

22. Neft, Cohen, and Korch, *Football Encyclopedia*, 456 and 473; *New Orleans Times-Picayune*, January 9, 1970.

23. Gruver, *American Football League*, 249; MacCambridge, *America's Game*, 269 (Robinson quotation).

24. Miller, *Going Long*, 347.

25. Steidel, *Remember the AFL*, 380; Miller, *Going Long*, 349 (Stram quotation); MacCambridge, *America's Game*, 269–270; Gruver, *American Football League*, 249–250 (Lanier quotation).

26. Steidel, *Remember the AFL*, 380.

27. *Kansas City Star*, January 28, 1970; Steidel, *Remember the AFL*, 380–381; Gruver, *American Football League*, 254 (Hunt quotation).

28. Neft, Cohen, and Korch, *Football Encyclopedia*, 493; Pro-Football-Reference.com, *1970 NFL Draft*, available at http://www.pro-football-reference.com/years/1970/draft.htm.

29. Pro-Football-Reference.com, *1970 NFL Draft*.

30. *New York Times*, January 17 and 21, 1971; Neft, Cohen, and Korch, *Football Encyclopedia*, 496; MacCambridge, *America's Game*, 277.

EPILOGUE

1. Pro-Football-Reference.com, *1958 and 1959 NFL and AFL Drafts*, available at http://www.pro-football-reference.com/years/1958/draft.htm and http://www.pro-football-reference.com/years/1959/draft.htm.

2. Greg Howard, "The Big Book of Black Quarterbacks," *Deadspin*, February 2014.

3. Greg Price, "Highest Paid NFL Quarterbacks: Top 10 Salaries for QBs in the 2014 Season," *International Business Times*, July 31, 2014.

4. Kurt Badenhausen, "The NFL's Highest-Paid Players, 2014," *Forbes*, August 2014.

5. *New York Times*, April 22, 2015.

BIBLIOGRAPHY

NEWSPAPERS

Boston Globe (Boston, Mass.)
Boston Herald (Boston, Mass.)
Buffalo Evening News (Buffalo, N.Y.)
Chicago Defender (Chicago, Ill.)
Cincinnati Enquirer (Cincinnati, Ohio)
Cincinnati Post and Times-Star (Cincinnati, Ohio)
Cleveland Plain Dealer (Cleveland, Ohio)
Cleveland Press (Cleveland, Ohio)
Dallas Morning News (Dallas, Tex.)
Dayton Daily News (Dayton, Ohio)
Houston Chronicle (Houston, Tex.)
Houston Informer (Houston, Tex.)
Houston Post (Houston, Tex.)
Huntsville Item (Huntsville, Tex.)
Kansas City Star (Kansas City, Mo.)
Lansing State Journal (Lansing, Mich.)
Los Angeles Sentinel (Los Angeles, Calif.)
Los Angeles Times (Los Angeles, Calif.)
Newark Star Ledger (Newark, N.J.)
New Orleans Times-Picayune (New Orleans, La.)
New York Daily News (New York, N.Y.)
New York Herald Tribune (New York, N.Y.)
New York Post (New York, N.Y.)
New York Times (New York, N.Y.)
Northwest Indiana Times (Munster, Ind.)

Oakland Tribune (Oakland, Calif.)
Pittsburgh Courier (Pittsburgh, Pa.)
Pittsburgh Press (Pittsburgh, Pa.)
San Diego Union Tribune (San Diego, Calif.)
San Francisco Examiner (San Francisco, Calif.)
San Jose Mercury News (San Jose, Calif.)
Springfield Sunday Republican (Springfield, Mass.)
Standard Times (New Bedford, Mass.)
St. Petersburg Times (St. Petersburg, Fla.)
USA Today (Tysons Corner, Va.)

BOOKS

Bennett, Lerone, Jr. *Before the Mayflower.* New York: Penguin Books, 1988.
Briscoe, Marlin, with Bob Schaller. *The First Black Quarterback: Marlin Briscoe's Journey to Break the Color Barrier and Start in the NFL.* Grand Island, Neb.: Cross Training Publishing, 2002.
Carroll, Kevin. *Houston Oilers: The Early Years.* Austin, Tex.: Eakin Press, 2001.
Eagles, Charles. *The Price of Defiance: James Meredith and the Integration of Ole Miss.* Chapel Hill: University of North Carolina Press, 2009.
Felser, Larry. *The Birth of the New NFL.* Guilford, Conn.: Lyons Press, 2008.
Gilchrist, Cookie, with Chris Garbarino. *The Cookie That Did Not Crumble.* Staten Island, N.Y.: U Are Superstar, 2011.
Gruver, Ed. *The American Football League: A Year-by-Year History, 1960–1969.* Jefferson, N.C.: McFarland, 1997.
Helyar, John. *Lords of the Realm: The Real History of Baseball.* New York: Ballantine Books, 1995.
Hine, Darlene Clark, William C. Hine, and Stanley Harrold. *The African American Odyssey.* Upper Saddle River, N.J.: Pearson–Prentice Hall, 2006.
Kriegel, Mark. *Namath: A Biography.* New York: Penguin Books, 2005.
Lombardo, John. *Raiders Forever.* New York: McGraw-Hill, 2001.
MacCambridge, Michael. *America's Game: The Epic Story of How Pro Football Captured a Nation.* New York: Random House, 2004.
———. *Lamar Hunt: A Life in Sports.* Kansas City, Mo.: Andrews McMeel Publishing, 2012.
Martin, Charles H. *Benching Jim Crow: The Rise and Fall of the Color Line in Southern College Sports, 1890–1980.* Urbana: University of Illinois Press, 2010.
Miller, Jeff. *Going Long: The Wild Ten-Year Saga of the American Football League in the Words of Those Who Lived It.* New York: McGraw-Hill, 2003.
Miller, Jeffrey J. *Rocking the Rockpile: The Buffalo Bills of the American Football League.* Toronto: ECW Press, 2007.
Morgan, Jon. *Glory for Sale.* Baltimore, Md.: Bancroft Press, 1997.
Neft, David S., Richard Cohen, and Rick Korch. *The Football Encyclopedia.* New York: St. Martin's Press, 1994.
Ross, Charles K. *Outside the Lines: African Americans and the Integration of the National Football League.* New York: New York University Press, 1999.
Ryczek, William J. *Crash of the Titans: The Early Years of the New York Jets and the AFL.* Jefferson, N.C.: McFarland, 2009.

Steidel, Dave. *Remember the AFL: The Ultimate Fan's Guide to the American Football League.* Cincinnati, Ohio: Clerisy Press, 2008.

Sweet, David A. F. *Lamar Hunt: The Gentle Giant Who Revolutionized Professional Sports.* Chicago: Triumph Books, 2010.

Tobias, Todd. *Charging through the AFL: Los Angeles and San Diego Chargers Football in the 1960s.* Paducah, Ky.: Turner Publishing, 2004.

Wolff, Rick, ed. *The Baseball Encyclopedia.* New York: Macmillan, 1993.

DOCUMENTS HOUSED AT
THE PRO FOOTBALL HALL OF FAME

ABC Press Release. *ABC Sports Page,* August 1, 1962.

———. "ABC-TV to Provide Exclusive Coverage of American Football League for 4th Straight Year," June 18, 1963.

———. "AFL Highlights: A Saturday Afternoon Roundup of Activities in the American Football League, Will Premiere September 7," June 21, 1963.

———. *AFL-TV, Pigskin for Profit, Television Age,* August 6, 1962.

———. "Forty American Football League Games Plus Championship Contest to Be Covered by ABC-TV Starting September 8," July 31, 1963.

AFL letter to Joe Foss. National Broadcasting Company, November 20, 1964, file titled "AFL and Television."

AFL Official Minutes. Memo No. 17, author AFL Assistant Commissioner Milt Woodard.

———. Memo No. 28, author AFL Assistant Commissioner Milt Woodard

———. Memo No. 33, author AFL Assistant Commissioner Milt Woodard.

———. Memo No. 97, author AFL Commissioner Joe Foss.

———. Memo No. 168, author AFL Commissioner Joe Foss.

———. Memo No. 221, author AFL Commissioner Joe Foss.

———. Memo No. 222 to Executives of AFL Clubs, author AFL Assistant Commissioner Milt Woodard.

———. Memo No. 230, author AFL Assistant Commissioner Milt Woodard.

———. Memo No. 236, author AFL Assistant Commissioner Milt Woodard.

———. Memo No. 245, author AFL Assistant Commissioner Milt Woodard.

———. Memo No. 251, author AFL Assistant Commissioner Milt Woodard.

———. Memo No. 260 to Executives of AFL Clubs, author AFL Assistant Commissioner Milt Woodard.

———. Memo to AFL Executive Committee, January 30, 1960, author AFL Assistant Commissioner Milt Woodard.

———. Memo to AFL Executive Committee, November 8, 1961, author AFL Assistant Commissioner Milt Woodard.

———. Memo to AFL Executive Committee, October 21, 1965, author AFL Commissioner Joe Foss.

———. Memo to AFL Presidents, General Managers and Coaches, December 13, 1961, author AFL Commissioner Joe Foss.

———. Memo to Members of Executive Committee, October 14, 1960, author unknown.

———. Memo to Officials of AFL Clubs, March 20, 1962, author AFL Assistant Commissioner Milt Woodard.

American Football League Players Association Minutes, January 16, 1966, AFL Players Association File.

Blair, Sam. "Boyette: Linebacker with All the Tools." *1968 Houston Oilers Magazine*, Houston Oilers file, July 1968.

———. "Stepping to the Roar of the Young Lions." *1968 Houston Oilers Magazine*, Houston Oilers file, July 1968.

———. "A Stroke of Luck for a Super Thief." *1968 Houston Oilers Magazine*, Houston Oilers file, July 1968.

———."Webster of the Oilers . . . All the Instincts of Greatness." *1968 Houston Oilers Magazine*, Houston Oilers file, July 1968.

"Chargers Busy during Off-Season." *Charge with the San Diego Chargers* 2, no. 1. LA/San Diego Chargers file, June 1963.

"Civic Stadium Ready for Bills' July 30 Pre-season Opener with Boston." *Buffalo Bills Bulletin* 1, no. 1. Buffalo Bills file, July 1960.

"Dimples Tell Coach Ramsey Pleased with Bills Q-Backs." *Buffalo Bills Bulletin* 1, no. 1. Buffalo Bills file, July 1960.

National Pro Football Hall of Fame. *The Longest Football Game Ever Played*, Kansas City Chiefs File.

Peebles, Dick. "Oilers Set to Open Training in Kerrville," *Gusher* 4, no. 7. Houston Oilers file, July 1969.

Pro Football Hall of Fame Series. *First A.F.L. Game*, Boston/New England Patriots file.

San Diego Chargers. *1963 Pre-season Press, Radio-TV Guide*, LA/San Diego Chargers file, June 1963.

ARTICLES

Boyle, Robert H. "Show-Biz Sonny and His Quest for Stars." *Sports Illustrated*, July 19, 1965.

Carroll, Bob. "The American Football League Attendance, 1960–69." *Coffin Corner* 13, no. 4 (1991): 1.

———. "The First AFL Game." *Coffin Corner* (Official Newsletter of the Professional Football Researchers Association) 2, no. 11 (November 1980).

Cimini, Rich. "Boozer Remembers Clarence Clemons," ESPN, June 20, 2011. Available at http://sports.espn.go.com/nfl/columns/story?columnist=cimini_rich&id =6682974.

———. "Floyd Little Chooses Cuse All Over Again," ESPN, May 26, 2011. Available at http://sports.espn.go.com/ncf/columns/story?columnist=cimini_rich&id=6596721.

Cobb, Barry. "Paul Brown Picks Younger Players for Baby Bengals." *Sporting News*, February 3, 1968.

Crippen, Ken. Interview with Marlin Briscoe. *National Football Post*, December 13, 2013.

Felser, Larry. "AFL Won't Unload Culls on Cincy." *Sporting News*, June 10, 1967.

Gill, Bob. "The Best of the Rest: Part One." *Coffin Corner* 5, no. 11 (1983): 3.

Hodges, Luther H., Secretary, U.S. Department of Commerce, and Richard M. Scammon, Director Bureau of the Census. "Current Population Reports Consumer Income," January 17, 1962. *Income of Families and Persons in the United States: 1960*, Series P-60, No. 17. Washington, D.C.

Little, Floyd, with Tom Mackie. "How Floyd Little Decided to Play Football at Syracuse: The Non-Hollywood Version." *Yahoo Sports*, January 11, 2013.

Maule, Tex. "The Sad Case of the Missing Quarterback." *Sports Illustrated*, November 26, 1962.

Nakoda, Zein. "New Orleans Citizens Boycott for U.S. Civil Rights, 1960–61." *Global Nonviolent Action Database*, Project of Swarthmore College, Peace and Conflict Studies, the Peace Collection, and the Lang Center for Civic and Social Responsibility, 2010. Available at http://nvdatabase.swarthmore.edu/content/new-orleans-citizens-boycott-us-civil-rights-1960-61.

Rhodes, Andy. "Monumental Change: Marker Commemorates Houston's First Sit-In, Dismantling of Segregation." *The Medallion* (Texas Historical Commission), January/February 2010, 2–3.

Rogin, Gilbert. "Run to a Title." *Sports Illustrated*, January 13, 1964.

Rosenthal, Harold. "Glib Wismer Wrapped in Riddle: Bumpkin or Victim of Bum Luck?" *Sporting News*, January 5, 1963.

Sara, Damali Binta. "Oakland Raiders QB: What Happened to Eldridge Dickey?" *Bleacher Report*, April 16, 2010.

Shrake, Edwin. "Almost All Alone at the Top." *Sports Illustrated*, December 25, 1967.

———. "A Break, a Wrench and a March of New Quarterbacks." *Sports Illustrated*, September 25, 1976.

———. "Thunder Out of Oakland: Unloved Al Davis and His Outcasts Jolted Houston and Climbed to Second in the AFL's Turbulent West." *Sports Illustrated*, November 15, 1965.

2011 Media Guide. West Texas A&M University, Canyon, Tex., 2011.

Vance, Lloyd. "Remembering Eldridge Dickey: A Pioneer before His Time." *Pro Football Researchers Association*, April 2007.

Yates, Brock. "Warts, Love and Dreams in Buffalo." *Sports Illustrated*, January 30, 1969.

UNPUBLISHED MATERIALS

Smith, Jennifer B. "An International History of the Black Panther Party." Ph.D. diss., State University of New York at Buffalo, 1997.

INDEX

Note: Page numbers in *italics* refer to illustrations.

Adams, Bud, 8, 9, 11, 42, 48, *112*, 121–122
Adams, K. S., 8
Adderley, Herb, 36, 94, 104
Addison, Tom, 97
"AFL Highlights," 57
Afro-American, 74–75
Agajanian, Ben, 33
Alcorn State University, 79
Ali, Muhammad, 65, 75, 133, 146
All-American Football Conference (AAFC), 5, 6, 11
Allen, George, 150
Alworth, Lance, 47, 58, 59, 72, 87
Ameche, Alan, 9
American Basketball Association (ABA), 128
American Football Conference (AFC), 159; divisions of, 144; drafts of, 159–160; NFL teams moved to, 144
American Football League (AFL): ABC agreements with, 38, 56–57; attendance and, 28–29, 56, 153; coaches of, 15 (*see also specific coaches*); commissioner of, 13, 14 (*see also* Foss, Joe); divisions of, 14–15; draft 1 of (1960 season), 13, 17–19, 20–21; draft 2

of (1961 season), 35–36; draft 3 of (1962 season), 41–43; draft 4 of (1963 season), 54–55, 71; draft 5 of (1964 season), 67–68, 71; draft 6 of (1965 season), 76–80; draft 7 of (1966 season), 88–90, 91–92; draft 8 of (1967 season), 105–106; draft 9 of (1968 season), 126–128; draft 10 of (1969 season), 143–144; expansion of, 84, 114–115; first exhibition games of, 22–23; first preseason of, 19–20; formation of, 1, 8–11; game clock of, 14; game schedule of, 14; Kennedy assassination response of, 62–63; Minneapolis franchise withdrawal from, 13; NBC agreement with, 66–67; New Orleans boycott by, 3, 65, 73–76; NFL fights with, 12–14, 94–95; NFL merger with, 92–97 (*see also* American Football Conference [AFC]); offensive penalty changes by, 50; season 1 of (1960), 22–23, 26–35; season 2 of (1961), 39–40; season 3 of (1962), 45–64; season 4 of (1963), 59–61; season 5 of (1964), 68–70; season 6 of (1965), 84–87; season 7 of (1966), 97–98, 100; season 8 of (1967),

Charles K. Ross is the Chair of the African American Studies Program and Associate Professor of African American Studies and History at the University of Mississippi. He is the author of *Outside the Lines: African Americans and the Integration of the National Football League* and the editor of *Race and Sport: The Struggle for Equality On and Off the Field.*